TESOL Technology Standards

Description, Implementation, Integration

Deborah Healey, Elizabeth Hanson-Smith, Philip Hubbard,
Sophie Ioannou-Georgiou, Greg Kessler, and Paige Ware

TESOL Teachers of English to Speakers of Other Languages, Inc.

Typeset in ITC Giovanni and Eurostile
by Capitol Communication Systems, Inc., Crofton, Maryland USA
Printed by United Graphics, Inc., Mattoon, Illinois USA
Indexed by Butler Indexing Services, Overland Park, Kansas USA

Teachers of English to Speakers of Other Languages, Inc.
1925 Ballenger Avenue, Suite 550
Alexandria, Virginia 22314 USA
Tel 703-836-0774 • Fax 703-836-6447 • E-mail tesol@tesol.org • http://www.tesol.org/

Technology Standards Task Force Members
    Deborah Healey (chair), *University of Oregon*
    Elizabeth Hanson-Smith, *California State University, Sacramento,* and *Computers for Education*
    Philip Hubbard, *Stanford University*
    Sophie Ioannou-Georgiou, *Cyprus Pedagogical Institute*
    Greg Kessler, *Ohio University*
    Paige Ware, *Southern Methodist University*

Publishing Manager: Carol Edwards
Copy Editor: Terrey Hatcher
Additional Reader: Rebecca Rauff
Cover Design: OmotoArt, Monterey, California

ISBN 9781931185721
Library of Congress Control Number 2011930573

Contents

List of Tables and Figures

Tables

Figures

Acknowledgments

The members of the TESOL Technology Standards Task Force hope that you find this book useful and that you will suggest vignettes based on your own experience to share online and in future volumes. We especially encourage those with an interest in other languages to contribute vignettes that fit their own settings.

Our thanks go to former task force member Volker Hegelheimer, Iowa State University, Ames, Iowa, USA, who was instrumental in work on developing the TESOL Technology Standards and the TESOL Technology Standards Framework Document.

We would also like to give credit to the TESOL Standards Committee, whose work substantively informed the TESOL Technology Standards Framework Document, and to the Book Publications Committee, whose work was instrumental in enabling this book to be published.

TESOL Standards Committee Members
Silvia Laborde, Liaison to the Technology Standards Committee
Supreet Anand   Paul Mahony
Geoffrey Crewes   Richmond Stroupe
Dorit Kaufman   Vilma Tafani
Erin Laverick

TESOL Book Publications Committee Members
Tim Collins   Robyn Brinks Lockwood
John Liontas   Hedy McGarrell
Linda Gerena   Lucie Moussu

Finally, thanks are also due to TESOL staff liaison John Segota, who took care of many logistical details.

TECHNOLOGY STANDARDS AT-A-GLANCE

Technology Standards for Language Learners

GOAL 1

Language learners demonstrate foundational knowledge and skills in technology for a multilingual world.

Standard 1: Language learners demonstrate basic operational skills in using various technology tools and Internet browsers.

Standard 2: Language learners are able to use available input and output devices (e.g., keyboard, mouse, printer, headset, microphone, media player, electronic whiteboard).

Standard 3: Language learners exercise appropriate caution when using online sources and when engaging in electronic communication.

Standard 4: Language learners demonstrate basic competence as users of technology.

GOAL 2

Language learners use technology in socially and culturally appropriate, legal, and ethical ways.

Standard 1: Language learners understand that communication conventions differ across cultures, communities, and contexts.

Standard 2: Language learners demonstrate respect for others in their use of private and public information.

GOAL 3

Language learners effectively use and critically evaluate technology-based tools as aids in the development of their language learning competence as part of formal instruction and for further learning.

Standard 1: Language learners effectively use and evaluate available technology-based productivity tools.

Standard 2: Language learners appropriately use and evaluate available technology-based language skill-building tools.

Standard 3: Language learners appropriately use and evaluate available technology-based tools for communication and collaboration.

Standard 4: Language learners use and evaluate available technology-based research tools appropriately.

Standard 5: Language learners recognize the value of technology to support autonomy, lifelong learning, creativity, metacognition, collaboration, personal pursuits, and productivity.

Technology Standards for Language Teachers

GOAL 1

Language teachers acquire and maintain foundational knowledge and skills in technology for professional purposes.

Standard 1: Language teachers demonstrate knowledge and skills in basic technological concepts and operational competence, meeting or exceeding TESOL technology standards for students in whatever situation in which they teach.

Standard 2: Language teachers demonstrate an understanding of a wide range of technology supports for language learning and options for using them in a given setting.

Standard 3: Language teachers actively strive to expand their skill and knowledge base to evaluate, adopt, and adapt emerging technologies throughout their careers.

Standard 4: Language teachers use technology in socially and culturally appropriate, legal, and ethical ways.

GOAL 2

Language teachers integrate pedagogical knowledge and skills with technology to enhance language teaching and learning.

Standard 1: Language teachers identify and evaluate technological resources and environments for suitability to their teaching context.

Standard 2: Language teachers coherently integrate technology into their pedagogical approaches.

Standard 3: Language teachers design and manage language learning activities and tasks using technology appropriately to meet curricular goals and objectives.

Standard 4: Language teachers use relevant research findings to inform the planning of language learning activities and tasks that involve technology.

GOAL 3

Language teachers apply technology in record keeping, feedback, and assessment.

Standard 1: Language teachers evaluate and implement relevant technology to aid in effective learner assessment.

Standard 2: Language teachers use technological resources to collect and analyze information in order to enhance language instruction and learning.

Standard 3: Language teachers evaluate the effectiveness of specific student uses of technology to enhance teaching and learning.

GOAL 4

Language teachers use technology to improve communication, collaboration, and efficiency.

Standard 1: Language teachers use communication technologies to maintain effective contact and collaboration with peers, students, administration, and other stakeholders.

Standard 2: Language teachers regularly reflect on the intersection of professional practice and technological developments so that they can make informed decisions regarding the use of technology to support language learning and communication.

Standard 3: Language teachers apply technology to improve efficiency in preparing for class, grading, and maintaining records.

PART I
Description

Part 1 introduces the technology standards, including why and how they were developed, the audiences they serve, and why teachers, students, administrators, teacher educators, and researchers should be aware of and use the standards. Also given in this section is a brief overview of the research that informs the standards to guide those who would like to understand why the standards are important for effective language teaching and learning.

Chapter 1

Introduction

This book extends and clarifies the *TESOL Technology Standards Framework Document* (2008). The framework document presented the Technology Standards for Language Learners and the Technology Standards for Language Teachers with the same goals, standards, and performance indicators as in the current document. This book, however, puts the standards into context by providing at least one vignette for each standard, elaborating on relevant research that informed the standards, and adding chapters targeted to teacher educators, administrators, and online teachers. Readers can assess their compliance with the standards by using the checklists for self-assessment and program assessment in Chapter 9.

This book helps students, teachers, teacher educators, administrators, and researchers better understand the technology standards and how they can be applied in the varied contexts in which language instruction occurs. Throughout this book, there has been a deliberate attempt to ensure that the standards and related information are applicable in a wide range of contexts: foreign language, second language, child, teen, adult, higher education, vocational education, language for specific purposes, and fully online programs; and in settings with low, medium, or high resources and access to communication technologies.

Throughout this book we use the phrase *available technology* rather than specifying particular resources. This is done deliberately so that those with little access to technology resources can apply the standards in their contexts, while those with a great deal of access to technology are encouraged to do as much as their resources will allow. The vignettes are often more specific in naming and describing resources because this level of detail helps others to understand the context and pedagogical use of technology more clearly. The vignettes attempt to offer free and open-source technology alternatives where possible, and in some instances they suggest technology for the physically disabled. We encourage teachers and teacher educators to use the vignettes as examples of how to use technology appropriately in language teaching. Although the vignettes tend to focus on English language learning and teaching, the technology standards can be applied to languages other than English.

Defining Technology

We use the term *technology* in this book to refer to systems that rely on computer chips, digital applications, and networks in all their forms. This includes not only desktop and laptop computers but also a wide range of electronic devices such as DVD players, data projectors, and interactive whiteboards. Our use of *technology* also includes computer-driven mobile devices such as cell phones, smart phones, personal digital assistants (PDAs), and MP3 players.

We also make frequent use of the terms *digital*, *electronic*, and *CALL*, or computer-assisted language learning. Although many alternative acronyms have arisen, such as TELL (technology-enhanced language learning) and CALI (computer-assisted language instruction), the acronym CALL has been the most consistently used. It appears in the names of professional associations and special interest groups such as TESOL's CALL Interest Section, APACALL, EuroCALL, PacCALL, JALTCALL, and WorldCALL. As a result, CALL is the term used consistently in this book to refer to the use of computers and digital technologies in language learning.

A glossary and a complete index in Part 4 further assist the reader in understanding the terminology and acronyms used throughout this book.

Organization of This Book

This book is divided into four major parts.

Part 1: Description

Chapter 1 introduces the technology standards and provides an overview of the rest of the book. **Chapter 2** references the second language acquisition and computer-assisted language learning research that informs the standards. This information comes from a rich and diverse research base that includes investigation into the teaching of individual language skills as well as insight into different environmental and delivery methods that have become common in language teaching and learning. Becoming familiar with the research base will help those who would like to understand why the standards are important for effective language teaching and learning.

Part 2: Implementation

Part 2, Implementation, provides the information needed to begin to implement the standards in teaching and learning.

Chapter 3, Technology Standards for Language Learners, includes three overarching goals, each with two to five standards, plus performance indicators that delineate how the standards are applied. Each standard includes at least one vignette to serve as an example of how the standards and indicators are put into classroom practice in a variety of settings.

Chapter 4, Technology Standards for Language Teachers, includes four overarching goals, each with three to five standards, plus performance indicators and at least one vignette for each standard. The goals and standards are not meant to be sequential. Standard 3 is not intended to be more difficult than Standard 2 nor easier than Standard 4, for example. Instead, the standards are intended to be complementary and, at times, overlapping because each focuses on a different goal.

Note: For a quick reference list of the goals, standards, and performance indicators minus the vignettes, see Appendix A.

In **Chapter 5**, the TESOL Technology Standards are compared to two other well-known technology standards documents:

- ISTE NETS: the International Society for Technology in Education's National Educational Technology Standards

- UNESCO ICT-CST: the United Nations Education, Scientific and Cultural Organization's Information and Communication Technologies Competency Standards for Teachers

Although there are many similarities among the three documents, all of which share an interest in technology in education, the TESOL Technology Standards are targeted to an international audience specifically composed of language teachers and learners. There is a clear focus in the TESOL Technology Standards on language pedagogy and learning, rather than solely on technology. Language educators who have used ISTE NETS can take advantage of the concordance to find TESOL Technology Standards that meet the demands of a standards-based curriculum and that are relevant to the more specific context of language teaching and learning.

Part 3: Integration

Part 3 offers guidance for specific categories of readers who are ready to make the technology standards a central part of their institutions, their teacher education and training programs, and their teaching. Separate chapters address teacher educators, administrators, and online teachers, and the section concludes with can-do checklists for self-assessment and program assessment.

Chapter 6, for teacher educators, examines the standards with a focus on implications for teacher preparation programs and in-service teacher training. This overview of the state of teacher preparation provides context for both the teacher and the student standards.

Chapter 7, for administrators, addresses ways to implement the standards across the curriculum in a variety of settings. It suggests global needs, such as ongoing teacher development with technology and appropriate compensation for teachers who serve as de facto or recognized technology experts. The vignettes in this chapter demonstrate how administrators in low-, medium-, and high-resource settings can help teachers meet the goals for the learner and the teacher standards.

Chapter 8 addresses the implications of the standards for fully online teaching and for teaching in a blended/hybrid environment, part face-to-face and part online. The fundamental premise is that good online teaching has the same overall characteristics as good teaching in a face-to-face environment, with a few shifts in focus. After a review of the underpinnings of successful online teaching and learning, the chapter examines the implications of each standard for online learning.

Chapter 9 provides checklists for self-assessment and program assessment for those who are interested in examining their own practice and settings. The self-assessments consist of a series of can-do statements that serve as behavioral objectives, based on the performance indicators in each standard. The program assessment is geared toward administrators and other stakeholders with an interest in ensuring that a program complies with the standards. These rubrics are designed to be aids to meeting the standards rather than absolute prescriptions, given the wide variety of available technology and pedagogical needs demanded by the different users of this book.

Part 4: Supporting Matter

Part 4 consists of a variety of supporting information.

The **Glossary** offers brief explanations for many of the technical terms used in the book, both from language pedagogy and from technology.

Appendix A is intended as a quick reference for the TESOL Technology Standards. It repeats all the goals, standards, and performance indicators for the teacher standards and the learner standards from Chapters 3 and 4, but minus the vignettes.

Appendix B cross-references three sets of language proficiency definitions referenced by the vignettes:

1. TESOL's *Standards for Adult Education ESL Programs* (2003)

2. TESOL's *PreK–12 English Language Proficiency Standards* (2006)

3. Council of Europe's Common European Framework of Reference (CEFR) for languages (2010)

Appendix C lists the vignettes from Chapters 3 and 4 by standard and gives the context, learner profile, and skill/focus area for each vignette, as well as suggesting the types of technology employed. Readers are encouraged to use these vignette tables to find examples of classroom practice in different contexts and using different technologies.

About the Authors and Contributors gives credit where credit is due, recognizing the Technology Standards Task Force that was responsible for the overall content of this volume; the Vignette Team members who edited, organized, selected, and wrote many of the vignettes; and the other individuals who contributed vignettes to this volume.

Finally, the **Index** is designed to help readers search quickly for information relevant to their particular contexts and to find specific topics of interest.

Chapter 2

Theoretical and Research Bases for the Technology Standards

This chapter is revised and expanded from the TESOL Technology Standards Framework Document *(2008). It offers an overview of research that informs the technology standards, as well as suggestions for using the standards in CALL research.*

Research in Computer-Assisted Language Learning (CALL)

The TESOL Technology Standards are informed by and best understood with background knowledge of the theory and research that have emerged in the field of CALL. There is currently no clearly articulated single theory specific to technology use in language teaching that could be used to inform these standards. Numerous scholars believe that the theoretical foundation for this field comes from a multitude of sources. Following Ellis (1999), Chapelle (2003, p. 56) takes the key concept of interaction and discusses three theoretical perspectives: the interaction hypothesis, sociocultural theory, and depth of processing theory. For each perspective, she demonstrates how a computer can help a language learner in some relevant way—by providing enhanced input, help for using language, and opportunities for increased attention to language, respectively. Those looking for a more unified view may find it in Egbert, Hanson-Smith, and Chao (2007). These authors take the position that "the hypothetical theory of CALL sounds not much different from an integrated theory of language acquisition; in fact, it is the same" (p. 1).

Levy and Stockwell (2006) reach a similar conclusion, noting that "with rare exceptions, CALL designers and language teachers are predominantly in the role of consumers as far as theory is concerned. For those in this group who see value in theory (and it must be said not all do), they review, select, and apply theories of language learning produced by others" (p. 139). Kern (2006) links this relationship of consumerism to a general issue in second language acquisition (SLA) theory: Citing Kramsch (2000), he observes, "it is important to bear in mind that SLA is itself informed by a rich variety of theoretical frameworks and has consistently resisted a single overarching theory" (p. 187).

The situation with research in the CALL field is similar. Egbert and Hanson-Smith (2007) attempt to unify the field by organizing their edited volume with results from a broad research base. In that volume, the introduction (Egbert, Hanson-Smith, & Chao, 2007) delves into eight optimal conditions for language learning. However, Levy and Stockwell (2006) identify six research strands with accompanying representative studies reflecting a "mix of approaches, methods, research tools, and procedures" (p. 157). An edited volume devoted specifically to CALL research (Egbert & Petrie, 2005) includes 12 chapters representing a wide variety of research perspectives and providing further evidence of fragmentation that is similar in many respects to divergences in SLA and general learning theory.

In addition to the work above, a strand of recent relevant literature centers specifically on language teacher education in the technology domain. Special issues of *Language Learning and Technology* (2002) and *Innovation in Language Learning and Teaching* (2009), along with edited volumes by Hubbard and Levy (2006b) and Kassen, Lavine, Murphy-Judy, and Peters (2007), focus on this area. Among the themes found in multiple contributions to this literature are the value of project-based learning, the importance of reflective learning, linkages to communities of practice, and development of teacher candidate portfolios (for more details, see Chapter 6 in this volume). Each of these edited volumes also includes a chapter on standards: Murphy-Judy and Youngs (2006) and Oxford with Jung (2007), the latter taking a highly critical view of current implementations.

Despite the large number of theories and research approaches, it is possible to identify three general themes that both support the need for the TESOL Technology Standards and identify necessary content for the standards themselves.

1. Research shows that there are important benefits to be gained from the use of technology in language learning and teaching.

Numerous studies looking at the effect of CALL on language learning support the integration of CALL in language teaching. A recent research synthesis by Grgurović and Chapelle (2007), looking at 200 experimental and quasi-experimental studies between 1970 and 2006, revealed that (a) computer instruction is slightly better than "traditional" instruction even under the most rigorous methodological conditions and that (b) "improvement is detected for CALL groups more often than not" (slide 24). Consequently, it is imperative that teachers be able to make decisions about the role of CALL in their pedagogy. However, only teachers with sufficient knowledge about CALL can make that decision wisely.

There is also evidence indicating important benefits of technology in language learning and teaching. These are found mainly in

1. improved motivation and development of positive attitudes toward learning and the target language (e.g., Meunier, 1997; Pennington, 1996; Warschauer, 1996),

2. improved learning outcomes (e.g., Brandl, 2002), and

3. improved retention rates (e.g., Ioannou-Georgiou & Michaelides, 2001).

Additional applications of CALL that have been studied include access to linguistic and cultural materials, opportunities for communication, provision of feedback, and learner motivation. Zhao's (2003) synthesis outlines efforts in these areas and calls for further research on comprehensive curriculum development, effective use of technology, classroom uses of technology, and empirical studies on how technology is used in schools.

2. Technology should be incorporated into teaching pedagogy so that students will not only effectively acquire a second language but will also develop electronic literacy skills.

Teaching our students language in its traditional media is no longer enough. Traditional literacies, such as reading and writing, are now only a subset of the skills a learner is required to develop in order to function efficiently. Increasingly, in everyday and professional life, people need the skills of electronic literacy, such as accessing, evaluating, and utilizing information (Warschauer, Shetzer, & Meloni, 2000).

Chapelle and Jamieson (2008) argue for an expanded view of English language teaching pedagogy, which now ought to include not only the learner, the English language, and the teacher, but also technology as an integral part. Chapelle and Jamieson articulate three assumptions of language learning on page 3 in the introduction to their book:

1. Guidance in learning a language is necessary.

2. English manifests itself in many varieties.

3. Teachers provide guidance and structure.

They explain that CALL may be able to provide opportunities to complement already-used teaching strategies. Specifically, CALL can foster skills development (reading, writing, listening, speaking), but it can also further language proficiency development by providing learners with the opportunity to practice these skills, which is, as recent research suggests, how language is learned (Lightbown & Spada, 2006).

Integration figures prominently in the current discussion of CALL, in writings by Levy and Stockwell (2006), Bax (2003), and others. Scholars debate certain aspects of the notion of integration and how to achieve it, but with the ubiquity of today's technology, it is difficult to justify not using CALL in language learning. It is, therefore, imperative that English language teachers integrate information and communication technologies (ICT) in the classroom so that students become proficient in communication not only within the traditional media but also within the framework of modern communication technologies (Lee, 2002, inter alia).

The use of technology in English language teaching and learning can also encourage the development of strategies necessary for modern survival: communication, collaboration, and information gathering and retrieval. Preparing students for the information society should be one of the fundamental aims of today's education (European Commission, 2001; Organisation for Economic Co-operation and Development, 2000; U.S. Department of Education, 2000). Ultimately, technologically skilled individuals benefit not only themselves but also their country of residence. Australia, for example, has already recognized the great importance to the country's economy of training individuals to work in an online environment (Australian National Office for the Information Economy, 1998, as cited in Davison, 2005).

Hubbard and Levy (2006a) emphasize the importance of CALL beyond the classroom, such as in the "research and development of a wide range of products including online courses, programs, tutors, and tools" (p. 9) and in the repurposing of off-the-shelf software. The common theme here is that technology is and should be used for language learning purposes.

3. Research shows that technology in learning is not being used to its full potential and that inadequate teacher training and learner training are some of the main reasons for this.

The importance of basing teacher training on standards and the detriment of not meeting the standards are discussed by Oxford with Jung (2007). They note that technology standards already exist for primary and secondary (preK–12) teachers and students in the United States, but indicate that the standards are routinely not being met in settings with English language learners, for reasons that include problems with schools of education, teacher educators, and institutional infrastructures. Oxford and Jung conclude with research-based advice aimed at solving this problem.

There are, therefore, significant benefits to language learning that can be achieved by using new technologies and by enabling students to obtain basic survival skills for the modern society and workplace. How many of these potential benefits are actually brought to the students, however, is questionable. Cuban (2001) gives evidence that computers are underused in today's classrooms. In general education and in language learning alike, Cuban writes, computers are mostly used for teacher preparation, and mainly for word processing. Even where computers are not used as expensive typewriters, and where teachers use them in instruction, traditional teaching techniques prevail. As a result, the technology's potential for developing critical-thinking skills and learner autonomy remains largely unrealized.

Cuban asserts that this is not due to limited access to technology. Rather, he suggests that it might be due to the way teachers use the technology, thus implicating teachers' inadequate training in the area of pedagogical uses of technology. However, teacher training must also include learner training. In other words, teachers who use CALL must be trained to teach learners how to use CALL programs, an issue discussed by Hubbard and Levy (2006a). Foundations for learner training in using technology for language acquisition, especially as it relates to developing learner autonomy, can be found in Barrette (2001), Healey (2007), and Hubbard (2004).

This need for increased training and proficiency in the use of technology is echoed by Kessler (2006), who points out that "teachers need to become more proficient in their understanding of CALL methodology, practices, history, and possibility" (p. 35). Along the same lines, Chapelle and Hegelheimer (2004) argue that "the resources offered by today's technologies for language learners and teachers provide valuable opportunity to rethink and perhaps reinvent what constitutes the knowledge base for L2 teachers" (p. 314).

Thus, with the weight of responsibility falling on the teachers and their work, the existence of the TESOL Technology Standards will play a positive role. The standards can help teachers and teacher preparation programs move forward and guide them in increasing the quality use of new technologies during instruction in ways that realize technology's potential. Further, developing an understanding of the growing body of CALL research will not only inform the interpretation and use of these standards but also contribute to future revisions to the standards.

Research has investigated specific domains within CALL, including telecollaboration, computer-mediated communication (CMC), tutorial CALL, online learning, and resource CALL. Across these domains we can observe pedagogical implications from the research in two ways: as they relate to the learning of language skills and as they relate to the role of the CALL environment. It is important for teachers to be aware of these studies because collectively they emphasize that integrating technology effectively into language classrooms requires more than simply laying knowledge of the technology on top of their basic classroom procedures. The studies cited here provide a foundation for meeting the targets of Teacher Goal 2, Standard 4: *Language teachers use relevant research findings to inform the planning of language learning activities and tasks that involve technology.* Table 2.1 provides a brief overview of some implications from research into individual language skills.

Research has also been conducted regarding the nature of various CALL task types and environments. Many of these studies provide guidance for ways in which teachers can use general and language learning software within specific contexts and language tasks. Some of the trends from this research are presented in Table 2.2.

Research in CALL has followed methodological trends in the broader area of second language acquisition (SLA). Survey results have been used often, typically to identify perceptions or attitudes toward some element of CALL. Comparative studies have been conducted in order to compare the integration of CALL into a curriculum with traditional teaching methods. Observational studies based upon language transcription have been conducted in order to analyze linguistic functions that may provide insight into SLA within CALL contexts. Some have recognized the limitations

Table 2.1. Trends in Research Into Individual Language Skills

Source	Implications From Research Into *Writing*
Bloch (2008)	The public nature of online writing provides motivation and accountability.
Selfe & Hawisher (2004)	Multiple literacies must be considered.
Ware & Warschauer (2006)	Automated Writing Evaluation (AWE) tools promote formulaic writing.
Chambers (2005)	Writing can be corpus-driven.
Liang (2010)	Collaborative technologies can support peer response groups.
Payne & Whitney (2002)	Extensive CMC writing can also enhance speaking fluency.
Source	**Implications From Research Into *Reading***
Chun (2006)	Availability of electronic texts allows for greater appropriateness of level and topic.
Cobb (2007)	Level and frequency of vocabulary can be adjusted for optimal learner retention.
Cobb (2007), Huang & Liou (2007)	Corpora can be used to enhance reading skills and vocabulary contextualization.
Source	**Implications From Research Into *Speaking***
Celce-Murcia, Brinton, & Goodwin (1996); Hincks & Edlund (2009)	Visual feedback can benefit speaking volume, rate, fluency, and pitch.
Tanner & Landon (2009)	Guided pronunciation readings can reduce errors related to pausing, stress, intonation, and overall comprehensibility.
Borras & Lafayette (1994)	Using subtitles can benefit oral proficiencies.
Source	**Implications From Research Into *Listening***
Grgurović & Hegelheimer (2007)	Subtitles and transcripts can support developing listening skills.
Verdugo & Belmonte (2007)	Digital stories can improve listening abilities.
Zhao (1997)	Learners benefit from control over speech rate.
Source	**Implications From Research Into *Form***
Hinkel & Fotos (2002)	Grammar can be learned through focus on form, acts of interaction, or samples of discourse.
Chapelle & Jamieson (2008)	Grammar material must be selected carefully, considering difficulty, requirements for production, and degree of instructional explicitness.
Pérez-Llantada (2009)	Grammar instruction can be corpus-based.
Kessler (2009)	Attention to form is increased during peer review.
Sauro (2009)	Varied forms of corrective feedback are valuable.

Table 2.2. Trends in Research Into CALL Environments

Source	Implications for *Synchronous Communication*
Smith (2003)	Text-based synchronous communication resembles speech.
Fiori (2005)	Synchronous communication with training helps develop grammatical competence.
Source	**Implications for *Asynchronous Communication***
Warschauer & Healey (1998)	Asynchronous communication allows for greater reflection.
Abrams (2006)	Asynchronous tasks benefit from varying degrees of teacher intervention.
Source	**Implications for *Hybrid/Online Language Learning***
Belz (2003), Warschauer & Kern (2000), Ware (2005)	Telecollaborative projects benefit from cultural orientation.
O'Dowd (2006)	Telecollaborative projects offer opportunities to increase intercultural communicative competence.
O'Dowd & Ware (2009)	Telecollaborative projects require careful group and task construction.
Compton (2009)	Online projects require unique teacher preparation.
González (2008)	CALL provides opportunities for exposure to authentic language.
Levy & Stockwell (2006)	CALL provides opportunities for extensive practice.
Source	**Implications for *Language Labs***
Kolaitis, Mahoney, Pomann, & Hubbard (2006); Winke & Goertler (2008)	Learner training is important for any environment.

of relying solely upon the textual output of a task and enhanced these practices with keystroke capturing (Fischer, 2007), student use of help menus (Grgurović & Hegelheimer, 2007), and screen capturing (Smith, 2003). Most recently, research has expanded into cognitive and perceptual observation. These emerging studies rely on psycholinguistic-based practices and data such as MRI data and heat maps produced by eye-tracking technology (Smith, 2010).

Conclusion

As we can see, CALL research and theory are informed by a diversity of academic investigation. We understand that technology has been identified as a beneficial component in language teaching and learning when properly incorporated into teaching pedagogy. This understanding recognizes that teachers require preparation to identify and integrate technology in their teaching pedagogy. We have learned that technology can be harnessed to strengthen language learning strategies, cultural knowledge, and individual language skills. This chapter highlights specific language-skill-related findings within the field of CALL. We have also learned how the integration of technology varies across different domains, task types, and environments. This variety of integration must be recognized for teachers to effectively address the technology standards. Finally, we understand the changes in methodological approaches within CALL. These can influence teachers' perspective on the research and contribute to their own reflective practices, including action research. This overview of theoretical and research bases that have informed CALL is intended to serve as support for integration of the TESOL Technology Standards. This review is not intended to be a comprehensive evaluation of CALL research. Readers who are interested in further exploration of CALL research would benefit from consulting the following resources.

Resources

Hubbard, P. (2005). *Survey of unanswered questions site*. Retrieved from http://www.stanford.edu/~efs/callsurvey/

Ohlrogge, A. & Lee, H. (2008) *Research on CALL and distance learning: A briefly annotated bibliography*. Retrieved from http://www.calico.org/DistanceEdBiblio.pdf

Siskin, C. B. (2005). *Selected bibliography for CALL*. Retrieved from http://www.edvista.com/claire/callbib.html

PART 2
Implementation

Part 2 provides the information needed to begin to implement the technology standards in teaching and learning. This section includes the goals and standards themselves, along with performance indicators and vignettes that provide examples of how others have implemented the standards. This section also includes a comparison between the TESOL Technology Standards and two other well-known technology-related standards: the National Educational Technology Standards (NETS) from the International Society for Technology in Education (ISTE) and the Information and Communication Technologies Competency Standards for Teachers (ICT-CST) from the United Nations Education, Scientific, and Cultural Organization (UNESCO).

Chapter 3

Technology Standards for Language Learners

This chapter contains three overarching goals and a total of 11 standards. Performance indicators and at least one vignette are included for each standard. The performance indicators and the vignettes pertain to a range of settings, English proficiency levels, and learner ages.

The Technology Standards for Language Learners consist of three overarching goals, each with two to five standards. The goals and standards are not listed hierarchically; each standard is independently important. The standards are not meant to be sequential. Standard 3 is not intended to be more difficult than Standard 2 or easier than Standard 4, for example.

Each standard includes four to six performance indicators that pertain to a range of settings—including high-access or low-resource; English as a second language (ESL) or English as a foreign language (EFL); face-to-face, hybrid, or fully online; child or adult; and general English or English for specific purposes (ESP), including academic English. Some performance indicators specify a particular setting, such as young learners or fully online.

For the examples that appear within the performance indicators, an effort has been made to avoid the use of technical language and the brand names of hardware and software. Using generic references throughout takes into account the rapidly changing nature of technology and enables this book to remain current.

The vignettes included with each standard are designed to put a human face on the standards, demonstrating how they are applied in real contexts. Each vignette includes examples of how the standard is applied in low-resource, low-access; medium-resource, medium-access; and high-resource, high-access settings. Across the standards, the vignettes cover a range of English proficiency levels and learner ages (children, teenagers, adults), as well as varied settings (including EFL, ESL, intensive English programs [IEPs], adult workplace English, academic and professional ESP, one-computer classroom, class-lab, and fully online). To be as immediately useful as possible, the vignettes include examples of current technology applications and websites, as well as reference to recent articles on the pedagogies involved.

Despite the specific contexts of the vignettes, the concepts and practices they illustrate can be applied over a much wider set of classroom and laboratory contexts. Readers are encouraged to envision how the technologies and activities illustrated in particular vignettes can apply in their own settings.

Each vignette is labeled with the following information:

Learner profile: Type of learner (adult, teen, young learner), age range in years, and language proficiency level (see Appendix B for level descriptors).

Context: Context in which the vignette is placed includes EFL/ESL/IEP designation, commercial school, blended, or all online.

Focus: Language skills practiced, approach, and the most important CALL tools used.

The vignettes provide examples and inspiration for teachers, teacher educators, and administrators who would like to do more with technology in language teaching and learning.

For handy reference, Appendix C contains tables listing the vignettes by goal and standard, along with their language focus and the technology used.

We encourage those who are working with technology in various contexts to continue to contribute their own vignettes to help expand the knowledge base available to educators. Follow the vignettes provided in this book as a template for organizing your vignette. Vignettes can be emailed to Deborah Healey, dhealey@uoregon.edu, for inclusion in an online repository.

Vignettes for Technology Standards for Language Learners

Goal 1: Language learners demonstrate foundational knowledge and skills in technology for a multilingual world.

Standard 1: Language learners demonstrate basic operational skills in using various technology tools and Internet browsers.

Performance indicators

- Language learners can perform basic functions on digital devices present in their learning environment: desktop computers, mobile/laptop computers, electronic whiteboards, mobile phones, MP3/video players (e.g., turning the device on and off; opening, closing, and resizing software windows; saving, editing, and organizing files and folders; copying, cutting, and pasting elements within a document; recognizing file types; launching and exiting software applications; and similar universal tasks).

- Language learners can perform basic browser functions (e.g., recognize hyperlinks, navigate forward and back, type in an address, use bookmarks, recognize the format of a URL [universal resource locator]).

- Language learners can recognize the format of an email address.

- Language learners can restart the digital device.

- Language learners recognize when they are and are not online.

- Language learners can use accessibility options as needed (e.g., zoom for visually impaired students, TDD, or telecommunications device for the deaf, Braille keyboard).

Each One Teach One
Learner Goal 1 Standard 1 Vignette

Learner profile: Teenagers, ages 13–18, Emerging/High Intermediate (Level 2, A2)

Context: Introduction of technology in an EFL secondary school

Focus: Students receiving their first computer lessons practice writing while learning basic computer operations through the "each one teach one" approach.

Background

EFL teenage students in a developing country's English-medium school have received their first computer access. They will be introduced to the computer in an "each one teach one" format, while the teacher and more experienced students become the coaches on the side. Before the lesson starts, the teacher has prepared a paper template of the computer keyboard (or an overhead transparency or slide, where a computer projector is available) with the basic function keys highlighted: e.g., Power switch, Ctrl (the Control key, or the Command key for Apple computers), Enter (Return), Backspace, Delete (sometimes Del), Shift. The teacher reviews these commands before students approach the computer, making sure they know the names in both English and their native language. The teacher has also prepared a "cheat sheet" with common software shortcuts (e.g., Ctrl-S for saving a file, Ctrl-C to copy, Ctrl-V to paste, etc.) for the word-processing or other software to be used. One sheet will be kept next to each computer. After basic commands are mastered, brightly colored posters with information about commands for specific software are hung around the room. These are created by the students themselves and are bilingual to assist in rapid access.

Using the paper template, the teacher takes two students to the computer, walking them through the basic commands, including opening and saving a word-processed file. The first student then sits at the keyboard and performs all the functions with oral directions (as needed) from the teacher, who does not touch the keyboard after the initial demonstration. Using the paper template allows the student to work at his/her level of comfort and prevents the teacher from inadvertently instilling computer phobia by preempting the initial exploratory movements. The initial essay prompt is to write three sentences in English describing the other student in the pair. This gives the student the opportunity to explore the QWERTY keyboard. The first student then stands behind the other student, who performs all the functions with the first student coaching as needed. Again, the first student must give only oral directions, using the template if necessary. Directions may be given in English or in the native language, depending on the level of the students, but the teacher uses English and encourages the students to coach in English while they are performing at the keyboard. Each student saves the electronic file to a folder created by the teacher on the computer. This folder will be the basis of the student's electronic portfolio.

During subsequent lessons, students will watch the teacher start the computer, and then log in to their own account (if appropriate), open a word processor or other software used in class, write a short essay or perform exercises as required, save a file to the appropriate folder, and exit the program. Students will be coached by each other in pairs, both orally and using the template, but the student coach will not take the keyboard away from the seated student. The teacher is consulted only when a problem arises, thus providing the teacher much-needed time to give attention to other students in the class who are working on other lessons. Students have multiple opportunities to observe computer operation before undertaking it themselves and have hands-on access with help for troubleshooting. Thus, they can overcome any computer phobia and can begin the process of mastery in a safe learning environment. After all students have used the computer, the teacher presents a short written or oral quiz, asking about the uses of the different function keys. A similar approach may be used each time a new program is introduced, including use of an Internet browser and email program. (For more on getting students started with the Internet, see Gaer, 2007.)

Technology Tasks

Low-resource, low-access setting

With one computer in the classroom, no Internet access, and no computer projector, students work in rotating pairs at the keyboard with the paper template in the "each one teach one" format described above. Once these two students seem comfortable, the first student returns to the class, and the second now becomes the coach to two new students, one seated at the computer and the other watching, as described above, and so on until the entire class has had a chance to use the computer and coach another student. The teacher creates a paper quiz on keyboard and computer functions. Students in pairs or triads access the classroom computer regularly to create drawings, write short papers, or engage in grammar exercises or games, which the teacher loads with a portable memory stick or creates at the computer with Hot Potatoes (Half-Baked Software, 2010, http://hotpot.uvic.ca) or a similar program.

Medium-resource, medium-access setting

With an overhead or computer projector, and one computer with Internet access for every three or four students, the teacher will introduce the basic activities of logging on, opening an application, typing, and so on, using an overhead projector (OHP) transparency, slideshow, or screencast video to highlight the most important keys and functions. Students will then move to the computers and use the "each one teach one" approach to perform the initial assignments. The teacher creates a short online quiz that students can take when they feel ready. The teacher then has students use their new computer literacy skills while performing a WebQuest (see Dodge, 2007, for existing quests) in which students follow links to specific locations.

When students are confident in typing links, following a trail of links, and using and creating bookmarks for their finds, they will be introduced to the local email application. They will review the sites they have found and compose email to each other, sending copies to the teacher, describing in brief the sites they have found.

High-resource, high-access setting

With a set of laptops or a computer lab and a projector, the teacher introduces the whole class to the basic function keys with a slideshow or screencast video (or an electronic whiteboard), highlighting the most important keys and functions within the word processor or other software program. The teacher then takes the students to the computer stations, where they follow the teacher from station to station. After viewing the activity at two or three stations, many students are able to continue on their own computer stations, where they work in pairs using the "each one teach one" approach to complete the assignments as above. The teacher creates a short online quiz that students can take when they feel ready. Students practice their new computer skills as above, using individual laptops to perform parts of tasks, and reporting back as a team.

See also: Learner Goal 1 Standard 3: Internet Safety for Children

Learner profile: Adults, ages 17+, Starting–Emerging/Low–High Intermediate (Level 1–2, A1–A2)

Context: ESL adult immigrant school in the U.S. where technology is available in or out of school

Focus: Students improve their reading–writing literacy in English while learning basic computer and word processor operations and practicing listening–speaking skills.

Background

In an adult education English language literacy context in North America, students often have access to computers and the Internet and can improve their English literacy skills while learning basic computer operations. Prior to any instruction in this area, the teacher assesses students' fundamental knowledge about computers. Students have a range from nonliterate in their native language to some functional literacy in English, and some have moderate visual disabilities, so computer skills can be evaluated in a variety of verbal or nonverbal ways such as a self-assessment, functional quiz, or observational activity. In the example below, 20 adult immigrant students representing five different languages are functionally literate in their native language and are enrolled as beginning English language students in conjunction with a life skills/study skills course.

Students first watch the teacher perform basic operating functions while the teacher speaks the commands out loud. These include turning the computer on and off, opening the word processor and typing in a new document, cutting and pasting, and saving a file. The teacher also shows how to use keyboard shortcuts to change font size for better readability (especially important for visually impaired students). Each student has a handout of the commands for a visual reference. Next, student volunteers read the commands on the list and watch the teacher perform the functions. Finally, students come up in pairs and perform the functions on the class computer as the teacher calls them out. Students are allowed time to discuss with one another before responding. In the final phase, students volunteer in pairs, alternating between the role of the one who gives the command and the one who performs the task in front of the class. For the visually impaired, the school has provided software (e.g., a text-to-speech reader, such as ReadPlease [ReadPlease Corporation, 1999–2005], and a speech-to-text writer, such as Dragon NaturallySpeaking [Nuance Communications, 2010]). By the end of the class session, students are thoroughly familiar with the commands orally, in writing, and as icons on the desktop and within the program. (For more help with tutorials for adult students, see Tips for Using Technology [Hopelink Education, 2009]; http://www.eastsideliteracy.org /tutorsupport/Tech/TechTips.htm.)

In subsequent lessons, the students watch video clips of people describing how to perform basic computer operations, including how to use a presentation program. Video tutorials may be found at many sites online, for example, at Microsoft 2007 Office Tutorials (Microsoft, 2007, http://www.officetutorials.com/). The teacher can also make her own tutorials at home using free screencast software. The teacher ensures that the tutorials include specific descriptions that will help the visually impaired students, who will also use a screen magnifier purchased by the school. The teacher has loaded these clips from a portable memory device if the Internet is not available in class and is careful to check for download permission first. In groups or pairs, students choose up to six new commands to peer-teach through video clips or graphics (e.g., from clip art or created with a drawing program) that show how the word processor or presentation software works. They use the teacher's or their own phone video camera, a video camcorder, or a class digital camera, if available, to record video of each other at the computer. They can also create videos with screencast software. The teacher demonstrates how to embed the art and video clips in their presentations. Then the teacher helps, or has more technologically experienced students help, each group complete a three-slide presentation demonstrating a basic computing function command illustrated with clip art, a picture drawn with the computer's graphics program, or a short video clip. The video demonstrations they create are archived for students in other classes to use as examples.

Technology Tasks

Low-resource, low-access setting

In a classroom with one computer and a data projector, students practice the computer and word processor commands as described above, watching the teacher perform them with the computer and projector. They later take turns in small groups or pairs using the classroom computer for creating their own art- or video-enhanced presentations. While the teacher helps students at the workstation, the other students work on other assignments. When the presentations are complete, the student groups present them to each other, using the class computer and projector with the teacher's help.

Medium-resource, medium-access setting

In a computer lab with no Internet connection, students follow the teacher's modeling of the functions and vocabulary as discussed above. After the teacher demonstration, students work in pairs at the computers, giving and carrying out commands for 10 more minutes while the teacher circulates around the class listening in on their activity. After every student has had a chance to type a few words and save a file in the word processor, the teacher provides a second demonstration related to the basic functions of presentation software, as described above. Each pair of students then creates and saves a three-slide presentation, as described above. Students walk around the class, and each pair demonstrates its show in turn.

High-resource, high-access setting

With Internet access for each student in a classroom lab and a video camera, students benefit from the teacher's modeling and guiding as above, with the addition of lessons on opening and closing the browser, getting online, using URLs, web safety, and so on. The teacher helps visually impaired students find and open a web page reader (e.g., BrowseAloud [TextHelp Systems, 2010], http://www.browsealoud.com /page.asp) and downloads it to one of the workstations for their use. After achieving familiarity with the basic operating functions and associated oral commands, students proceed with word-processing and presentation software, creating their demonstrations, as they work in pairs at the computers over several lab sessions. They use art found on the web or clip art on their computers. They may also go to other tutorial sites to study more advanced uses of software and web tools. They present their work, either through the computer projector or as a gallery walk, as described in the other settings above.

See also: Learner Goal 1 Standard 1: Each One Teach One

Standard 2: Language learners are able to use available input and output devices (e.g., keyboard, mouse, printer, headset, microphone, media player, electronic whiteboard)

Performance indicators

- Language learners demonstrate understanding of the layout of a standard English keyboard.

- Language learners can change the keyboard layout between different languages as needed.

- Language learners demonstrate understanding of where available media, devices, and other peripherals go (e.g., CDs or DVDs go into slots or CD/ DVD drives, portable memory devices go into universal serial bus (USB) ports, cables connect only where they fit and work).

- Language learners can operate available peripherals (e.g., printers and scanners) at a basic level.

- Language learners can operate relevant classroom technologies (e.g., data projectors, electronic whiteboards) and personal technologies (PDAs, mobile phones, MP3/video players) at a basic level.

Learner profile: Teenagers, ages 13–18, Developing–Expanding/Low–High Advanced (Level 3–4, B1–B2)

Context: Blended instruction, ESL

Focus: Students become familiar with basic hardware operations while practicing oral skills in a prepared speech involving note taking, writing, and speaking.

Background

In an ESL class with 12 students representing four languages, students prepare a 5- to 7-minute speech about their favorite native-language song. Before the assignment is begun, the instructor gives a class demonstration on multimedia setup (e.g., how to connect devices by cable or wireless to their computer; how to embed a recording in their presentation as needed) and a short speech on a favorite song to provide an example. The teacher points out how to reference sources and reminds students about appropriate citations.

To activate native-language schemata and promote fluency, the instructor asks that students include a summary of the lyrics, why they enjoy the song, and information on the artist. Students will then prepare speeches in English that include this information. They may use notes in English to help their oral performances. The other students take notes and ask questions after each presentation. Students use a variety of media and hardware, and they practice how to connect different devices with cables or wireless, how to open and close media players, how to run security software, and how to use the computer projector, if available. (For more on using music to teach language, see Beasley and Chuang, 2008.)

Technology Tasks

Low-resource, low-access setting

In a classroom with one computer and one set of speakers, students are assigned their presentations as homework. The teacher asks that each student bring a copy of the song via a CD/DVD, MP3 player, or portable memory device. During a student's assigned turn, he or she will come to the front of the class, load the chosen media (with teacher assistance, if needed), and open the song with the proper media software. Once the speech is finished, the student will be expected to properly close running software and remove the media hardware.

Medium-resource, medium-access setting

In a computer lab with no Internet connection, the instructor assigns students the presentation as homework. The students are to discuss why they enjoy the song and provide photos or video clips that illustrate their feelings or ideas about the music.

They download the media at an Internet café or from their mobile phones. Students then prepare the summary and biography using presentation software. Each slide will include a short text description or comment. If equipment is available, students may add a short clip from the song via their recorder or MP3 player, with proper attribution. With teacher assistance, as needed, students use the scanner to copy photos and mobile devices to upload clips (e.g., with cables or wireless) as they work in the lab. More experienced students help those who are just beginning to use the media devices and software. Students are required, prior to speaking, to set up their song for play at the end of the speech and to load their presentation, which has been saved to the computer. Four students will be selected to give speeches at computer stations in the four corners of the room, with the remaining students listening to each speech via a gallery walk from computer station to computer station in small groups. Students cycle through turns until everyone has spoken.

High-resource, high-access setting

In a classroom lab with computers for all students, Internet access, and computer projector, students have been assigned to create an online blog (web + log) that will include media (linked or uploaded from a digital camera, scanner, or mobile device) that presents their interpretation of a favorite song; students are also asked to link their summary and biography to the song or lyrics online. Before the oral presentation, students are asked to post questions or comments on the blogs of three classmates. The teacher assists them with the media, browser, and blog operation, as needed. In class, students show their blog via the computer projector (or in a gallery walk as in the previous section) and explain why they chose particular images or media. After giving their speech and playing their selected song, students answer any remaining questions that have not been posted and answered on their blogs.

See also: Learner Goal 2 Standard 2: Peer Biographies

Based on a concept submitted by Jeff Kuhn.

Standard 3: Language learners exercise appropriate caution when using online sources and when engaging in electronic communication.

Performance indicators

- Language learners are cautious when opening attachments and clicking on links in email messages.

- Language learners have security software running on their own computers and other devices and keep it current (e.g., antivirus and firewall software).

- Underage students do not provide personal contact information except as directed by the teacher; adult students exercise caution.

- Language learners exercise caution in computer-mediated communication (CMC) (e.g., log out/off when leaving an email account or a public computer; protect personal information).

- Language learners demonstrate their understanding of the fact that placing any information or content online can become part of a permanent record.

- Language learners identify examples of false and potentially malicious information that exists online.

Internet Safety for Children
Learner Goal 1 Standard 3 Vignette

Learner profile: Young learners, ages 9–12, Emerging–Developing/High Intermediate–Low Advanced (Level 2–3, A2–B1)

Context: ESL classroom and/or lab with Internet access

Focus: Young learners expand their use of oral and written language through international projects while learning about basic safety issues on the Internet.

Background

Just as they do with real-life dangers, students learn to assess the risks of accessing Internet sites. They learn to evaluate statements made online, whether people are who they say they are when engaging in online communications, and how much information about themselves they should give. The language teacher gradually introduces Internet security management so that young learners will eventually be able to make appropriate decisions when they are at home or using the web in some other unsupervised location. Lessons begin with highly managed access to the Internet: The teacher creates a set of bookmarks that students are allowed to use. Computers are arranged in the class or lab so that the monitors are visible to the teacher or lab assistant, and student activity can be easily viewed. Young learners are given cartoons showing various situations in which they must determine the real and the false, e.g., the Big Bad Wolf pretending to be Grandmother. The teacher leads a discussion in which students brainstorm safety rules based on typical childhood warnings such as "Don't talk to strangers" and discuss "What if . . ." situations (e.g., "What if someone online asks for your telephone number?" or "Do people always tell their real name and age on the web?").

These lessons are reviewed whenever students are going to explore the web. The teacher reminds students not to click on ads or commercials. The teacher and students brainstorm rules for safe web use and create colorful posters (these may be bilingual for ease of access) to remind themselves to be cautious. Students are taught to ask for adult assistance whenever a site requests a password or personal information, and parents are given information packets in their home language about Internet safety to use at home. The teacher uses the brochure and posters from the Council of Europe explaining children's rights (Council of Europe, 2010a) and has students use an online safety game on the Internet, such as Through the Wild Web Woods (Council of Europe, 2009, in 14 languages; http://www.wildwebwoods.org).

Whether in a classroom or lab, the computers are placed where the teacher can easily see the monitors, and pairs or triads of students work as a team to perform a WebQuest (a guided search through Internet sites; Dodge, 2007) about Internet safety for children. (For sample links, see Internet Safety: Using Our Seat Belt Online [Najarian, n.d.], http://questgarden.com/81/47/9/090502174626/.) Students take notes or print out their findings, if possible, to use in writing their reports. The teacher helps students understand bookmarks and helps them develop an organization for bookmarking the sites that the team finds.

As students become Internet savvy, the teacher will assign them work on an international collaborative project (both email and web-based) at a safe site, such as iEARN (2011, http://www.iearn.org) or GLOBE (UCAR Community Programs, 2010, http://www.globe.gov; the teacher must attend a GLOBE workshop beforehand). The teacher assists students in logging on and in using resources at the main site, demonstrating these processes with a computer projector (where available) to the whole class before students access their computers in pairs or triads to upload materials. The teacher trains students to help each other with site access, as needed, and reminds them not to give out passwords or personal information while browsing. Students are instructed to seek adult assistance whenever a site demands a password or personal information. The teacher assists students in logging off the computers completely so that their data remains safe. Students evaluate their team's work at the end of each activity. (For a description of the GLOBE program, see Kennedy, 2006.)

Technology Tasks

Low-resource, low-access setting
With one computer, Internet access, and, if possible, a printer in the classroom, pairs or triads of students take turns performing the WebQuest, taking notes on paper (or printing out their findings, if possible) to use in writing their reports. At the beginning of the rotated computer use, the teacher reminds students of safety precautions. When the WebQuest tasks are completed, students change places with another pair or triad and begin writing their reports at their seats. The teacher monitors the screen occasionally as students work. Students join an international group project as a whole class, with teams performing various parts of their joint task.

Medium-resource, medium-access setting
With a computer projector and several students sharing multiple computers in the classroom or a lab, students are led through the discussions and web search activities previously described, alternating access to the computers in teams with individual work on paper for their projects.

High-resource, high-access setting
With an interactive whiteboard (or computer and projector) in the classroom and a fully equipped lab with Internet connections, teachers prepare students for access to the projects previously described by leading safety discussions and demonstrating the site access in the classroom before students proceed to the lab. During lab time, students work in pairs or individually, with the teacher monitoring their computer screens. Students take notes in the target language using a word-processing program and/or print their findings to use in writing their reports.

See also: Learner Goal 1 Standard 1: Each One Teach One;
Learner Goal 1 Standard 4: Basic Troubleshooting and Safety

Standard 4: Language learners demonstrate basic competence as users of technology.

Performance indicators

- Language learners can perform basic troubleshooting operations (e.g., check for power, see if the monitor is turned off, restart safely, check the volume on media).

- Language learners can search for a file.

- Language learners can access a help menu, where available.

- Language learners ask for technical help when appropriate.

- Underage students call an adult when they have found offensive or inappropriate material, turning off the monitor if on a computer; adult students realize that they may need to turn off the computer to exit some websites.

Learner profile:	Adults, ages 18+, Developing–Expanding/Low–High Advanced (Level 3–4, B1–B2)
Context:	Hybrid/blended face-to-face instruction, supported by web-conferencing instruction via phone or computer, and individual practice online.
Focus:	Mid-level restaurant workers at a fast-food chain learn workplace ESL targeted to their future employment and promotion.

Background

Management shift employees who work in a fast-food chain attend classes from their place of employment. Innovative multiple-site design allows them to take classes during their regular shift and count them as part of their work hours, which allows them to conveniently access the class and maintain work and personal commitments. The work-based curriculum focuses on critical-thinking skills and problem-solving tasks. Adult students participate in monthly face-to-face training sessions at their work site, where they are first introduced to and then review ways to operate computers, especially log-ins, passwords, and keyboarding skills. Students are taught basic troubleshooting, such as checking for appropriate volume with keyboard controls and accessing the help menu. Students use a typing program on CD for further practice and complete communicative homework assignments, including typical workplace ESL tasks such as answering the phone, taking messages, and asking for clarification. Students practice dialogues using transcripts of typical workplace conversations, and they read and discuss passages from the employee manual. The teacher helps them create individual folders where they can store files recording their progress in writing and speaking. The teacher also helps them understand the differences between the various file types that they are saving into the folders that constitute their portfolios. (For further descriptions of restaurant programs, see Jaschik, 2009, and Migration Policy Institute, 2010.)

Technology Tasks

Low-resource, low-access setting

With computer access available at their workplace and a tape recording device or mobile phone, students complete the activities just described and create a portfolio including speaking and writing tasks. For example, they might create files of tape recordings or mobile phone recordings of typical workplace dialogues or answer a phone call from the instructor and write down the message, which they then type and save as a file.

Medium-resource, medium-access setting

With relatively easy access to the Internet at home or at work, students complete online homework assignments posted at a class wiki or blog. These include listening and short-phrase writing tasks based on weekly lessons targeted to the workplace setting. Students are taught to access websites with care, to protect their personal passwords, and to avoid sites that may have deceptive advertising or spamming potential. Students understand that they may have to shut down their computer to escape from some sites.

High-resource, high-access setting

With high bandwidth Internet access, students engage in videoconferencing on the web, with one to three ESL learners participating from each restaurant. The instructor leads class and paired activities during web conferencing, including short dialogues for oral practice, and discussion of short readings taken from the employee manual. Students engage in pronunciation practice with tape or mobile technology as described previously.

See also: Learner Goal 1 Standard 1: Computer Basics

Based on a concept submitted by Ingrid Greenberg.

Learner profile: Teenagers, ages 13–18, Emerging–Developing/High Intermediate–Low Advanced (Level 2–3, A2–B1)

Context: EFL blended classroom/lab with Internet access

Focus: Young learners practice computer safety and understand netiquette while taking part in an international collaborative project that will help them practice reading and writing skills.

Background

Teenagers in an EFL setting are practicing computer skills and learning about safe ways to use the Internet to prepare for a collaborative project at an international educational site, such as iEARN (2011, http://www.iearn.org). While students are already somewhat familiar with computer hardware, they are learning how to do some basic troubleshooting and how to problem-solve with easily accessible tools, such as the computer's Help menu. They also are learning about Internet etiquette (netiquette) and ways to be responsible online while preserving their own privacy.

Using large paper templates of the computer keyboard and monitor provided by the teacher, students locate the power key of their monitor and of the computer processor itself (in newer machines these may be the same), as well as the function keys to change monitor brightness and sound level. They take turns demonstrating, for example, how to find a file on their computer using the appropriate pull-down menu or shortcut key (Control-F or Command-F) and how to move it to a different folder. They point out the Help function in the menu bar. These templates are then posted on a wall for future reference.

In a separate lesson, students explore the Help menu on their own computers with the aid of a teacher-made set of questions, such as "What do I do if the computer freezes?" (search "frozen" in advance to prepare for such a situation) or "How do I log into/out of my computer?" (search "user information"). In a whole-class session, students discuss when such functions will be needed and what kinds of vocabulary they might use for alternate searches. Where the Internet is immediately available, students demonstrate their knowledge of similar functions on the web, e.g., logging into a password-protected site, shutting down the browser, searching the Help menu of their browser. Students also discuss Internet privacy, how to avoid the temptation of flashing ads, and when not to click on a promising, but dubious, commercial.

Students discuss netiquette, the rules of polite, respectful communication across international boundaries (see Netiquette for Kids [Boston Public Library, n.d.], http://www.bpl.org/kids/netiquette.htm), and they create a list of important features of netiquette for themselves. They take a netiquette quiz based on their discussion. Students also play a game at Internet Safety for Teenagers (Verschoor, 2010; http://

jenverschoor.wordpress.com/2010/07/29/internet-safety-for-teenagers-through-games/), which raises their awareness of safety and privacy issues. Students learn to turn off the computer if they cannot get rid of offensive distracters.

Students are now ready to join an international collaboration. They use what they have learned to log into the collaborative site, transfer information files to their partner school, and communicate respectfully with partner students in other countries. The teacher helps them decide on a project that they can share with another class at the same or similar language level. Students create a personal or (with the help of the teacher) group log-in identity on the class computer and give the log-in information to the teacher for safekeeping. The teacher reminds students to use what they have learned about safety when they are web surfing at home or on a public computer and to remember to use the rules of netiquette as they participate in the international project. (For more on tasks for collaborative learning, see Hanson-Smith, 2007.)

Technology Tasks

Low-resource, low-access setting

With one computer in the classroom and limited Internet access, the students take turns using the computer in small groups and assist each other in finding the appropriate function keys and performing the searches required, referring to the paper templates as needed. Students play the Internet Safety for Teenagers game in small groups.

Medium-resource, medium-access setting, and high-resource, high-access setting

With several computers (either in the classroom or with lab time), a computer projector (or electronic whiteboard), and Internet access, the teacher will demonstrate the various function keys and help students prepare posters for reference. Students then take turns demonstrating their knowledge of the function keys, procedures for logging in and out, finding help files, etc., in the safety of their school or classroom before joining the international online collaboration. Students are asked to find out more information about netiquette by searching the web, and they take an online quiz.

See also: Learner Goal 1 Standard 1: Each One Teach One;
Learner Goal 1 Standard 3: Internet Safety for Children

Goal 2: Language learners use technology in socially and culturally appropriate, legal, and ethical ways.

Standard 1: Language learners understand that communication conventions differ across cultures, communities, and contexts.

Performance indicators

- Language learners identify similarities and differences in local and global communication.

- Language learners demonstrate understanding of multiple ways that computer-mediated communication (CMC) can be (mis)interpreted (e.g., using appropriate register, turn-taking, respecting expected length and content of messages, considering literal versus rhetorical meaning).

- Language learners show sensitivity to their use of communication conventions, according to the context (e.g., not using all caps [capital letters], waiting for lag time in synchronous communication, using turn-taking cues, checking spelling).

- Language learners conform to current social conventions when using technology in communication (e.g., social conventions in the classroom may restrict cell phone use).

- Language learners can identify cultural variables at play in interpreting and responding to a message.

Learner profile: Teenagers, ages 13–18, Developing/Low Advanced
(Level 3, B1)

Context: ESL integrated-skills class in a North American combined
middle school–high school technology program

Focus: Immigrant students from a variety of countries explore cross-
cultural communication using various language skills and
digital media.

Background

Middle and high school students in ESL classes in North America are often from a
wide variety of cultural groups and from different countries of origin. As a four-week
project, teachers would like these students to get to know each other by exploring
different cultural aspects such as the way people greet each other in different
languages (verbally and with gestures and body language). Students use technology
in order to find their similarities and differences and to begin the exploration of
cross-cultural communication while practicing listening, speaking, reading, writing,
and digital literacy. Students create a slideshow using Microsoft's PowerPoint
(Microsoft, 2010a) or a free slide maker such as Impress from Openoffice.org (2010,
http://www.openoffice.org) with audio and video files as well as text. They present
their findings orally while showing their presentations to an adult audience at family
night. The teacher leads a discussion on the classroom conventions of teamwork,
such as turn taking, ways to show respect for others' opinions, and ways to arrive
at consensus. Students create a checklist to use in their teams. The teacher models
how to use various tools, such as video and still digital cameras, a scanner, and
computers, and how to upload files from various peripheral devices. The teacher sets
up a student-friendly organizational structure of folders on the computer for each
team of students. The teacher explains and demonstrates how to cite Internet and
library resources. An I-search format (see Macrorie, 1988) may be used for the team
as a whole, indicating what is already known, what needs to be learned, and how
information is to be found.

Students begin away from the computer, sitting in mixed language groups and
exchanging cultural information concerning the ways people greet each other in
various languages, including conventions they use with mobile media and the
Internet. Students record each other, creating audio or video files to insert into a
slideshow presentation. Away from the computer, they meet regularly, creating a
flowchart with their ideas for content presentation and planning what areas will
need further research on the Internet and in the library. Students keep notes of
their work (either on paper or online), and the teacher checks their notes regularly,
assisting them with English and with their presentation plan. The teacher's

questioning strategies will help students think about cultural differences and what communication conventions are appropriate both face-to-face and more globally.

The students then build the slideshow on their team computer, each student working with one or more slides, inserting video, text, graphics, and audio. Teams also discuss how they will present their show and evaluate what they have learned about other cultures through this experience. The teacher coaches them as they practice their oral presentations in English. Students present the slideshows at family night, explaining orally in English what their group was attempting to accomplish with their show and what they learned through the experience. A recording (e.g., on a CD, DVD, or memory stick) of each show is created as an archive or part of a digital portfolio of each team's work. (See "Learn Basic Computer Skills: How to Burn a CD in Microsoft Windows" [Safronoff, 2007], http://www.youtube.com/watch?v=EXn3ha6X3Vg.)

In the evaluation phase, the teacher asks students several questions that will help them process the importance of bridging cross-cultural communication differences and assess the value of the various tools they have used: Did you enjoy the creative process? What did you learn from it? How well did the team work together? Did cross-cultural differences prevent you from communicating easily at any point? How could you make communication easier? If you could do the activity again, would you do it the same way or differently? Why?

Technology Tasks

Low-resource, low-access setting
With one computer in the classroom, one headset, and one digital camera (with video capability) available to the school, student teams take turns creating or loading files onto the computer while other teams plan the sequence of slides and their content or research in the library. The teacher checks students' written notes regularly as part of their English development and to be sure their plans are workable. The teacher (or students) may find digital images appropriate to the presentations and load them on the computer from a portable disk or through mobile media. If a school computer projector is not available, a computer monitor may be hooked to a TV for viewing at family night. The digital archive recording is created either on the class computer or on the teacher's computer at home. The evaluation survey is done on paper.

Medium-resource, medium-access setting
With one computer for every four to six students, Internet access, and several digital cameras, students begin away from the computer as described in the Background section. If computer access is frequent, teams build their flowchart with a wiki (a quick and easy web page) or an online mind-mapping tool. Individual students are asked to blog regularly about their group's work. The teacher regularly checks their notes and blogs, both for language instruction and to help with problems in their plan. The teacher presents the evaluative questions with an online survey tool to collect statistics about the activity.

High-resource, high-access setting

With a fully networked lab and one computer per student, Internet access, and several digital cameras and video recorders, students begin away from the computers, discussing their project, their roles on the team, and how the work will proceed, as previously described. Students use wikis, blogs, and mind-mapping tools, with the teacher checking their work regularly. Students create individual slides on their own computers to be added to the group project (e.g., by emailing or transferring their slides to each other over the network before assembling the final show).

See also: Learner Goal 1 Standard 1: Each One Teach One

Based on a concept contributed by Elizabeth Hanson-Smith, Jennifer Brown, and James Perren, and revised from the original Technology Standards Framework Document.

Learner profile: Adults, ages 19+, Developing–Expanding/Low–High Advanced (Level 3–4, B1–B2)

Context: EFL blended classroom

Focus: Adult students learn more about the conventions of social interaction in the target culture, while practicing listening and speaking.

Background

In an adult EFL setting, the instructor wants students to learn about the conventions of personal interaction in different settings (e.g., at a store, at a family dinner, at the bank). The teacher has students interact with each other first in their native language (if the class is monolingual or has groups from the same native language), taking on different roles. Students then analyze their communication choices and engage in role-plays on the same topics in English. Where possible, the teacher brings a native speaker to class to engage in conversation and to respond to students' questions about social interactions. Students record their role-plays and have the opportunity to review their own performances repeatedly to revise and correct them as their language capability develops. Where the Internet is available, students take part in tandem learning on one of the many free sites available. (For more on tandem learning, see Lewis, 2003, and Elia, 2006.)

Technology Tasks

Low-resource, low-access setting

With access to video or audio recorders or a classroom computer, but no access to the Internet, students watch several video clips with social interactions selected by the teacher. After discussing the key points, which they place on a checklist or rubric, students record their role-plays using digital recorders or recording software, such as Audacity (2010, http://audacity.sourceforge.net), on the class computer. Students review their role-plays and analyze the success of the interaction using the rubric. Students edit and rerecord as needed.

Medium-resource, medium-access setting

With access to video or audio recorders and limited access to the Internet, students search for examples of introductions and other social interactions in movie trailers, for instance using the Internet Movie Database (IMDb.com, 2010, http://www.imdb.com) and video sites such as Real English (Marzio School, 2010, http://www.real-english.com). Students work in small groups to analyze their samples; they are then assigned a new topic or setting by the teacher, record their own role-plays, and analyze them, comparing them to their original samples. They upload their role-plays to a class blog or podcast, where their classmates can watch and make comments.

High-resource, high-access setting

After initiating the topic of social conventions and discussing situations that occur in one or two movie or video excerpts as in the settings previously described, students use Internet and video chat with native speakers in the target culture. Students are assigned to regularly access a free, social, tandem language learning site (e.g., Tandem Server Bochum [BrammertsRuhr-Universität Bochum, 2005], http://www.slf.ruhr-uni-bochum.de/index.html, or Palabea [Palabea, 2009], http://www.palabea.net/). The teacher assigns them specific topics to discuss with their native-speaking interlocutors. Students are asked to request permission from interlocutors to record their sessions with a desktop recording device, such as Audacity (Audacity Development Team, 2010, http://audacity.sourceforge.net), so they can archive and review their interactions.

In preparation for speaking to native interlocutors, students find online samples, record their own samples, and upload them as already described. They engage in video chat role-plays with native speakers (individuals playing different roles or as part of a tandem learning setting), using the topics suggested by their teacher. Students analyze their interactions, taking notes if they are unable to record the discussion. Once they have collected adequate information, they prepare a presentation for the rest of the class. Their native speaker partner can also be virtually present, if possible, using Internet telephony such as Skype (Skype Technologies, 2010; http://www.skype.com), to answer potential questions raised by the rest of the class.

Standard 2: Language learners demonstrate respect for others in their use of private and public information.

Performance indicators

- Language learners demonstrate their understanding that public information in one community may be considered private in other communities.

- Language learners demonstrate their understanding that images may carry different connotations in different communities (e.g., pigs as symbols of prosperity vs. unclean animals).

- Language learners use communications and digital media tools ethically and responsibly (e.g., they don't secretly videotape others and post the videos on public sites).

- Language learners practice legal, responsible, and ethical use of technology systems, information, and software (e.g., they don't make and distribute illegal copies; they document sources as appropriate).

- Language learners accommodate different communication styles online.

Learner profile: Teens/adults, ages 13+, Developing/Low Advanced (Level 3, B1)

Context: EFL listening–speaking class in secondary school

Focus: Students gain understanding of cultural customs while studying grammar and practicing listening, speaking, and reading skills.

Background

An EFL teacher feels students would benefit from exposure to the ideas and customs of other countries, but teaching in the native culture/country of the students has required the teacher to look to technology to provide access to the cultural customs of different regions that are not available to students locally. This module begins with the class away from technology. The teacher begins class by asking if it is acceptable to put your feet on the table. The teacher then introduces the use of infinitives to discuss cultural norms (e.g., "It's rude to put your feet on the table"), and the class brainstorms cultural norms of their own country. The students also look at the nuances of modals for making suggestions (e.g., *should/shouldn't, could/couldn't*), practicing with each other in role-play pairs. Students then seek out cultural norms from other countries or regions as assigned by their teacher, using information gathered, for example, from Wikipedia's (2010b) site on cultural faux pas (http://en.wikipedia.org/wiki/Faux_pas).

Using the think-pair-share strategy, students report back and discuss in groups the differences or similarities between their culture and the other cultures assigned by their teacher. In this activity students first brainstorm ideas alone (think), then they are asked to share these ideas with a partner (pair), and finally the pair presents some ideas to the group (share). Next the groups script out a scenario of a foreign exchange student from their assigned culture coming to their school. The scenario consists of an orientation for the new student regarding what the local community considers public and private information (including visual information) as contrasted with cultural norms in the student's home country. Students perform their role-plays while recording them for later analysis. The teacher reminds them to incorporate the grammatical forms they have been studying. Eventually each individual student will perform a short, more formal speech summarizing what has been learned about different cultural customs. Classmates will evaluate each other's performances, including accuracy of speech. (For more on think-pair-share, see Ledlow, 2001.)

Technology Tasks

Low-resource, low-access setting

In a one-computer classroom with no Internet access, the teacher prints out several Wikipedia articles, dividing them into sections for students to use in small groups. (With Internet access at home or in a public place, students take turns and work in small groups to find information on Wikipedia, skimming the articles their teacher has suggested.) Students take notes, and if a printer is available, they print appropriate parts of the Wikipedia article to share with the class. Students use the Wikipedia information in their think-pair-share exercises, role-plays, and speeches (but students are not allowed to read from the notes or printouts during these activities). The oral performances are recorded for later analysis, using recording software such as Audacity (Audacity Development Team, 2010, http://audacity.sourceforge.com) with a microphone attached to the computer, using a digital camera or recorder, or using a cell phone.

Medium-resource, medium-access setting

In a classroom with several computers, a projector, and Internet access, after students have completed the Wikipedia search the teacher finds a series of videos on YouTube (2010) that feature cross-cultural mishaps, by using the search terms "cross-cultural differences," "cultural faux pas," and the like. The teacher bookmarks these at each computer station (e.g., by emailing the addresses to herself first). After viewing the videos in small groups while taking notes, the students do a think-pair-share exercise on the cross-cultural mistakes that were made. The students then script out a scenario of a friend offering the video's protagonist an analysis of what went wrong and perform their role-plays and speeches as previously described.

High-resource, high-access setting

With one computer for each student, students are assigned the Wikipedia search, but with each student using a computer station. They then share their findings and perform the activities described in the medium-resource setting. The recordings are then uploaded to a podcast site for comment by classmates. If possible, natives of the culture presented in the podcasts might be invited to listen and comment on whether they agree with the presentations.

See also: Teacher Goal 1 Standard 3: Podcasts and Podquests

Based on a concept submitted by Jeff Kuhn.

Learner profile: Adults, ages 17+, Expanding–Bridging/High Advanced+ (Level 4–5, B2–C1)

Context: Intensive English Program in the United States with technology access readily available

Focus: Students practice integrated skills while creating a peer biography to share online that will respect others' cultural values.

Background

The Intensive English Program (IEP) offers an elective in which students practice integrated skills by interviewing each other and creating short biographies as part of a class project. They are expected to ask each other about their families, share photos, and create a short biography that describes significant moments in their partner's life. The elective course includes 19 students from 12 different countries, including countries in Latin America, the Middle East, and Asia, and a wide range of ages. The resulting class biography compilation is very popular and is shared widely around the IEP and in the community as a whole.

The teacher brings in photos, short readings, and video clips that can help start discussion about culturally sensitive topics (e.g., people in swimsuits at the beach or a child in the bathtub). The teacher then leads a discussion with students about what might be appropriate for display on the web. As a result of the discussion, the students set ground rules, guided by the teacher, about what kinds of graphics they will use in their biographies and the topics they will address. They realize that standards of modesty and privacy vary a great deal in the class. Since families will also see the biographies, students are careful to double-check with each other before including photos, text, or other information that might be embarrassing. They agree not to send any part of a biography outside of the classroom until after the class as a whole reviews the final project and agrees that it is ready for distribution. (See also Wikipedia's (2010b) site on cultural faux pas, http://en.wikipedia.org/wiki/Faux_pas, which may be used to clarify cultural guidelines.)

For their project, students interview each other in order to create a short biography with photos. They work in groups of three; each student takes a turn as interviewer, interviewee, and note-taker. Students may want to record the interviews, using audio or video recorders, for ease in creating the written text. After interviewing each other to get ideas about significant moments in their lives, the student groups decide together how to structure the biographical material. They use free timeline software such as TimeGlider (Mnemograph, 2010; http://timeglider.com/) or Timelinr (Sundar, n.d.; http://veerasundar.com/timelinr) to help them organize their project and focus on the most significant events in the biographies; the teacher downloads and prints timelines where the Internet is not available to students. Once all the raw material is collected, the students work together to interview each other and create peer biographies. Students are encouraged to be creative in their use of illustrations and cover art for the biographies, using free graphics editing software, either on the computer or online. The digitized photos and draft biographies are stored on a private class computer or school website with access only for class members as they undergo review and revision. Students are very careful not to post any personal information about others on their own public social networking sites. Any student can request that a photo be removed from the private site and not included in the public compilation.

All class members are expected to view others' biographies in near-final form and offer comments and suggestions about the information included, coherence of the project, and any privacy issues, following a checklist they have created with the teacher's help. Students also discuss appropriate ways to make comments about others' creative work. Once the final versions have been approved by each group and the teacher, they are put onto a CD or DVD and uploaded to the public IEP site for distribution. Students agree not to post any information other than their own on any other public site such as Facebook (2010, http://www.facebook.com). (For more on writing tasks, see Hedge, 2005.)

Technology Tasks

Low-resource, low-access setting
With one computer in class, students proceed as described in the Background section. They use digital cameras or cell phones with photo capability in class or outside of class to take pictures, and the teacher will scan any photos not in digital form. If there is no private server to protect student information, sharing the information online may not be appropriate. The teacher prints out a timeline template for students to use on paper. Students may use Gimp (Gimp Team, 2010; free download at http://www.gimp.org), which the teacher can load on the class computer using a portable memory device. The teacher creates files on the computer for each student team's project where students can load their photos, work on drafts, and create their biographies, which can be printed out to take home.

Medium-resource, medium-access setting
Students have access to computers at the IEP once a week. Internet access is readily available on campus, and many students have their own computers and Internet access at home. Students access facilities at multiple locations, use the IEP's scanner, and check out digital cameras. The teacher prints out timeline templates for student groups to use on paper. Students work in pairs, taking turns interviewing and responding to questions. They use the scanner to scan the photos from home that are not in digital format and edit photos as needed using online tools such as Picasa (Google, 2010h; http://picasaweb.google.com) or Photoshop Express (Adobe, 2010; http://www.photoshop.com). They assemble all their materials into their written biography. Drafts are posted on the class website or wiki for review.

High-resource, high-access setting

Where computers and Internet access are available all hours of the day and night on campus, students are expected to produce biographies of each other, interspersing photos with the text. They focus on significant events in each partner's life, using timeline software online as an organizing tool. They find background information and supporting graphics online, scan print photos, and take additional photos of each other as needed, using the digital editing tools previously described. They peer-edit the documents on a class wiki.

See also: Learner Goal 2 Standard 2: Think-Pair-Share;
Teacher Goal 3 Standard 3: Rubrics in English for Science

Goal 3: Language learners effectively use and critically evaluate technology-based tools as aids in the development of their language learning competence as part of formal instruction and for further learning.

Standard 1: Language learners effectively use and evaluate available technology-based productivity tools.

Performance indicators

- Language learners use technology-based productivity tools as aids in production (e.g., word processing, presentation software, and web-design software; associated applications such as spell-checkers and thesauri; templates for preparing presentations, newsletters, and reports; tools to assist in brainstorming and creating graphic organizers).

- Language learners use technology-based productivity tools as aids in comprehension (e.g., translators, electronic dictionaries).

- Language learners apply criteria to evaluate the appropriate use of particular technology tools for specific language learning tasks.

- Language learners use technology-based productivity tools collaboratively and individually in order to enhance their language learning competence.

Family Stories
Learner Goal 3 Standard 1 Vignette

Learner profile: Very young learners, ages 6–8, Literacy–Starting/Beginning Literacy–Low Intermediate (Level 1 and lower, A1 and lower)

Context: ESL elementary school or newcomers' program

Focus: Students work to improve their vocabulary/reading comprehension with productivity tools.

Background

In an elementary ESL context, young learners are working on improving their reading competence by creating and illustrating a story about families. The students have learned basic vocabulary by looking at images of family groups representative of U.S. families and of families from the students' backgrounds (Mexico, Ukraine, and Somalia) from photos that students have brought to class and from images the teacher has downloaded from the Internet. Depending on the classroom level of access to technology, students themselves use technology-based productivity tools (e.g., Microsoft's PowerPoint or a free slide maker such as Openoffice.org's Impress (Openoffice.org, 2010, http://www.openoffice.org) in various ways to aid both their comprehension and their language production as they create an illustrated story about a family. Students from different countries will negotiate meaning and what they feel is important to use in the story.

Away from the computer and with the whole class, the teacher first models an example story using photos that the learners have brought to class, then models the sentences they might use, e.g., "This is Tanya" and "She is the [daughter]." (The students finish the sentences orally.) The teacher then uses the computer to demonstrate how to open and use a word-processing file created with key words and phrases related to the lesson on families. Students work in small groups to create sentences for their stories and come to the computer to dictate them to the teacher, who types them with the word processor, adding them to the file with key words.

Subsequently, the teacher demonstrates how to copy and paste these phrases into a slideshow presentation (one sentence per slide) to create sentences like those modeled earlier on the projector. The students help the teacher decide which illustrations to add to each slide by dragging and dropping (or using the >Insert function) from a collection of images from clip art or from the Internet that the teacher has prepared and saved into a folder on the computer. Several students are asked to come forward to use the keyboard and mouse until all students seem confident in what is expected of them in the creation of a presentation and use of the interface.

The teacher then puts students into cross-cultural groups of three to create their own presentations. One student is the writer, one student is the decider, and a third student is the checker. Students help each other compose descriptive sentences or a short narrative about the family grouping they choose to illustrate using the words and phrases they have just reviewed. They select illustrations to add to the story, and they dictate sentences to each other to type (hunt-and-peck) into the program. Students then use the presentation program and word processor to create and save their presentation, assisted by the teacher or by more technology-savvy students. Each group ends with a story of at least four pictures and at least four sentences. The groups practice reading the final story that they have created, and then present it to the class, each student reading a slide in turn. In a large class, groups pair up to share their stories with their partner group. The teacher later prints the stories and gives them to the student groups so that they can share their illustrated stories with one another to practice reading. (For more about writing stories with children, see Wright, 2003.)

Technology Tasks

Low-resource, low-access setting

With one computer in the classroom and a data projector or whiteboard, but no Internet, the teacher models the illustrated story, first with a photo and then with the productivity tools discussed in the previous section. The students work on their demonstrations in triads, and they take turns going to the computer to select an illustration from the teacher's folder and work on their sentences. Meanwhile, the rest of the class is assigned other activities. If students are already somewhat familiar with keyboarding, the teacher lets them type and copy and paste (or drag and drop) words and images with supervision.

Medium-resource, medium-access setting

With a computer and Internet access for every three students, students first watch the teacher's demonstration and then work in groups of three at the computer, as described, to create their presentations. The teacher circulates among the workstations, helping students find the right phrases and use the keyboard. The students present their stories to the class, and the teacher prints the stories for further practice as in the Background section.

High-resource, high-access setting

With a networked set of laptops, one per learner, and a projector for the teacher, the teacher demonstrations proceed as previously described, with students watching away from the computers. The teacher then sends the demonstration to the students' monitors for them to use as a model while they work on their own presentations in triads sharing one computer. The students choose and download one or more additional images from the teacher's folder on the school's file server to include in their slideshow and add the URL on the final slide. Each pair's final illustrated story is, in turn, presented to the whole class orally using the lab's data projector.

See also: Learner Goal 1 Standard 1: Each One Teach One; Goal 2 Standard 2: Peer Biographies

Standard 2: Language learners appropriately use and evaluate
available technology-based language skill-building tools.

Performance indicators

- Language learners employ age- and proficiency-appropriate vocabulary and pragmatics/body language during collaborative work that uses technology.

- Language learners demonstrate that they know when to ask for help in order to achieve their language learning objectives when using technology.

- Language learners decide when to use language software and devices as available and appropriate to enhance specific skill areas (e.g., vocabulary, grammar, and pronunciation practice software; MP3 recorders).

- Language learners critically evaluate Internet resources as available and appropriate to enhance their language learning (e.g., web-based listening exercises, online sentence jumbles).

Learner profile: ESL adult education–immigrant (blended learning), adults ages 17+, Literacy–Starting–Emerging/Low–High Intermediate (Level 1–2, A1–A2)

Context: ESL classroom for working adults with access to computers and Internet

Focus: Adult students access comprehensive programs supplemented by language games and exercises related to their work

Background

Adult learners often have access to technology in labs and school libraries, or at work sites or in their own classrooms. A higher level of technology allows them to access software or online sites developed specifically to meet their need for further skill practice and greater English proficiency. Adult learners with this kind of technology access can utilize interactive language games and exercises more purposefully for out-of-class use with a teacher's guidance. For example, with the help of the teacher, adult students can create learning objectives and use interactive software or Internet sites that allow them to expand on their textbook and classroom activities, to practice specific language skills, and to develop grammar and vocabulary related to their work experience. They use these learning tools independently and seek other exercises, games, and activities that help them continue language development after their graduation from basic classes.

A series of activities can illustrate how adult learners can use a teacher's help to maximize their use of technology. First, students can be assisted by the teacher in formulating specific personal objectives (e.g., not just "I want to learn English," but rather "I will use three new words this week" or "I will write down what I think someone said and ask about it in class"). Students then access the lessons, exercises, or learning games suggested by their teacher. To ensure they have a successful learning experience, the teacher assists students in using the CD/DVD folder or in getting online, registering and using a password, and finding appropriate exercises and games, either with in-class demonstrations with a data projector or whiteboard, or for a wholly online class, with a videoconferencing tool.

Students are asked to use the exercises or games independently (or in pairs or triads, if they use a lab during class times) about 30 minutes per day, viewing the videos or other prompts several times, reading with the script and performing the exercises, e.g., writing a short essay. Students speak out loud with the dialogues even if they don't have a microphone to record and compare. Students keep a learning journal with new expressions and bring questions to class or post them to the class discussion forum. At frequent intervals throughout the term, the teacher leads a whole-class discussion on what students are finding in the exercises and any problems that may have arisen. The teacher uses a visual checklist to help students express their problems nonverbally if needed. Students are encouraged to evaluate their lessons, games, and tools and choose those that give them the right kinds of practice for their needs. The teacher develops short tests and quizzes (either paper or online) to supplement the programs and to ensure that learners access them at regular, frequent intervals. The teacher also confers with students individually (either face-to-face or, in a distance class, online) to see if they need further help in meeting their objectives. For more on using comprehensive video programs, see the U.S.A. Learns Webcast at http://www.usalearns.org/teacher/webcast.html; requires free teacher registration, or available through the Outreach and Technical Assistance Network (OTAN, 2010b). For language learning games, see Interesting Things for ESL Students (C. Kelly and L. Kelly, 1997–2010; http://www.manythings.org/).

Technology Tasks

Low-resource, low-access setting

With access to classroom computers or a lab, students in pairs or triads use the CDs/DVDs that accompany their textbooks. The teacher helps students select the exercises that will benefit their learning goals and assists them with the activities described in the Background section. The teacher also creates a paper self-report checklist and a quiz for each unit or set of exercises that students complete. If students have access to the Internet outside of class, the teacher also recommends that they use one of the many free Internet sites for further exercises, such as Randall's Cyber ESL Listening Lab (Davis, 2010, http://www.esl-lab.com/) or Real English (Marzio School, 2010, http://www.real-english.com; with many job-related videos), or games and podcasts at Interesting Things for ESL Students (C. Kelly and L. Kelly, 1997-2010; http://www.manythings.org/). The teacher assists them in finding the appropriate level and type of exercises.

Medium-resource, medium-access setting

With headsets and stable bandwidth in the school lab or classroom, or with easy access to the Internet in public sites or at home, students regularly access a free, comprehensive language learning site, such as U.S.A. Learns (OTAN, 2010a; http://www.usalearns.org; for low-level students) or English for All (OTAN, 2003; http://www.myefa.org/; for higher-level beginners), both of which have vocabulary and integrated skills activities focused on work and job-related scenarios. Students use the program individually or in pairs to complete exercises. The teacher downloads and prints free supplemental text materials, or the school may purchase the videos on CD and print materials from the Outreach and Technical Assistance Network (OTAN, 2003, 2010a) in order to use them at free-standing workstations, as well as individually. The teacher monitors student activities using a paper self-report checklist and quiz for each unit, or uses the program's management system to see which activities students are completing and how often they access the program. Students may also access the programs as independent learners. Students access language games at Interesting Things for ESL Students (C. Kelly and L. Kelly, 1997–2010; http://www.manythings.org/) suggested by their teacher to provide further practice and motivation in learning vocabulary and grammar items.

High-resource, high-access setting

With high bandwidth, headsets, and easy access to the Internet, a class of students use ANVILL (A National Virtual Language Lab; Yamada Language Center, 2010, https://anvill.uoregon.edu/anvill2/), a speech-based toolbox for language learning. (See the ANVILL Webinar at https://anvill.uoregon.edu/anvill2/node/4255 for full information.) The teacher creates a course designed specifically for the class. Lessons are centered around the practice of oral/aural language but incorporate voiceboards (both audio- and video-capable), live chat, oral quizzes, and so on. Students use the tools to chat with each other, and the teacher encourages them to analyze body language and gestures as well as oral pronunciation as they work. The teacher records (or finds) and places audio- and video-based lessons at the class site (e.g., linked from the discussion board) using the online resource to expand on classroom materials. Students respond interactively with voice or writing to readings and activities, for example, embedded videos from elsewhere on the web, and they build their own audiovisual projects using the simple recording tool. The teacher can also insert audio corrections into students' speech recordings. The teacher creates voice chat rooms to hold office hours or to allow student groups to work and plan together. Students also access listening games and podcasts at Interesting Things for ESL Students (C. Kelly and L. Kelly, 1997–2010; http://www.manythings.org/), as suggested by their teacher.

See also: Learner Goal 3 Standard 2: E-dictionaries

E-Dictionaries
Learner Goal 3 Standard 2 Vignette

Learner profile: Young learners, ages 9–12, Starting–Emerging/Low–High Intermediate (Level 1–2, A1–A2)

Context: EFL classroom for young children

Focus: Young students learn new vocabulary items and develop language learning strategies such as use of electronic dictionaries, goal setting, and evaluation of learning resources.

Background

In a primary EFL classroom, the teacher guides students in using appropriate dictionaries so that students can improve their own vocabulary and develop learning strategies that can help them independently improve their learning over time. If the class is large, the teacher will have aides or parents assist in the classroom or lab. The teacher sometimes uses one or two students who are very good in technology as classroom helpers.

Students are asked to decide in pairs or groups what they think the key vocabulary items were in the unit they have just covered, relating to the theme of "home." The teacher brings to class a poster-size picture of, for example, a room in a house or a cutaway house as a visual aid, or displays the poster on the class computer projector. Once the key vocabulary items are identified, the students are encouraged to include them in their personal picture dictionaries. The children write each vocabulary item in their personal word-processing file and include a picture that illustrates the meaning of the word, copying or dragging and dropping from clip art files on the desktop, or from a folder of images created by the teacher. Depending on their language level, students also add a sentence or phrase that includes the new item or word.

Next, students are asked to point to pictures of other objects in the poster whose names they would like to learn but that were not included in the unit they studied, thus allowing for personalization of learning and development of learner autonomy. These might be additional furniture items, for example, or objects similar to those students have in their own rooms. The teacher or other students help identify the names of these items in English, and the students then research them in digital dictionaries, adding the items to their personal journals with illustrations and short sentences.

Finally, students work in pairs or groups to prepare activities using the additional vocabulary items they have learned, for example, a short dialogue or narrative, or vocabulary games. Vocabulary activities can be used later by their classmates. (For more on using dictionaries for vocabulary learning, see Gu, 2003.)

In the review of the lesson, the teacher asks the children to evaluate the print and e-dictionaries they used. The students individually complete the rubric shown in Table 3.1 and then join in a class discussion that concludes with a ranking of the dictionaries used.

Technology Tasks

Low-resource, low-access setting

In a classroom with one computer but no Internet connection, after deciding on the key vocabulary items for the unit or thematic area, the students work to include these items in their personal picture dictionaries. They can either draw pictures or find pictures to represent the vocabulary items from clip art collections on their class computer or pictures from CD/DVD dictionaries.

Later, when students choose the additional vocabulary they would like to learn within the specific unit, they use personal or school print picture dictionaries or CD/DVD dictionaries from the school library. Once they choose the words they would like to learn, they write them in their personal picture dictionaries and illustrate them with pictures as described in the Background section. The pairs or groups take turns designing this section of their personal dictionaries using mind-mapping software—such as Kidspiration (Inspiration Software, 2008) or FreeMind (2010)—installed on the class computer.

Finally, the teacher uses the students' vocabulary journals to create activities that can help them practice the new vocabulary items. The teacher installs software on their computer downloaded from the Internet to a portable memory device (e.g., XWord Interactive Crossword Puzzles [Greaves, 2010], http://vlc.polyu.edu.hk/XWord/xword .htm) or creates games online and prints them (e.g., from PuzzleMaker [Discovery Education, 2008], http://puzzlemaker.discoveryeducation.com/). Once the activities are ready, they are photocopied and given to the whole class as homework or saved as additional resource activities to be used by fast finishers. Some of the pairs or groups may be technologically ready to use the class computer to prepare electronic versions of their activities themselves.

Medium-resource, medium-access setting

In a class that can schedule time in a computer lab connected to the Internet, with one computer for every three students, the teacher starts the lesson away from the

Table 3.1. Rubric for Assessing Dictionaries

Name of Print or Online Dictionary	Easy to Use?	Quality of Interface	Variety of Vocabulary Items	Nice Pictures?
	Very good	Good	OK	Not so good

computers, with the children deciding on the key vocabulary items and the additional vocabulary items they would like to learn, as previously described. Then in groups of three they work at their computers to illustrate the new vocabulary items using mind-mapping software installed on the computers, such as Kidspiration (Inspiration Software, 2008) or FreeMind (2010). Their work is then printed for the students to include in their personal dictionaries.

Afterward, the students use CD/DVD or online dictionaries (e.g., Enchanted Learning, [Enchanted Learning, 2010], http://www.enchantedlearning.com/Home.html, or the Visual Dictionary Online [Merriam-Webster, 2010], http://visual.merriam-webster .com/) to write and illustrate the new vocabulary items they have selected, and they return to Kidspiration or a similar program in order to create the pages for their personal dictionaries. Finally, students work online with easy interactive exercise makers, such as Quia (2010, http://www.quia.com/web, if the school has purchased it) or free programs such as Puzzlemaker (Discovery Education, 2008, http:// puzzlemaker.discoveryeducation.com/) or Tools for Educators (2010, http://www .toolsforeducators.com/) to design simple activities, games, or puzzles with which to practice their selected vocabulary items. They use instruction sheets with clear step-by-step directions illustrated with a number of screenshots, which they can refer to if they need help. The class has aides they can address for help as well as the teacher. The students may complete their evaluation rubrics online, but they bring their results to class for the final discussion and evaluations.

High-resource, high-access setting
In a classroom where the students have their personal laptops connected to the Internet, the children away from the computers discuss the key vocabulary items of the unit as described. The children then add the key items in their personal e-dictionaries and use clip art, drawings, online resources recommended by their teacher, or illustrations saved for them in a folder to illustrate the meanings of the words.

The students then use a range of online dictionaries to further investigate the specific thematic area (e.g., "home") and choose new words they would like to learn. They add the words to their personal e-dictionaries, writing and illustrating them as described. Finally, they work with easy interactive exercise or puzzle makers (e.g., Puzzlemaker, Quia, or Tools for Educators) to design simple activities or worksheets with which to practice their selected vocabulary items as described.

The teacher then uploads the activities the students have prepared to the class section of the school website so that the rest of the class can access them. The children are asked to complete some of their classmates' activities as homework. Finally, the children are asked to choose some of their work (either e-dictionary pages or vocabulary activities) and upload it to their online portfolios. The students complete their evaluation rubric online and bring a printout of it to class for the final discussion and evaluations.

Learner profile: Adult students, ages 17+, Beginning–Emerging/Beginning–High Intermediate (Level 1–2 and lower, A1–A2 and lower)

Context: ESL class with multiple languages at an adult school held during the day in a local community center

Focus: Adult students practice language skills (listening, speaking, reading, and writing) while learning about the various community resources that may be of help to them and their families.

Background

Adult learners need to become aware of various resources within their community, such as information and services from city hall, the local library, or the employment office. The teacher organizes learners in groups and assigns each group a task based on a community resource, for example, calling their phone line to get information. Students practice dialogues before making an appointment to connect with a service representative. The teacher helps them use appropriate greetings, body language, and eye contact. They also practice phrases to ask for clarification of information and to respond when their respondent doesn't understand them. Students make note of what phrases they will need to know and pool their knowledge, with the teacher's help, about politeness formulas. The teacher uses these questions to form the basis for grammar, vocabulary, and pronunciation exercises. Where the Internet is available, the students also do research online, visiting the community resource's website to gather more information about the service provided. Eventually, students visit the community resource location to gather brochures and pamphlets and to get information in person. They then create presentations in their groups and share with the whole class what they have learned about the services offered. The class discusses the best ways to obtain community information. (For more on using community resources, see Jewell, 2006.)

Technology Tasks

Low-resource, low-access setting

With no computer in the classroom and only occasional Internet access, e.g., from home or a community center, students use their mobile phones to access a local community resource. In each group, one student uses the phone's speaker feature so that all can hear the greeting and the phone tree options for the community resource. The other students in the group write down what they hear and discuss it. If they get a real person, they ask a question they have previously brainstormed. Students who have Internet access will bring information acquired on the Web to class to add to their group's final presentation.

Medium-resource, medium-access setting
With the help of a document camera and data projector, students present paper-based materials and printouts they have collected at a local community resource while they communicate to the group what they have learned. Students may connect their cameras or download images from their mobile phones to the projector and show photos of, for example, the City Hall and its directory of departments. These texts and digital images become part of their group's final presentation.

High-resource, high-access setting
With a computer lab, students ask the teacher to help them identify search terms to locate community resources. They create slide shows and interactive quizzes to present what they have learned and check for their peers' understanding. Each group creates a wiki page about the assigned local community resource and embeds interactive elements such as audio, video, and practice activities related to the topic. The wiki becomes the basis for the group's final presentation.

See also: Teacher Goal 2 Standard 1: Blended Learning for Adult Students

Based on a concept submitted by Branka Marceta.

Standard 3: Language learners appropriately use and evaluate available technology-based tools for communication and collaboration.

Performance indicators

Language learners communicate in appropriate ways with those from other cultures and communities using digital tools.

- Language learners actively encourage others to fully participate in conversations that use technology-based tools in a language learning context (e.g., simulations, mobile phones, CMC [computer-mediated communication] tools).

- Language learners use criteria to determine which technology tools function best as a means of collaborating with others for specific types of language learning (e.g., comment function in word processors, wikis, interactive whiteboards, CMC tools).

- Language learners use and critically evaluate the use of particular digital resources to communicate ideas effectively to peers or a wider audience (e.g., blogs, podcasts, movie-making tools).

- Language learners use available technology individually or collaboratively to create content to share with peers or a wider audience, online or offline.

Learner profile: Teens/adults, ages 12+, Developing/Low Advanced (Level 3, B1)

Context: EFL integrated skills classroom with access to technology

Focus: Students practice speaking, writing, thinking skills while using new technologies

Background

Students in an intermediate EFL class are encouraged to consider how technology can be used to assist the needs of language learners like themselves and provide opportunities to use English outside their textbooks. The students are encouraged to use English to navigate new technology via menus and instructions, and to practice writing, thinking, and speaking skills while they take learning a step further toward technology incorporation in their studies.

Students first examine advertisements (either in paper or on the web) for various types of technologies (such as digital cameras, MP3 players, presentation software) to analyze the language and visual presentation of ads and commercials. They then use this analysis as the basis for creating their own presentation or sales pitch, describing the merits of a particular technology for collaborative language learning. Students use graphics programs, audio technology, and, in a high-access setting, video, to create their commercials. The class debates the relative merits of the various technologies to create collaborations, and they discuss technical, creative, and oral skills aspects of their project, creating a checklist or rubric as they proceed. Once the projects are completed, students present their work at an in-class exposition or awards competition which is judged using their checklists. Students also mount their work at online sites and invite other classes to view the presentations. (For more on using podcasting and video projects, see Yeh, 2007.)

Technology Tasks

Low-resource, low-access setting

In a classroom with one computer, a microphone, and speakers, students in groups of four to five receive a packet of materials, e.g., magazines, advertisements, and images of various technologies collected by the teacher. Each group is given the task of selecting a specific technology and then creating a poster presentation and sales pitch describing the merits of the technology in language learning. Students use the graphics program or digital images saved on the computer and record the accompanying sales pitch. Once the projects have been completed, the students present their work at a classroom exposition, taking turns using the computer for presentation. The class discusses the merits of each group's work, using their checklists. For added verisimilitude, their teacher and two other language teachers, acting as visiting presidents of famous universities, visit each poster presentation and decide which technology to buy for their school based on organization of information, visual appeal, grammaticality, and oral proficiency.

Medium-resource, medium-access setting

In a computer room with five computers, microphones, and speakers for each, and Internet access outside of class, students work in groups with a choice of technology (or are sent to websites with illustrations of the technologies) and are assigned the task of creating a radio sales pitch for their product that emphasizes its function as an aid in collaborative communication. After submitting a script to the teacher to check for language and appropriateness, the students record their radio commercials, either at a podcast site such as PodOmatic (2010, http://www.podomatic.com), if the Internet is available, or on their local computers. Upon completion of the project, the class listens to the commercials and hosts an awards ceremony with awards such as best pronunciation, best grammar, best voice actor/actress, and so on, using their checklists. If the projects are posted to a podcasting site, other classes are invited to add comments or to answer a poll based on the checklists.

High-resource, high-access setting

In a computer lab with a computer for each student, Internet, and a computer projector, plus video or digital cameras available, students watch a variety of video commercials at YouTube (YouTube, 2011, http://www.youtube.com), for example, or at product websites and discuss in small groups their opinions of the ads. Each group is then given a piece of technology (or is sent to websites with illustrations of the technologies) and assigned the task of brainstorming ideas on how it could be used to assist collaboration among language learners. Following this activity, the students are asked to create a commercial of their own, pitching the ideas brainstormed using digital cameras, mobile phone video, or webcams, as available, to create video/ audio products. Upon completion of the project, one class is devoted to "Oscar night," when students view the commercials with the computer projector and vote on awards, using their checklists, in categories such as grammaticality, best actor/ actress, most creative use of assigned technology, and overall best commercial. If the commercials are mounted at a blog or video site like Vimeo (2010, http://vimeo .com/), other classes may be invited to join a group, add comments, or respond to a poll based on the checklists. (Vimeo and other video sites also sponsor video contests where students can submit their work.)

See also: Learner Goal 2 Standard 1: Cross-cultural Communication; Teacher Goal 1 Standard 3: Podcasts and PodQuests

Based on a concept submitted by Jeff Kuhn.

Standard 4:   Language learners use and evaluate available technology-based research tools appropriately.

Performance indicators

- Language learners employ technology to locate and collect information from a variety of sources.

- Language learners employ strategies to evaluate online information.

- Language learners document source material appropriately.

- Language learners determine which technology tools to use to organize information from research (e.g., moving information around in the word processor, using a database or spreadsheet).

ESP for Architecture
Learner Goal 3 Standard 4 Vignette

Learner profile: Adults, ages 17+, Bridging (Level 5, C1)

Context: EFL online or blended course at a university or professional school, English for Special Purposes (ESP)

Focus: Students practice authentic speaking and writing skills in a collaborative presentation for an authentic audience in a professional field.

Background

Students in an online English for Architecture class are learning to use the Internet for research and to evaluate and present information as if they were working on an architectural team in a prospective place of employment in their field. Their assignment helps them practice English while learning about a period of architectural style. They find images from a particular architectural style, either on the web or by taking pictures of specific buildings with their own cameras or mobile phones, and assemble a presentation to be given in English wholly online for peers and invited guests. Planning and execution of the presentation mimic the kinds of team effort and language skills students will be required to use in their projected future employment. Students work in groups of three to five to prepare a research plan in English, which is checked at frequent intervals by the ESP instructor, who helps with English vocabulary and structure as well as checking on progress. Team members choose various roles with differing responsibilities, such as text editor, image editor, assembly editor. (Roles will change in various team configurations throughout the course; if students are widely dispersed globally, the teacher may need to create groups that are geographically compact.)

The students' instructor helps them find image resources and related professional reference material. Students consult an online dictionary of technical terms, such as Archiseek (Clerkin, 2010, http://www.archiseek.com/), to ensure they are using appropriate vocabulary. Students are given examples of correct ways to cite online resources in their field, and they document all their materials. Individual students use blogs to describe their work processes and any difficulties they may encounter as they work in a team, so that the teacher can monitor their interactions and assist in vocabulary and other English skill development as needed. A practice presentation at an online venue (e.g., Wiziq [AuthorGEN, 2010], http://www.wiziq.com) gives the teacher the opportunity to correct students' oral language efforts without the pressure of the final performance. (If students and audience are widely dispersed, they may need to present several times in order to include everyone.)

While watching the practice presentations, students take notes critiquing each other's oral performance, which they share in their online forum. Following the final presentations to an authentic audience of peers and teachers recruited from the instructor's community of practice, students will write in their blogs, evaluating the technology tools they used and the sources of their materials based on feedback they received from the audience, using a rubric developed in discussion with their team and the online instructor. (See González, 2008, for further discussion of an architecture ESP course.)

Technology Tasks

Low-resource, low-access setting
With lower bandwidth Internet access, students email parts of their presentation to each other. Images are uploaded or linked to a wiki, where appropriate textual descriptions can be added. Students take turns editing their sections of the presentation and convene in a live text chat venue and view the wiki together for the practice sessions and final presentations.

Medium-resource, medium-access setting
With higher bandwidth and headsets, presentation slides may be uploaded to a free photo/video site to be shared, discussed through an online forum, and eventually turned into an online slideshow or video. Students take turns editing their sections of the presentation, which takes place using an audio/video live chat venue.

High-resource, high-access setting
With high bandwidth, headsets, and webcams, students use an audio/video chat venue with webcam capability that allows the audience (who may be at other locations on the campus or at a distance) to see the presenters, ask questions, and discuss their work with them.

See also: Learner Goal 3 Standard 3: Making Commercials

Based on a concept submitted by Dafne González.

Evaluating Web Sources
Learner Goal 3 Standard 4 Vignette

Learner profile: Adults, ages 17+, Developing/Low Advanced (Level 3, B1)

Context: Intensive English Program (IEP) reading–writing class at a North American university

Focus: Students practice critical thinking while reading resources on the Internet and writing research papers.

Background

Students in a college IEP setting come from various countries, but this is their first experience in the United States. They have some competencies in analyzing the credibility of a text, but these vary, depending on their prior learning. During class discussion, students are given a short time to critically analyze print items representing a spectrum of reliability, such as *The Washington Post* and *The National Enquirer*. They discuss which is a good news source and which is not, and start a checklist of criteria. Students in groups are then given copies of the *New York Post*, *USA Today*, and *The New York Times* and continue to work on their criteria. Then the class comes together and discusses the criteria and what makes a good resource. (For more on search strategies, see Google for Educators: Google Web Search [Google, 2010d], http://www.google.com/educators/p_websearch.html.)

In a subsequent session, students compare printouts of several web pages, some from sources similar to those above and some from less reliable sources, such as extremist groups or groups with vested commercial interests. Using the criteria they have created, students decide in groups whether particular sites are reliable or not. The class then comes together and discusses what is important about evaluating websites, as compared to print resources. Discussion includes points such as what the domain names mean (*.org*, *.edu*, *.gov*, *.com*, and others), who owns a site (private individual, research institute, school district, etc.), whether hyperlinks are active, time stamps of last updates to the website, the amount of advertisement on a given site, whether the site is copyrighted, and whether a contact can easily be found. Students learn how to find out who owns a site (e.g., at easyDNS, 2010,, http://www.easywhois.com) and look at previous versions of the site at the Internet Archive: WayBackMachine (Internet Archive, 2010; http://www.archive.org). Printouts or screenshots of results from these sites are shared with the class. Students also look at what sites are linked to and from the site they are evaluating, and discuss what this implies about the site's reliability. In groups, students continue to develop their checklists to include website evaluation comparable to their ideas for evaluating texts. Then they use the new criteria to examine websites within the framework of the technology access they have. Students make their own paper copies of the reliability criteria the class devises, and keep their copies with them as they access the Internet when they are doing research. The teacher gives them a handout with appropriate referencing formats, which they discuss during the course of their research so that sources will be accurately cited.

Papers are written using a word processor at the lab or on a home computer or laptop. Students include a checklist whenever they turn in a research paper, indicating how well their Internet resources met the criteria. (For more on web page validity, see Davis, Ferenz, & Gray, 2010.)

Technology Tasks

Low-resource, low-access setting

With one computer in the classroom and access to the IEP lab on campus outside of class, students will work from print copies of the newspapers and news magazines. Printouts from websites are also used for discussion. Students in small groups accessing the computer will use website and link searches to discover additional ways to evaluate documents found on the Internet.

Medium-resource, medium-access setting

With several computers and adequate access to the Internet, all resources are electronic, including online versions of the newspapers and news magazines. Students group around the computers to do the activities and keep an electronic document with their search criteria available on the desktop.

High-resource, high-access setting

With one computer per student and broadband access in a networked lab with a course management system (CMS), students begin with the assessment of paper documents to develop their criteria, as described, but they then work on their own computers and are grouped electronically within the CMS to develop a group list. During the project, students communicate via text chat or video/audio chat within the CMS and collaborate through a wiki or with language lab software as they develop their checklists. With a CMS, students can keep the electronic list on display in the chat as they work. The teacher can "look in" on their chat and view a transcript of their interactions to ensure that all students are participating fully. (For more on electronic grouping, see Liang, 2010.)

See also: Teacher Goal 3 Standard 3: Rubrics in English for Science

Based on a concept submitted by Steve Sharp.

Standard 5: Language learners recognize the value of technology to support autonomy, lifelong learning, creativity, metacognition, collaboration, personal pursuits, and productivity.

Performance indicators

- Language learners select the most appropriate available technology for independent language learning and can provide reasons for their choices.

- Language learners demonstrate the ability to set language learning goals and objectives that employ technology, with a teacher's support or independently.

- Language learners can use technology to monitor their progress (e.g., record keeping within programs, electronic portfolios), with a teacher's support or independently.

- Language learners can express themselves using technology (e.g., creating digital media as works of art)

- Language learners provide reasons for the value of technology in maintaining communication for personal and professional purposes and having access to authentic material that supports their language learning.

- Language learners use technology to work in English more effectively (e.g., using an electronic dictionary when it is more efficient than using a paper dictionary)

Learner profile: Teenagers, ages 13–18, Emerging–Developing/High Intermediate–Low Advanced (Level 2–3, A2–B1)

Context: A sheltered/content-based Science Concepts class with Internet access

Focus: At-risk adolescents learn to use an appropriate open-source tool and collaborative learning for academic vocabulary development.

Background

The teacher is aware of the importance of vocabulary development in a sheltered Science Concepts class and wants to empower students to use technology for knowledge and self-efficacy. The teacher also knows that technology is motivating for adolescent students. The students have access to CD/DVD dictionaries in the school lab and library, but the teacher also introduces open-source software and websites because students can access them freely from home or community computers. Open-source online Wiktionary (Wikimedia, 2010; www.wiktionary.org) is useful to preview a lesson and to allow students to learn vocabulary in a comprehensive way. By becoming aware of the information offered by Wiktionary as well as its ease of access, students become more self-sufficient in accelerating their own vocabulary development and become aware of a lifelong learning tool.

In addition, the teacher attempts to encourage a community of learners, in which students and teachers share information and skills. As students read their science text, they make notes about the words they are not sure of or would like to know more about. In class, students work in pairs, looking up the words they are both unsure of and cross-checking those they agree on. Classmates take notes and ask questions when each pair reports back to the class. Students keep their notes and a record of the new words, e.g., in a vocabulary journal, and are expected to use the new vocabulary in subsequent writing assignments and oral discussions/presentations. If students are unable to find a particular word or phrase in Wiktionary, they write a description of it, using the required format, to submit for publication. Students are encouraged to explore linked references from the Wiktionary pages as well. Eventually, students use their vocabulary journal to help write a paper on an assigned subject or to work on a collaborative project with their peers. (For more on vocabulary journals and notebooks, see Board of Education, San Diego County, 2007; and Feldman & Kinsella, 2005.)

Technology Tasks

Low-resource, low-access setting

With Internet access outside the classroom, the teacher prints and copies key vocabulary from Wiktionary for an upcoming lesson. The teacher models analysis of the information from Wiktionary by presenting a few examples and demonstrates on an overhead projector (or chalkboard) the pronunciation using IPA, the part of speech, and the number of different meanings. The teacher asks students which meaning may be relevant to the upcoming lesson. Pairs of students then use a printout of one key word in a matrix and prepare a presentation of each aspect: the pronunciation in IPA, the part of speech, the number of different meanings, and which meaning is relevant to the upcoming lesson. Before each pair of students presents its key word to the class, the partners practice their presentation with teacher assistance—especially the pronunciation of the word, which each student should master. (If Internet access is available at home or in the school lab, students may also use an online talking dictionary, such as HowJSay.com, Boyer, 2010, http://www .howjsay.com/, for pronunciation help.)

Medium-resource, medium-access setting

With one computer in the classroom, Internet access, and, if possible, a computer projector or electronic whiteboard, the teacher models the uses of Wiktionary by demonstrating how to look up key vocabulary, discussing the importance of precise spelling, showing the multilingual translations and the academic definition, and, if possible, clicking on the pronunciation. Each feature, such as spelling and translations, is documented on the board for reference. Students in pairs take turns at the computer and look up key vocabulary while discussing each feature listed on the board. They present their findings to the class and save their notes for their vocabulary journals.

High-resource, high-access setting

In a networked computer lab, with one computer and a headset for each student, the teacher models the uses of Wiktionary before students go to the computers. The teacher posts a list of key vocabulary from the students' textbook on the wall or board or hands out copies. The teacher then shows how to access and use Wiktionary in a step-by-step process. At each step, the teacher involves students' awareness and engages them. The procedure is modeled, discussed, and documented on the board for reference. The teacher discusses the information on the site, focusing on two aspects: the audio file and translations. At the computers with headsets, students click on the audio file and practice pronunciation. Students in pairs are assigned one or more words and subsequently collaborate to present their words to the class.

See also: Teacher Goal 3 Standard 2: Readability in Academic Texts

Based on a concept submitted by Ann Kennedy.

Google Earth
Learner Goal 3 Standard 5 Vignette

Learner profile: Adults, ages 17+, Expanding–Bridging/High Advanced+ (Level 4–5, B2–C1)

Context: IEP integrated skills class in North America

Focus: Students gain understanding of the value of technology for personal and professional purposes while practicing all four language skills.

Background

An advanced IEP class is coming to a close, and the teacher wants the students (a) to recognize the range of English that is used around the world by native and nonnative speakers and (b) to recognize how technology can help them expand their own understanding as well as contribute to others' understanding of the variations of English. The instructor has decided to use maps as a visual platform for students to conceptualize the use of English worldwide and to contribute their own reflections about language variation to a collaborative, publicly accessible forum. There are 15 students in the class representing six nationalities.

Working in groups, students are assigned a country and then locate places of interest in their assigned country, which might include their or their parents' hometowns. They create maps with placemarks indicating places worth a visit in their assigned country, using either a graphics program on the computer, or, where the Internet is available, Google Earth (Google, 2010b, http://earth.google.com). Their placemarks will include short descriptions in English and will demonstrate at least one example of a phrase or sentence in a local variety of English. Students find these examples by locating local online newspapers, stories, or blogs by local people written in English. After creating their maps, students display them to their classmates, who help with peer editing and ask questions that can be clarified in later revisions. The groups then return to the computer for revision and editing. Once the maps and edited placemarks are finalized, they are displayed again.

In a culminating discussion, students analyze the map project and what they have learned about other countries (and their own), about their classmates, and about English variation. They also discuss the strengths and limitations of the technology they have used and how it can increase opportunities for communication with other English speakers around the world. The electronic versions of the maps, both first and second drafts, are included in each student's personal e-portfolio. (For more on educational uses of Google Earth, see Herring, 2008; and Google, 2010c.)

Technology Tasks

Low-resource, low-access setting

In a classroom with one computer and no Internet access, using personal access to the Internet, the teacher downloads map images of countries around the world on a portable device and uploads them to the class computer for students to work on in groups. After brainstorming the places they will describe, each group uses the computer's drawing program to mark four places on their map that would be of interest to their classmates. If the teacher has access to a scanner, the students bring in photos to add to their map. They write on the map graphic a brief description in English of each place, using a print dictionary or an electronic dictionary on the computer. The teacher brings in printouts from online sources and leads a discussion on aspects of local Englishes. The teacher also prints out pictures students have brought from home, using the school's printer if one is not available in the classroom. If audio sources are available (CDs or student recordings), they can also be used, giving the students the chance to hear varieties of English. Next, the student groups place their maps on the wall, and the class does a gallery walk in which students write notes (on sticky notes) as the groups take turns presenting their map and pictures. In order not to interrupt the presentations, the audience members later tag other students' maps with their questions, comments, or edits. The student groups then revise their maps to address their classmates' questions. The finalized maps are placed on display around the room for the culminating class discussion.

Medium-resource, medium-access setting

In a fully equipped computer lab that is only available twice a week, with reliable Internet access, students in groups perform the brainstorming and begin writing their descriptions on paper away from the computer. In the next class, held in the computer lab, students do an online search for pictures, videos, or audio samples to accompany their descriptive passages, or they record their own video testimonials using audio software like Audacity (Audacity Development Team, 2010, http://audacity.sourceforge.com). In subsequent lessons, the instructor gives a demonstration on making placemarks on Google Earth (Google, 2010b, http:// earth.google.com) and then circulates around the room as students create their own placemarks using the photos, videos, and audio files. The next lesson is held in a standard classroom, and the class works on organizing speeches, with the task of creating a speech that ties all their placemarks together. Meeting once again in the computer lab, the students record their speeches into a Google Earth tour (using free downloadable software). When the class meets in the lab again, the students watch the tours. Students then hold their culminating discussion back in their standard classroom.

High-resource, high-access setting

In a fully equipped computer lab with Internet and computer projector, following a teacher demonstration, students are asked to make a series of placemarks tags on Google Earth for their assigned countries, including all aspects described in previous sections. Students include photos, video or audio clips, and writing. Over the next week, as students collect their material, the teacher helps them piece it all together in a Google Earth tour. For their final class, students watch each other's tours and see, via Google Earth, the reach of their potential English-language network, as they hold their culminating discussion.

See also: Teacher Goal 1 Standard 3: Adapting Technology for Writing Instruction

Based on a concept submitted by Jeff Kuhn.

Chapter 4

Technology Standards for Language Teachers

This chapter presents four overarching goals and a total of 14 standards. Each standard includes performance indicators and at least one vignette. Some of the standards include additional performance indicators to distinguish expert-level skills. As in the learner section, the vignettes pertain to a range of settings and learner types.

The Technology Standards for Language Teachers consist of four overarching goals, each with three or four standards. Each of the 14 standards is accompanied by 5–11 performance indicators. As in the learner standards, the teacher goals and standards are not listed hierarchically or sequentially; each standard is independently important.

The performance indicators in the teacher section indicate standards that all teachers should meet. Some of the standards include additional performance indicators for technology experts. These teachers have a high level of technological ability, experience, and pedagogical knowledge. Teachers serving as technology specialists should be able to meet the expert performance indicators in settings that rely heavily on technology.

This chapter includes one or two vignettes for each standard. The vignettes are designed to demonstrate how the standards are applied in real contexts and to encourage appropriate use of technology by teachers, teacher educators, administrators, and others. Each vignette includes examples of how the standard is applied in low-resource, low-access; medium-resource, medium-access; and high-resource, high-access settings. Across the standards, the vignettes cover a wide range of teacher and learner types and settings. Some of the vignettes in the teacher section show administrators, teacher educators, and fully online teachers making decisions related to technology use. To be as immediately useful as possible, the vignettes include examples of current technology applications and websites, as well as reference to recent articles on the pedagogies involved. The vignettes included here do not, of course, illustrate all the possible ways in which the standards can be applied.

Every effort has been made to represent different teacher populations (e.g., teachers of young learners, teacher trainers, tertiary language teachers). Most teachers, as well as teacher educators and administrators, will find vignettes in which they will recognize themselves and their context. We hope this familiarity will help make the standards more meaningful. At the same time, educators should imagine how these practices can enrich their own. Although not all vignettes will be relevant to every educator, we believe that they will still enable the visualization of the performance indicators and offer ideas that can easily be transferred to other contexts.

Each vignette is labeled with the following:

Teacher profile: This includes a description of the teacher (teacher, teacher educator, teacher trainer) and profile of the students, including type (adult, teen, young learner), age range in years, and language proficiency level (see Appendix B for level descriptors).

Context: This is the context in which the vignette is placed. It includes EFL/ESL/IEP designation, commercial school, blended, or all online.

Focus: This includes language skills practiced, approach, and the most important CALL tools used.

Table C2 in Appendix C lists the vignettes by goal and standard.

We encourage those who are working with technology in various contexts to continue to contribute their own vignettes to help expand the knowledge base available to educators. Follow the vignettes provided in this book as a template for organizing your vignette. Vignettes can be emailed to Deborah Healey, dhealey@uoregon.edu, for inclusion in an online repository.

Goal 1: Language teachers acquire and maintain foundational knowledge and skills in technology for professional purposes.

Standard 1: Language teachers demonstrate knowledge and skills in basic technological concepts and operational competence, meeting or exceeding TESOL technology standards for students in whatever situation they teach.

Performance indicators

- Language teachers perform basic functions with available digital devices in order to accomplish instructional and organizational goals (e.g., turning the device on and off; opening, closing, and resizing software windows; saving, editing, and organizing files and folders; copying, cutting, and pasting elements within a document; recognizing file types; launching and exiting software applications; and similar universal tasks).

- Language teachers prepare instructional materials for students using basic technology tools (e.g., word-processing software, presentation software, and software that creates Internet resources).

- Language teachers exercise appropriate caution when using online sources and when engaging in electronic communication. (See Learner Standards Goal 1 Standard 3 for some examples.)

Teacher profile: Teacher of very young learners, ages 3–6, Literacy/Beginning Literacy

Context: Beginning EFL/CLIL (content and language integrated learning) classroom in a state primary school

Focus: A teacher uses technology in order to enhance teaching and enrich the student learning environment.

Background

A teacher works in a state school that is implementing the CLIL (content and language integrated learning) approach in order to improve the EFL learning environment of young primary school students. The instructor teaches in the foreign language to very young children who are just beginning to learn that language, but their school has a rather limited range of foreign language resources. The teacher uses technology to enhance their classroom in various ways. For example, CDs or DVDs provide the children with more linguistic and content input. The children sometimes gather around the computer to view a story or animated song, and they sometimes interact with animated storybooks and interactive CDs or DVDs in the English corner at the back of their classroom.

Often the teacher cannot find print materials, and so uses copyright-free pictures downloaded at home and transferred with a memory device to the class computer. The teacher pastes the pictures into presentation software to create visually enhanced presentations for the class. The children then sit in their chairs in a circle around the computer and view and discuss the presentation.

The teacher organizes the materials in folders, exchanges materials with an email group of local colleagues, and often downloads flash cards or creates board games and card games from teacher resource websites such as Tools for Educators (2010, http://www.toolsforeducators.com) or DLTK's Educational Activities for Children (DLTK's Sites, 2010, http://www.dltk-teach.com). The teacher also frequently visits resource sites such as A to Z Teacher Stuff (2010, http://www.atozteacherstuff.com) to find lesson plans and ideas for the class.

Finally, in order to create authentic and stimulating contexts for the students and also to involve parents, the teacher sometimes video records students' role-plays of various songs or just the children singing a song or narrating a story. The teacher then prepares CDs or DVDs with the material and sends it home—or, if the parents give their permission, uploads it to the school or community website.

Technology Tasks

Low-resource, low-access setting

In a classroom with one computer but no projector or Internet, the teacher prepares materials at home. To teach the story *Brown Bear, Brown Bear* (Martin & Carle, 1967, 1970), the teacher looks for ideas at educational resource websites and downloads flash cards from ESL Flashcards (ESLflashcards.com, 2010, http://www.eslflashcards .com) to help with introducing the new vocabulary. The teacher does not have a big book to present the story to the class, and so scans the pictures from the book or uses similar pictures from DLTK's Sites (2010) Crafts for Kids to create a slide presentation. The teacher uses the slides like a book, changing them as if turning the pages of the book, while the children sit around the computer as the story is read aloud to them.

Next, the teacher gives the children a handout prepared with the various pictures from the story. The children cut out the pictures and place them in the right order. At the end of the lesson, the children sing the story to the tune of a familiar song (e.g., "Frère Jacques"). Later, during free activity time, the children can practice the new vocabulary by playing card games or a board game, which the teacher has prepared with the help of materials downloaded from Tools for Educators. In the follow-up lesson, the teacher video records the children singing the song in order to put the recording in their portfolios and on a CD or DVD that the children will take home at the end of the term.

Medium-resource, medium-access setting

In a classroom with a computer for every three students, a projector, and some Internet access, the teacher carries out the lesson as described previously but with the children following the story with the help of the projector. The teacher might also use animal sounds from the Internet (e.g., from Sea World's Animal Sounds Library, SeaWorld Parks & Entertainment, 2010, http://www.seaworld.org/animal-info/sound-library /index.htm) so that the children can listen to and identify animal sounds.

During their free activity time, the children can draw the animals from the story using Paint or other drawing software, work on interactive CDs or DVDs, or view a presentation of the story with narration recorded by the teacher to supplement the visuals.

In the follow-up lesson, the teacher records the children narrating parts of the story on an MP3 device. The teacher then uses the audio recordings and the children's drawings with a video editor (e.g., Windows Movie Maker [Microsoft, 2004] or iMovie [Apple Computer, 2009]) in order to create a digital video presentation in which the children narrate the story. The presentation is included in the children's portfolio and copied on a CD/DVD that the children can take home at the end of the term. The teacher also uploads the presentation, after obtaining parents' permission, on the school or community website.

High-resource, high-access setting

In a classroom with one computer, a projector, and a good Internet connection, the lesson can be carried out as previously descibed. In the follow-up lesson, the teacher can record individual students or student pairs narrating their favorite parts of the story using Voki (Oddcast, 2010; http://www.voki.com/) or a similar program, in which the students can choose a personalized avatar. The students choose their favorite avatar and then record their narration. The teacher uploads the recording to the school or community website. Although Voki provides safety for the children, because their images are not shown online, the teacher still asks for parents' permission before uploading and sends an informative leaflet to parents detailing how Voki will be used. The teacher also invites the parents to watch the Voki presentations and give feedback to their children.

See also: Learner Goal 3 Standard 1: Family Stories

Teacher profile: Technology-using teacher of experienced university EFL teachers, native speaker or Bridging–Mastery/High Advanced (Level 5+, C1–C2)

Context: University with lab and technical support staff

Focus: A teacher who uses technology is asked to prepare a workshop for colleagues to help introduce technology into the language curriculum.

Background

An experienced teacher who uses technology in language courses has been asked to provide an introduction to CALL for other teachers at their university. The teacher often uses productivity software, such as a word processor for writing reports, spreadsheets for maintaining a grade book, a presentation program for projects, and email software at home. Thus, the teacher is familiar with basic functions such as turning devices on and off, opening and closing files and folders, using search mechanisms, and launching and exiting software and a browser. To prepare for teaching a CALL course to colleagues, the teacher visits with the university instructional technology department to ensure familiarity with how computers work in the lab (e.g., how to access the Internet or local intranet, and what software will be available for the class). Well in advance of the first day, the teacher requests that audio technology be installed, and the university agrees to supply several computer stations in the lab with headsets and appropriate software. The university technology support professionals also demonstrate the assistive computer devices that are available for students with disabilities. The teacher practices plugging in the equipment and adjusting it in preparation for showing the teachers how to use it. Where an intranet or Internet access is available, the teacher also requests university server space to create an online forum where teachers (and later their students) can write about their projects and ask questions about their work. The teacher communicates regularly with individual colleagues. One or more of the workshops focuses on technology safety, for example, setting computer or Internet passwords, avoiding giving out personal information, using virus-checking software, and determining the reliability of information collected on the web. The teacher reminds colleagues that when they supplement their computer work at home or in an Internet café, they should virus-check their portable devices before loading files onto the school's computers.

In the course of the school term, the new teacher-trainer asks colleagues to complete several different kinds of projects directly related to their work, depending on the technology available to them. These include a team presentation using slideshow software to examine pedagogical aspects of some software or Internet sites, for example, how to use a word processor for pedagogical purposes, a project requiring a web search for images and text, a podcast audio recording, a collage using an online graphics program, a review of a CALL lesson website or lesson software, or a WebQuest, based on their own interests and access to technology. Colleagues are also asked to create an online or paper rubric to evaluate each other's projects as well as their own (see PBL Checklists [ALTEC, University of Kansas, 2009], http://pblchecklist.4teachers.org/checklist.shtml). They collect all their projects in an electronic portfolio. These projects represent the types of activities the teachers may require of their own future students, and they give ample practice in basic file and computer management while using typical CALL productivity tools and teaching software. As the semester progresses, the teachers begin working collaboratively on specific activities, handouts, website links, and so on, that they will use with their own students. By the beginning of the semester in which they will use the lab, all the teachers have completed a set of materials to help students access the lab for language learning and have helped archive them for others to use as well. (For online courses for professional development, see TESOL's Online Education Programs [TESOL, 2010], http://tesol.org/s_tesol/seccss.asp?CID=244&DID=1716; and TESOL CALL Interest Section [2010a], Electronic Village Online, http://evosessions.pbworks.com/.)

Technology Tasks

Low-resource, low-access setting

With only one or two computers in the classroom and no Internet access, teachers work in teams, taking turns, and they supplement their work with a home computer or at a public Internet café or community center. The teacher–trainer brings printouts of web pages to class as exemplars and creates folders on the class computer to hold the teams' electronic portfolios. Teachers use printouts of the presentations and other activities they have created, and they use home or public computers to download and save the web pages onto portable devices to bring to the classroom. Portable media are virus-checked before copies are made to the classroom machine. These activities give the teachers ample practice in overcoming the limitations of their setting and in practicing safe computing while they prepare classroom materials.

Medium-resource, medium-access setting

With a small lab with headsets and modest Internet access, teachers are able to complete all the suggested activities more easily. The teacher–trainer helps them create a checkout system so their students will be able to borrow and return the headsets. The teachers supplement their work with a home computer or at a public Internet café or community center, either sending files to themselves for download at the lab or saving them to a portable device to bring to the university. The teacher–trainer regularly accesses the online forum or a virtual office space such as Tapped In ([SRI, 2010] http://www.tappedin.org), either from home or at school, in order to motivate the teachers to complete their tasks.

High-resource, high-access setting

With several university labs, broadband Internet access, and a computer/projector set up in the classroom, teachers are able to use open lab times to access the forum, email, and a virtual office space (e.g., Tapped In), and they complete their projects using the Internet. The teacher–trainer uses the projector to demonstrate how the projects will be shaped and provides examples of websites to visit for their pedagogical studies. Online lessons are sampled by everyone in the lab, with comments from the whole class at the discussion forum, before teachers begin their reviews. The teachers save their reviews of websites and software in a wiki set up by the trainer; this archive will help remind them of the content when they begin to use the Internet with their own students. The teachers are encouraged to set up their own virtual offices and to create links to websites and downloadable materials that they can begin using immediately with their own students.

See also: Learner Goal 3 Standard 4: Evaluating Web Sources; Teacher Goal 3 Standard 3: Rubrics in English for Science

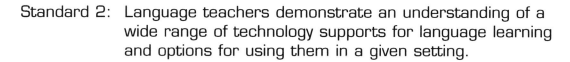

Standard 2: Language teachers demonstrate an understanding of a wide range of technology supports for language learning and options for using them in a given setting.

Performance indicators

- Language teachers identify appropriate technologies to support a range of instructional objectives.

- Language teachers use evaluation tools to analyze the appropriateness of specific technology options.

- Language teachers share information about available technology with colleagues.

- Language teachers use online technology as available to deliver instructional or support material.

- Language teachers locate and can adapt a variety of digital resources.

Teacher profile: A nonnative-English-speaking (NNES) teacher working with a native-English-speaking (NES) aide in a class for teenagers, ages 13–18, Expanding–Bridging/High Advanced+ (Levels 4–5, B2–C1)

Context: EFL class with some access to technology and the Internet for classroom teachers

Focus: The teacher seeks to improve the students' speaking and pronunciation skills using the available technology.

Background

A native-English-speaking (NES) teacher's aide in a small provincial center has been tasked with helping the nonnative-English-speaking (NNES) teacher implement more communication practice in a high-intermediate EFL class by drawing on different types of technology support. Although a native speaker of English, the aide has not had pedagogical training. The nonnative speaker is a former teacher of another language. While possessing a strong understanding of pedagogy and English grammar, the teacher lacks confidence in speaking skills and so is reluctant to introduce speaking and pronunciation activities into class. The NNES teacher is familiar with basic word processing and Internet search skills and has used technology to support students' reading and writing skills, but is now interested in learning to use technology to support students' listening and speaking skills. The teacher and the aide analyze the language objectives for the upcoming unit and discuss the range of choices available for students who have various levels of familiarity with technology. As they try out several of their ideas over a six-week period, the teacher and the aide meet regularly to discuss the challenges and successes of each of the technology supports. The teacher suggests that they write a blog to share their insights with colleagues. (For more on developing listening–speaking skills, see Barrett, 2007.)

Technology Tasks

Low-resource, low-access setting

In a classroom with no computer, the teacher has a laptop and occasional Internet access outside the school setting. Many of the students at the school have small, inexpensive MP3 players with recording capability, so the teacher's aide encourages the use of these mobile devices for language practice. The NNES teacher decides to create dialogues that the students can practice and record in pairs or small groups. The teacher has written the dialogues and so can listen to the responses with a fair amount of confidence. Once the students' dialogues have been submitted, the teacher and the aide listen to them together via audio editing software, such as Audacity (downloadable free at http://www.audacity.com), on a laptop. By using Audacity they can isolate particular pronunciation issues and suggest audio corrections to give back to the students. Working together in this way also gives the NNES teacher fluency and accuracy practice and exposure to the pronunciation issues of the students. The teacher and the aide save the MP3 files with corrections to be uploaded to their students' devices in class.

Medium-resource, medium-access setting

In a classroom with a computer and projector, the teacher and aide have been looking at how suprasegmentals and word linking can be used to boost student speaking speed. The students are fans of karaoke, so the teachers decide to work with the idea of "movie karaoke." They select several movies and use an Internet search or transcription to find and print out the dialogue of individual scenes. In class, they play a movie scene (on DVD, if the Internet is not available) and the class watches without scripts. The class watches and listens to the scene a second time while following along with a script. For the third viewing, the class is encouraged to read aloud with the actors on screen. Finally, the teacher asks for volunteers to come to the front of the class to be the voices of the actors on screen; they read the script with the sound turned off in the video, mimicking the body language and gestures of the actors as they recite the dialogue. The teacher ends the class with a native-language lecture on how words are linked in English. With this new understanding of linking, the next class is devoted to further movie karaoke and practice.

High-resource, high-access setting

In a computer lab with 10 computers and reliable Internet access, students have access to digital cameras or video cameras. In a unit focusing on the future tense, the teacher seeks to incorporate more speaking practice for the students and has considered working with the weather. The aide suggests they visit a weather forecast site, such as The Weather Channel ([Weather Channel Interactive, 2010] http://www.weather .com), and prepare questions for the class that will require the use of the future forms. In class, students work in pairs to view the weather forecast site for various locales, including their own; students are asked to note down the weather for the coming week and take notes answering the questions. They take turns responding orally to the questions in a whole-class discussion. For homework, the student pairs go outside and use their cameras to shoot a weather report for the coming week where they use the future tense terminology learned that week. The student pairs report back, showing their forecasts and evaluating each other's reports. The teacher and the aide later review the students' productions together, making recorded comments and isolating dominant pronunciation issues for each student.

See also: Teacher Goal 1 Standard 3: Podcasts and Podquests

Standard 3: Language teachers actively strive to expand their skill and knowledge base to evaluate, adopt, and adapt emerging technologies throughout their careers.

Performance indicators

- Language teachers utilize technology tools to expand upon a conventional activity.

- Language teachers keep up with information through a variety of sources (e.g., books, journals, mailing lists, conventions).

- Language teachers participate in a relevant community of practice.

- Language teachers explore the possibilities inherent in emerging technologies with a critical eye.

Adapting Technology for Writing Instruction
Teacher Goal 1 Standard 3 Vignette

Teacher profile: ESL teacher of teenagers, ages 13–18, Developing–Expanding/ Low–High Advanced (Levels 3–4, B1–B2)

Context: ESL class in a U.S. secondary school

Focus: A teacher uses technology to expand on writing activities such as peer editing and publishing for teenage ESL students, who are partnered with an elementary class.

Background

As part of in-service training, a secondary ESL teacher attends a TESOL online conference focused on implementing the TESOL PreK-12 standards in the classroom. Because the conference did not focus specifically on technology implementation, the teacher decides to explore how technology is used in teaching languages by reading articles in practitioner journals related to teaching with technology (e.g., *Language Learning & Technology*, http://llt.msu.edu/; and the *TESOL Journal*, 2010, http://www .tesol.org ->Publications >TESOL Journal, free to members online). The teacher also joins a community of practice mentioned at the conference. Online colleagues encourage the teacher to try new technologies and offer their classes for learning partners. The teacher decides that summary writing is an area in the curriculum that would benefit from technology implementation and digital media. The curriculum has a strong focus on expository writing because students must learn how to read complex texts in their content-area classes, such as science, social studies, and language arts. However, the students are not typically motivated to read in depth, and they find the task of summarizing laborious. The teacher decides to have students create nonfiction picture books about their topic for an audience of a partnered elementary class offered by a colleague from the online community of practice who teaches at a nearby school.

In this activity, the secondary school students must read, process, and organize information from complex texts that extend topics they are learning in their content-area classes. They then use summaries of the content to create books appropriate to the elementary class audience. The teacher first meets with each of the content-area teachers who express an interest in the project to develop a set of appropriate materials and a list of websites where students can conduct research on a topic that interests them and relates to content they are studying in one of their core classes. The teacher also arranges with the partnering elementary classroom teacher for the secondary students to read their books to the younger students. In this way, the teacher provides the older students with opportunities to demonstrate their understanding of a content-area topic of their choice in the context of practicing their expository writing for an authentic audience. At the conclusion of the project, the teacher discusses the shared successes and problems with the partner teacher and with the online community of practice, who share their ideas for improvement. (For more on project-based learning, see Boss and Kraus, 2007.)

Technology Tasks

Low-resource, low-access setting

With only one or two computers in the classroom and no Internet access, the secondary teacher develops a collection of CD-ROM materials downloaded from the Internet or found in relevant books and journals related to several content-area topics. The students team up in pairs to work on a particular topic of interest. Their task is to locate, read, and organize information about their topic in order to write a nonfiction book for young (7- to 8-year-old) learners. As a whole-class activity, the teacher helps students read and analyze several short nonfiction picture books. They list features of this genre and together create guidelines for what to include in their texts. After breaking into teams and writing their texts, the students take turns at the computer using word-processing software to format their books with different fonts, clip art, color, and their own illustrations made with the computer's drawing program. The teacher prints the books and puts each one in a spiral binder for the elementary classroom teacher. At the appointed time, the teenage ESL students read their books to the elementary students.

Medium-resource, medium-access setting

With a computer lab in the school that has headsets and modest Internet access, the teacher reserves the lab once a week for several weeks so that students can complete the activities suggested in the low-access setting, using CD-ROMs and informational websites that the teacher has previously bookmarked. The students then use a book-making website such as the Stapleless Book ([National Council of Teachers of English, 2010] http://www.readwritethink.org/classroom-resources/student-interactives/stapleless-book-30010.html) to create their nonfiction picture books. They use a free recording program such as Audacity (downloadable at http://audacity.sourceforge.net) to create audio files after they have practiced reading their texts aloud. They print and send the books and audio files to their partner elementary class. If the partner class is nearby, they also go to the elementary classroom to read aloud, as suggested previously.

High-resource, high-access setting

With broadband Internet access in the lab and a set of digital cameras available for checkout, the teacher has students complete the assignment described in the medium-access setting and also adds an additional layer: the students take turns recording videos of each other reading aloud from their picture books. They discuss features of read-alouds (pace, prosody, gestures, etc.) and develop a rubric for helping each other read well. After practicing under the teacher's guidance, the students take turns reading and video recording alternate pages of the text. Using the computers' video editing software, the students splice together the segments to create a short video clip to post to an education-oriented video site (e.g., TeacherTube [2010], http://www.teachertube.com) so that the partnering teacher can have the elementary students read along with the videos in class. If the partner class is nearby, students also go to the elementary classroom to read aloud, as previously suggested. The videos create a permanent archive that can be used in subsequent years.

See also: Teacher Goal 4 Standard 2: CALL Professional Development; Teacher Goal 1 Standard 3: Podcasts and PodQuests

Teacher profile: EFL teacher of teenagers/adults, ages 13+, Expanding–Bridging/ High Advanced+ (Levels 4–5, B2–C1)

Context: EFL school classroom

Focus: An EFL teacher joins communities of practice to keep abreast of developments in technology and language learning, in particular technologies for listening practice.

Background

A teacher of EFL students seeks to keep abreast of new technologies in the field. The teacher tries to attend conferences whenever possible, but funding for international travel is difficult and local conferences offer few new ideas. To compensate for infrequent travel, the teacher has joined a number of international online communities and special interest sections of English language teachers who are involved with and interested in technology (e.g., TESOL's CALL Interest Section [2010b], http://www.call-is.org/info/). The teacher has a computer at home, but can also go to local Internet cafés or the local library to access the online discussions of the community via email. When possible, the teacher also participates in synchronous video- or audioconferencing and is regularly involved in interesting discussions evaluating emerging technologies in language learning. The teacher often carries out online research about technologies that seem promising for the local context and tries to find out more about their implementation in language learning and teaching. When possible, the teacher tries to access the specific technologies in order to experiment with them by using them with the online community, colleagues from the local professional association, or colleagues at school.

The teacher regularly briefs local colleagues about this work. When trying out a particular technology, the teacher presents it to and discusses it with these colleagues. In situations where a specific technology seems promising for the local context, the teacher prepares a carefully designed trial of implementation with students. In such a case, all the factors relevant to the context must be considered. These include training students, obtaining permissions, and considering time requirements (class length and syllabus fit).

The teacher evaluates the implementation and also asks students for their feedback. If the initial implementation brings about positive results and evaluations, and if the technology fits the needs of the students and adds value to their learning situation, the teacher will continue using it. Sometimes the teacher decides not to implement technology because it could not satisfy the teaching objectives or it does not bring added value to the students. In either case, the teacher shares the project locally and reports findings to online colleagues.

In this scenario, the teacher has decided to try out podcasting in order to provide authentic listening in the target language. Even in a low-access setting, digital media allow for extensive listening and comprehension tasks. (For more on audio activities, see Barrett, 2007.)

Technology Tasks

Low-resource, low-access setting

With a computer in the classroom but no projector or Internet access at the school, the teacher's international colleagues discuss technologies that might not be appropriate to use, but they are always willing to help out with ideas. The teacher has been very interested in integrating podcasts into traditional courses because the authentic listening opportunity would be beneficial to language students and would offer them a wider variety of listening tasks than the recordings accompanying their textbook. The teacher spends time on the Internet at the local library to find suitable podcasts for class. The teacher then downloads a selection on a portable memory device and prepares listening tasks based on it. The teacher uses the class computer and speakers to play the podcast for the students to listen to and complete the tasks as a whole-class activity. After repeating the process several times, students are asked to evaluate the podcasts. They also take listening tests at regular intervals to determine their progress. The teacher's goal is to help them become independent listeners to authentic materials.

Medium-resource, medium-access setting

With a computer lab and Internet, but low bandwidth and unreliable access, the teacher learns about developments in technology through the online community. The teacher always has to assess the relevance of new technologies to the local setting and their practicality, effectiveness, and overall value for the teaching situation at hand. The teacher explores technologies that seem promising and are recommended by colleagues but reevaluates them in relation to the local context and curricular goals.

The teacher has evaluated podcasts and decided to implement them with the students. Having to deal with the problem of bandwidth, the teacher decides to create a podquest. This is a "treasure hunt" search of interesting and historic local sites found by listening to audio directions using podcasts that have been downloaded beforehand and saved on the computer hard disk. Enough students own MP3 devices (e.g., iPods or other mobile devices) that there is one for each group, and the teacher transfers the podcasts to these devices. Students read instructions, find the building or site mentioned, and then listen to the audio directions while viewing the building. At some sites, they are told to pick up a brochure, ask the attendant a question, read a timetable, or some other task. They then answer a short quiz on their mobile device. The group must answer all questions correctly (and listen again if they have an incorrect answer) to get directions to the next site. When all groups have finished the activity, the students discuss their experiences, and the teacher evaluates their progress as previously described. (See Reinders, 2007; and Using iPod as a Tour Guide [Apple Computer, 2006], http://developer.apple.com/hardwaredrivers/ipod/iPodNoteReader Guide.pdf.)

High-resource, high-access setting

With a high-speed Internet lab available and computers, Internet access, projector, printer, and scanner in each classroom, the teacher holds classes in the computer lab once or twice a week. Recently the teacher has been experimenting with podquests as a way to help students get the most out of podcasts. The teacher prepares podquests so that students can carry them out while in the computer lab (i.e., with student answers hyperlinked to podcast sites containing further treasure hunt instructions; see Reinders, 2006).

See also: Teacher Goal 2 Standard 3: Practice for Speaking Test

Standard 4: Language teachers use technology in socially and culturally appropriate, legal, and ethical ways.

Performance indicators

- Language teachers demonstrate sensitivity to the similarities and differences in communication conventions across cultures, communities, and contexts.

- Language teachers show an awareness of their role as models, demonstrating respect for others in their use of public and private information.

- Language teachers show awareness and understanding when approaching culturally sensitive topics and offer students alternatives.

- Language teachers conform to local legal requirements regarding the privacy of students' personal information.

- Language teachers conform to local legal requirements regarding accessibility.

- Language teachers conform to local legal requirements regarding fair use and copyright.

- Language teachers follow local guidelines regarding the use of human subjects for research.

- Language teachers demonstrate awareness that electronic communication is not secure and private, and that in some localities, email may be subject to "open records" laws.

- Language teachers seek help in identifying and implementing solutions related to legal requirements.

- Language teachers protect student privacy (e.g., not inappropriately putting student email addresses, biodata, or photos online; fully informing students about public sharing of blogs and websites; using password-protected sites when possible).

- Language teachers respect student ownership of their own work (e.g., not sharing student work inappropriately; not requiring students to post their work publicly).

Teacher profile: Faculty and staff at an intensive English program (IEP) for adults, ages 17+, Developing–Bridging/Low–High Advanced+ (Levels 3–5, B1–C2)

Context: University IEP in the United States

Focus: Faculty and staff conduct a mandatory review of guidelines for the Family Educational Rights and Privacy Act (FERPA).

Background

A U.S. university-based IEP is under a university mandate to follow strict guidelines related to student privacy as per the federal Family Educational Rights and Privacy Act (FERPA). A committee consisting of IEP teachers and front office staff has been tasked with creating IEP-specific rules and guidelines to help ensure compliance with FERPA. Teachers have downloaded a copy of the university's guidelines related to FERPA, prepared by university attorneys. The FERPA committee has divided up different parts of the act related to the following:

- teachers' use of personally identifiable student information, including student record keeping and grade books

- front office procedures

- communication with students, sponsors, and family members

The FERPA committee uses a questionnaire to assess faculty and staff beliefs about student privacy and knowledge of FERPA. The committee realizes that most teachers are not in compliance and that the front office has compliance issues as well. For example, some teachers are posting grades or graded papers in a publicly accessible space (typically outside their door). Teachers are using email for discussions about students, freely sharing information about students' family issues and other private information. The front office keeps student records in a locked cabinet, but all the teachers know where the keys are and can access them after hours.

The FERPA committee has presented a few workshops for faculty and staff on privacy issues, using materials such as FERPA Resources (n.d.) and the Forum Guide to the Privacy of Student Information (National Forum on Education Statistics, 2006), and all have realized that some changes will need to occur in how information is disseminated. Once those changes are in place, faculty are given an orientation to FERPA, which includes a template they can use in email about students, warning that the confidential information is only for the direct recipient and is not to be forwarded. They are expected to use this template on all their email messages that have information about students. Student orientation for new learners includes a short presentation about student rights and responsibilities related to private information.

Technology Tasks

Low-resource, low-access setting

With a low level of access to the Internet (e.g., an email system) and online student record keeping on an internal server or intranet, the major privacy concerns revolve around paper documents. These include not only admissions and visa records, but also teachers' paper grade books and student papers with grades and comments. Even though much of the work is on paper, many teachers store grades in digital form, in spreadsheets. As the front office moves more records to digital form, they password-protect all computers that hold student information. Teachers have the password so that they can access student records from a computer in the front office. Graded papers are to be handed back to the students directly, not left in an area where anyone has access. Administrators encourage teachers to begin accepting and responding to papers electronically so that graded, printed versions do not need to be distributed to students. These safeguards may take some time to put into place, due to resource constraints.

Medium-resource, medium-access setting

Where the Internet or private intranet is readily available in teacher offices and labs, most student records are moved to electronic form, and teachers have access to them via a password-protected computer in the front office. In order to respond to teachers' needs for information about students, administrators consider how to set up online access using encryption in order to allow teachers to view student records without violating FERPA. Teachers are strongly urged to accept and respond to homework in electronic form in order to protect student papers with grades on them. The IEP website has been set up so that there are private areas for file sharing in each class as well as a public space for each class.

High-resource, high-access setting

With readily-available Internet access at all times, access to a local intranet, and a sophisticated course management system (CMS), IEP faculty and staff are better positioned to protect students' privacy (see Blackboard [2010], http://www .blackboard.com, or Moodle.org [2010], http://www.moodle.org; for a comparison of CMS systems, see EDU Tools [2010], http://www.edutools.info/). After the FERPA committee makes its recommendations, an online version is posted on the IEP website, and all new faculty are expected to take a short online quiz on FERPA issues before beginning work. All student records are in electronic form in the university-wide record-keeping system, with student grades also kept in a password-protected location on the IEP server. Faculty members have different levels of access to the records, depending on their role in the institute: Administrators can see all records; advisors can see grades and some admissions information on the university-wide server and the IEP server; teachers can see grade records on the IEP server. All faculty and staff are strongly encouraged to use only the university email system in discussions about students, not third-party commercial systems, where the email server is not under university control.

The IEP generally uses the password-protected, encrypted university CMS for online discussion and file sharing. The system also provides a drop box for assignments so that students can see their own graded work but not anyone else's. Students have password-protected access to their grades at any time through the CMS. Email messages that include private information for specific students are sent through the email program on the CMS whenever possible. Students are warned that forwarding their mail to a third-party email system may make their messages vulnerable to being read.

Goal 2: Language teachers integrate pedagogical knowledge and skills with technology to enhance language teaching and learning.

Standard 1: Language teachers identify and evaluate technological resources and environments for suitability to their teaching context.

Performance indicators

- Language teachers identify the technological resources (e.g., hardware, communication technologies, digital material, courseware) and limitations of the current teaching environment.

- Language teachers identify appropriate technology environments (e.g., lab, one-computer class, online, independent use) to meet specific learning/ teaching goals.

- Language teachers evaluate technology environments for alignment with the goals of the class.

- Language teachers evaluate technological resources for alignment with the needs and abilities of the students.

Teacher profile: ESL teachers of adults, ages 19+, Emerging–Expanding/High Intermediate–High Advanced (Levels 2–4, A2–B2)

Context: ESL adult school with a variety of technology access in a blended environment

Focus: Teachers collaborate in learning how to use technologies with their students while enabling the students to also help their families learn English.

Background

An ESL adult school with students from 15 countries has recently been given a new multimedia lab to assist in language teaching and learning. Several classrooms have also been given one or two computers and projectors to use for instructional purposes. One classroom has a digital whiteboard, and some classrooms also have wireless access to share the lab's Internet capabilities. The teachers have invited a local online CALL instructor to visit their school for three workshops, and this instructor has helped them use several different productivity tools and find good free websites with online lessons to create a fully blended learning environment. The teachers seek to explore these various tools further and have decided to work in teams of three, each team visiting one or more sites per week, trying out tools, and examining software. The teams report their best finds during a monthly teachers' meeting, which is held in the lab so that new sites and software can be tried out immediately.

The teachers use an evaluation rubric that the CALL instructor helped them develop to analyze and organize information. (For help with rubrics, see Burston, 2003; and Schrock, 2007.) They also use a wiki set up by the instructor to archive their reviews of the tools and sites they have explored, with active links so that others can try them out. Some teacher teams decide to explore ways to use the one-computer classrooms, while others work on effective activities for the large lab. Information about and instructions for software or sites are printed out and kept in a file for additional convenience.

Teachers encourage students with computers at home to use language learning sites with their families so that others too will have a chance to practice in private. They make copies of the instruction sheets for students to take home. In the one-computer classrooms and in the lab, students are often paired so that newcomers to the computer have a more expert partner to help out as they perform the required activities at the keyboard, adjust the headset volume, and so on. This also gives students practice as teaching guides for their families.

At the end of the term, the teachers review the information collected at their wiki in order to evaluate the tools, software, and Internet sites they have used. They discuss the success of various materials with different levels of students and the fit to the curricula of different classes. They organize into new teams for new explorations.

Technology Tasks

Low-resource, low-access setting

With a one-computer classroom and a data projector, teachers use presentation slides for explanations of grammar, usage, and vocabulary. They can easily edit their presentations or add material while they teach, for example, by typing in student responses while the class is watching. In their software review research, they find a number of tools that can be installed on the computer and used by teams of students, either for additional practice/discussion exercises or to create their own flash cards or learning games. Student teams take turns using the computer while other groups of students work on different lessons. In very low-level classes, teachers use an electronic whiteboard when possible to help students become familiar with keyboard functions of the computer hardware or to explain how to use a piece of software before students try it on their own.

Medium-resource, medium-access setting

In a one-computer classroom with Internet and projector, teachers have students access publishers' websites, which provide additional language practice activities and exercises to accompany their textbooks. Students work in small groups, taking turns at the computer, to complete the activities while quietly discussing their answers. Teachers find that these interactive exercises are highly motivating, and they also use them during full lab time. They project the initial lesson for each chapter for the whole class to watch so that students will be prepared to use the lab effectively. Teachers also select software training videos found through searches on TeacherTube ([2010] http://www.teachertube.com/) or on a teacher training site such as Russell Stannard's (2010) TTV (http://www.teachertrainingvideos.com/). Students watch these videos as a class (for example, how to use a word processor) in preparation for activities in the lab. Teachers also select several listening–speaking sites, such as Randall's ESL Cyber Listening Lab ([Davis, 2010] http://www.esl-lab.com/) or Interesting Things for ESL Students ([Kelly & Kelly, 2010] http://www.manythings .org/), so that students can try out the activities in a whole-class setting before accessing them in the lab with headsets or at home.

High-resource, high-access setting

To use the full multimedia lab, teachers first prepare their students with the activities suggested previously so that they come to the lab ready to sit down and work. Where advance preparation has not been possible, students initially sit away from the computers around a large table in the center of the room and view their activity preparation on the computer projector, on an overhead projector, or on paper with teacher explanation. Students who are already familiar with computer functions may be asked to prepare a screencast video to help instruct newcomers; they can use free or inexpensive screencasting software (see Comparison of Screencasting Software at Wikipedia, 2010a). This activity provides authentic practice in speaking while creating a useful electronic product.

See also: Learner Goal 3 Standard 2: Interactive Language Games and Exercises; Learner Goal 1 Standard 1: Each One Teach One

Standard 2: Language teachers coherently integrate technology into their pedagogical approaches.

Performance indicators

- Language teachers demonstrate understanding of their own teaching styles.

- Language teachers review personal pedagogical approaches in order to use technology to support current teaching styles.

- Language teachers demonstrate their understanding of the potential and limitations in technology.

- Language teachers embed technology into teaching rather than making it an add-on.

- Language teachers engage regularly in professional development related to technology use.

- Language teachers evaluate their use of technology in teaching.

Performance indicators, expert level of technology

- Language teachers work around the limitations in available technology to achieve instructional goals.

- Language teachers support peers in their professional development with technology. (Informal support may be unpaid; formal support should be paid.)

Teacher profile: Secondary school ESL teacher of teenagers, ages 16–17, Developing/Low Advanced (Level 3, B1)

Context: 10th-grade ESL language arts class

Focus: Teacher fosters communicative, interactive language learning in technology-supported settings for a content-based English class.

Background

In a 10th-grade ESL language arts class in a U.S. high school, recently arrived native-Spanish-speaking students are developing English proficiency. The teacher self-describes as someone who likes to encourage students to develop verbal skills conversationally, but wants them to learn how to contribute to academic discussions as well. Aware that open-ended opportunities to participate in large class discussions about literature can be intimidating and challenging, the teacher ensures that the pedagogical approach used allows for multiple low-anxiety opportunities to participate. Literature response groups, author's chair, and think-pair-share are activities used on a regular basis. With self-awareness of current teaching styles, the instructor decides to use technology to support these academic discussions about literature. In this lesson, the teacher has the students prepare for and participate in literature response groups to ensure that they discuss ideas with one another rather than simply listening to the teacher's comments (adapted from the ESL Standards for PreK–12 Students [TESOL, 1997], pp. 122–123). They first participate in a fishbowl discussion activity:

- Students sit in inner and outer circles. The inner circle discusses a poem, and the outer circle takes notes on their peers' interactions.

- The teacher facilitates a reflective discussion with the students about which observations represented positive ways to participate in group discussions.

With technology, the language teacher adds several layers to this lesson, including transcripts of discussions by poets and critics in electronic media. (For more on teaching literature with technology, see Hanson-Smith, 2009.)

Technology Tasks

Low-resource, low-access setting

Without a computer in the classroom, but with a recorder or MP3 player available, the teacher uses the Internet at home or in the school's lab to find a recording and the transcript from an online written discussion in which native-English-speaking peers have discussed a poem (see, for example, a video clip from the movie *Dead*

Poets Society [Haft and Weir, 1989]). After the ESL students have read the poem, they listen to the recording of the discussion while reading copies of the transcript. Then they underline and discuss different ways of exchanging ideas: agreeing, disagreeing, adding comments. Students listen to the teacher read the poem again, then read the transcript and make notes to share in their subsequent fishbowl class discussion. Outside of class, they look up any words that are unfamiliar to them in an online dictionary or a paper dictionary.

Medium-resource, medium-access setting

With one computer and a data projector in the classroom, the teacher presents a pre-reading activity with the projector, asking for ideas about a poem based solely on the title. Students discuss their ideas before reading the poem, which is then displayed using the projector. Students listen to various interpretations of the poem on audio recordings that the teacher has located and bookmarked on the Internet (see, for example, Poets.org [Academy of American Poets, 2010], http://www.poets.org/). They also watch and discuss several short clips of literary critics discussing the poem, and with the help of transcripts they create a "phrase guide" of language features that they notice in how the literary critics argue their points. They use these phrase guides in their own fishbowl discussions in class. As in the setting above, they look up any words in the poem or discussion that are unfamiliar to them.

High-resource, high-access setting

With the ESL students in a networked computer lab, with a computer and headset for each student, the language teacher further adapts this lesson. Before discussing the poem orally in class, the ESL students log on to the class blog that the teacher has created. The blog includes the text of the poem (with hyperlinked definitions of difficult vocabulary and links to critical discussions, videos, and their transcripts) and an audio file of the poem that students can read and listen to multiple times at their own pace. With the poem before them on the desktop, students use a discussion forum to share their comments about the poem. (In a large class, the students are divided into groups and respond on different threads.) The online setting allows quieter class members more time to think and respond, and it prevents more orally proficient students from dominating the whole-group discussion. After a period of time online, the language teacher asks students to pair up with a partner from another group (sharing one computer) and scroll back through the online discussions to find and list two comments with which they agree and two comments with which they disagree. The students then use these prepared comments to continue the discussion in an oral, face-to-face format. At the end of class, the teacher saves the discussions into individual files so that they can be used several months later to help students monitor their language progress.

See also: Learner Goal 3 Standard 5: Sheltered Science Concepts

Standard 3: Language teachers design and manage language learning activities and tasks using technology appropriately to meet curricular goals and objectives.

Performance indicators

- Language teachers demonstrate familiarity with a variety of technology-based options.

- Language teachers choose a technology environment that is aligned with the goals of the class.

- Language teachers choose technology that is aligned with the needs and abilities of the students (e.g., language learning-focused software, productivity tools, content tools).

- Language teachers demonstrate awareness of students' level of digital competence.

- Language teachers ensure that students understand how to use the technology to meet instructional goals (e.g., teach students how to evaluate online resources).

- Language teachers enable students to think critically about their use of technology in an age-appropriate manner.

Performance indicators, expert level of technology

- Language teachers adapt technology-based activities and tasks to align with the goals of the class and with the needs and abilities of the students.

- Language teachers create an appropriate technology environment to meet specific teaching and learning goals.

- Language teachers operate with an understanding of the underlying structure of the technology in use.

- Language teachers demonstrate the ability to draw on a wide range of functions in technological resources.

- Language teachers identify more than one approach to achieve an objective (e.g., a backup plan for when the technology is not working).

Practice for Speaking Test
Teacher Goal 2 Standard 3 Vignette

Teacher Profile: EFL teacher of teenagers/adults, ages 16+, Developing–
Bridging/Low–High Advanced+ (Level 3–5, B1–C2)

Context: EFL test-preparation class in a private school or IEP

Focus: Students practice speaking (accuracy and fluency) and
pronunciation with a variety of online tools in preparation for
a standardized online test.

Background

The instructor of an EFL test preparation class seeks to lessen the anxiety the students
have with the speaking section of the computerized test. In class the students generate
only short utterances due to the pressure of speaking in front of the class. The teacher
wants to provide speaking opportunities for students that reduce the pressure they
feel about responding "on the spot" while preparing them for the test they will take
to enter a North American university. The teacher provides a weekly set of questions,
based on the question types found in a major computerized online English ability
test like the TOEFL, or Test of English as a Foreign Language (Educational Testing
Service, 2010). Early in the term, the teacher explains how the online recording works
and supervises the students' initial trials. For the first few weeks, students may attempt
each question as many times as they like. In subsequent weeks, the students are given
a fixed amount of time to respond to the audio questions with their own recordings.
The students are given the rubric (in print or online) used to evaluate their speaking
in the standardized test assessment, and the technology provides an easy method to
rerecord until they are satisfied with their corrections.

The teacher wants to create a catalog of speaking samples (an audio e-portfolio)
of each student that can be used to evaluate improvement in fluency and accuracy.
Meeting students individually for recorded interviews is impractical, so the teacher
experiments with a variety of technology-based options. During the course of the
school term, the teacher also reviews the audio recording archive of each student
at regular intervals, referring to the rubric to clarify the comments made on the
recording. The teacher suggests online venues for further practice, such as Randall's
ESL Cyber Listening Lab for pronunciation ([Davis, 2010] http://www.esl-lab.com/)
or VOA Special English files at ManyThings.org for accuracy and intonation ([Kelly
& Kelly, 2010] http://www.manythings.org/voa/scripts/). The teacher explains the
relationship between listening and good speaking skills. The teacher helps students
find other podcasts on topics of general interest to help with further practice. In
class, the teacher discusses the value of rerecording and elicits students' ideas about
their e-portfolio construction process. (For more about creating and using audio and
podcasts, see Jobbings, 2005.)

Technology Tasks

Low-resource, low-access setting

In a classroom with no computer, but where students have access to a full-resource computer lab (with headsets and Internet access) at a scheduled time each week and computers at home, the teacher posts three questions in a podcast constructed specifically for the class (see PodOmatic [2010], http://www.podomatic.com). Students may also use mobile devices to access the podcasts. The questions are based on question types found on a major computerized English ability test like the TOEFL (Test of English as a Foreign Language [Educational Testing Service, 2010]). Students are given a fixed amount of time to submit their audio answers via the podcast. For sample questions, see the TOEFL iBT Speaking Practice Tests ([Renshaw Internet School of English, 2009] http://www.english-itutor.com/TOEFL_iBT_speaking_tests .html) or EnglishClub.com ([2010] http://www.englishclub.com/esl-exams/ets-toefl-practice-speaking.htm). The teacher records audio comments (either on a mobile phone or on a laptop) about students' pronunciation, fluency, and accuracy, and emails them to the individual students to protect their privacy. Students rerecord themselves, incorporating corrections.

Medium-resource, medium-access setting

In a classroom with no computer, but where students have access to a full-resource computer lab three times a week with audio recording/editing software such as Audacity ([Audacity Development Team, 2010] http://audacity.sourceforge.com), headsets, and an email system, at regular intervals in the lab class, the teacher gives students the speaking questions and asks them to record responses with the audio software. The teacher then listens to the students' submissions and, with the sound editing function of the software, splices pronunciation corrections and fluency and accuracy comments directly into student responses and emails the files back to them. Students rerecord as in the previous sections.

High-resource, high-access setting

In a fully equipped computer lab with Internet access and a course management system (CMS) like Moodle ([Moodle.org, 2010] http://www.moodle.org) that students can access anytime, the teacher posts speaking questions or podcasts to a class discussion forum set up specifically for this purpose. Students use the built-in audio recording software in the CMS to answer. The teacher records responses and the students rerecord as previously described. Students use the CMS to create e-portfolios of their work.

See also: Learner Goal 2 Standard 1: Social Interactions; Teacher Goal 1 Standard 3: Podcasts and Podquests

Workday Interviews
Teacher Goal 2 Standard 3 Vignette

Teacher profile: Teacher of adults, ages 17+, Developing–Bridging/Low–High Advanced+ (Level 3–5, B1–C1)

Context: North American IEP integrated skills class with an emphasis on listening and speaking

Focus: Students practice language activities with an authentic informant and find out more about working in North America.

Background

Aware of the importance of authenticity in practicing language skills, especially at the more advanced levels, an IEP teacher wants a small class of students to interact with North American cultural informants and learn about their typical workdays while practicing speaking and listening skills. Informants might include doctors, janitors, and technicians. The preliminary lesson consists of a review of materials about typical workdays using videos of authentic speakers and accompanying listening exercises at Real English ([Marzio School, 2010] http://www.real-english.com). This preparation allows students to explore the vocabulary and syntax of speaking about the workplace and prepare questions for the informant. They also read short descriptions of the workday at LifeWorks ([Office of Science Education, U.S. National Institute of Health, 2004–2010] http://science.education.nih.gov/LifeWorks.nsf/Interviews), which will give them the basis to write their own questions.

The teacher assigns a variety of interviews for students to read and look at so that they will have different points of view to discuss. In small groups, students share what they have found and brainstorm a list of questions. The groups report back to the whole class, and the teacher helps them select the most appropriate questions. Students are assigned or select a specific question to ask, but they must also prepare a follow-up question. The teacher ensures that the work described in the interviews they study will not be the same as that of the informant, so that students will have to ask questions and respond in a more impromptu fashion. Students then meet with the informant. In a class without technology, this could only be a face-to-face meeting with the interviewee, which might be difficult to arrange. If the class has access to technology, however, the informant does not have to be physically present in the classroom and can in fact be anywhere in the world. Materials generated during the interview are recorded (with the informant's permission, arranged in advance by the teacher) and accessed later for further language practice.

Following the question-and-answer session, students are assigned their homework—to write the answers to their specific questions and at least three other interesting points they learned. They access the recording to practice their questions again, and to listen to the speaker's pronunciation and vocabulary. They share their most interesting linguistic and social discoveries orally in a subsequent class session and write up their experiences. The teacher asks them to discuss any difficulties with the technology and how they might improve their questions in a subsequent interview. (For more on telephony and cross-cultural communication, see O'Dowd, 2006.)

Technology Tasks

Low-resource, low-access setting

In a classroom with no computer or audiovisual facilities, but with access to a computer lab elsewhere on campus, students view the Real English videos and perform the exercises outside of class. The teacher prints out one interview from LifeWorks for each student, choosing interviews that are not about the same job as the interlocutor's. Students use the teacher's mobile phone to speak to the interlocutor. The recording can be made with a simple cassette or digital recorder, with the microphone held to the phone. At a prearranged time, the instructor calls the informant on a mobile phone. Once the informant answers, the instructor puts the phone on its "speakerphone" setting so that the students can interact with the informant through this medium. Students are requested not to simply read their questions, but to interact live with the interviewee. Students may make multiple copies of the interview or listen together in pairs or small groups outside of class.

Medium-resource, medium-access setting

With a single computer, data projector, speakers, and Internet access in the classroom, students watch a video that the teacher has found on YouTube (e.g., Nico's Workday [2007], http://www.youtube.com/watch?v=99IYG_xsAYA) or a comparable video at Real English in which an informant describes his or her job. The brainstorming of questions is done in a word processor on the computer and projected to the room. The phone call is made through Skype ([Skype Technologies, 2010] http://www.skype .com) or another Internet-based telephony provider and played through the room speakers for clearer sound. Students working in pairs take turns at the class computer writing up their interviews in a class blog or wiki online, and they also access the Internet outside of class to write comments and questions on their peers' entries.

High-resource, high-access setting

With Internet access for each student and a school course management system (CMS) like Moodle, students are asked to go to LifeWorks or Real English and select three interviews to review. They then summarize key points they learned and post related questions in the class discussion forum online that their teacher has set up for this purpose. As in the previous scenario, students interact with the informant on Skype ([Skype Technologies, 2010] http://www.skype.com) or, if the interlocutor has Internet access, in their CMS audio chat room. For homework, students post the answers to their questions and three other interesting points they learned on their blogs or, for further speaking practice, in a podcast. (For examples of students writing and talking about their projects, see Zeinsteijer, 2006.)

See also: Learner Goal 2 Standard 2: Think-Pair-Share

Standard 4:   Language teachers use relevant research findings to inform the planning of language learning activities and tasks that involve technology.

Performance indicators

- Language teachers demonstrate familiarity with suggestions from research for classroom practice using technology.

- Language teachers use a variety of avenues for getting information about research related to technology use (e.g., communities of practice, conferences).

- Language teachers demonstrate understanding of the temporal nature of research findings related to technology use (i.e., that technology changes over time, so older research may not be applicable to current settings).

- Language teachers demonstrate awareness of multiple research sources and perspectives that inform technology use.

- Language teachers discern which findings about technology use are most appropriate for their situation.

- Language teachers share relevant research findings about technology use with others.

- Language teachers identify the context and limitations of research about technology use and do not apply findings inappropriately.

Performance indicators, expert level of technology

- Language teachers demonstrate their understanding of relevant research findings related to technology use for language learning.

- Language teachers identify gaps in current research about technology use.

- Language teachers help others recognize the context and limitations of research about technology use.

- Language teachers produce and disseminate research related to technology use.

Teacher profile: University teacher of pre-service and in-service teachers enrolled in graduate school, ages 20+, native speakers of English or Bridging–Mastery (Level C1–C2)

Context: ESL teaching methods course in a North American university for secondary school teachers to obtain TESOL certification

Focus: Teachers explore practices that apply pedagogical research to technological innovations that support language learning for newcomer immigrant secondary school students.

Background

In a teacher education class focused on ESL teaching methods, student teachers pursuing an initial or supplemental teaching certificate in TESOL have a fieldwork, or hands-on, component in which they combine their research with volunteering in practical teaching situations. These fieldwork experiences take place in various ways throughout the duration of a course, such as offering individual face-to-face tutoring sessions or tutoring online with ESL students.

Each week the teachers read and discuss relevant research that their instructor provides and that they locate through various Internet and library sources. Because their teaching contexts involve high numbers of newcomers (recent immigrants with limited experience with English), the course focuses on sheltered practices for supporting students in understanding the content of secondary subject areas while also learning basic structures of English. A part of their discussion concerns how to use technology in ways that might augment pedagogical strategies that are useful with newcomer students. In the weekly fieldwork component of the class, the in-service teachers utilize various technologies in their one-on-one tutoring of adolescent ESL newcomers. In addition, the teachers share their experiences on a password-protected class-based website (e.g., a wiki or their course management system blog), where they post lesson plan ideas, materials, and multimedia projects.

At the end of their teacher education course, teachers prepare and submit a critical evaluation of which technology tools were most appropriate for their particular tutoring context. Their final lesson plans, recordings, and transcripts are included in their personal electronic portfolios. They also select one or more of their critiques of the research and/or the technology they used to be included in the portfolio. (For a short form for software review, see Schrock, 2007, or ICT4LT CALL Software and Website Evaluation Forms, 2009.)

Technology Tasks

Low-resource, low-access setting

With one computer in the classroom and limited Internet access, teachers read and discuss in groups research articles pertaining to adolescent newcomer students and assist one another in modifying their plans for instructional delivery to accommodate students with beginning-level English. The course instructor (or a designated group member) assembles their ideas for modifying instructional delivery for ESL students and publishes these ideas on the course website. The teachers then choose from among these ideas and use them in their individual face-to-face tutoring sessions with an ESL student. (The consultation can also take place online if both student and teacher have Internet access, e.g., with personal or community center computers or through mobile phone technology.)

Medium-resource, medium-access setting

With several computers and adequate access to the Internet, including access on their own computers at home, teachers read assigned recent research and then discuss it in small groups to determine how they will work with their ESL students in the weekly tutoring session. After assisting one another with this idea exchange, they post a draft lesson plan to their class wiki or blog. They solicit written comments and discussion on their final lesson plans from the other student teachers. Where students are at some distance from the teachers, instead of face-to-face tutoring, the teachers apply the strategies they are studying in weekly online tutoring sessions using the chat feature within the school's course management system.

High-resource, high-access setting

With one computer per teacher, headsets, webcam, and broadband access, teachers each create a video or audio recording, explaining how and why they made lesson plan modifications, and then publish the video or audio file to the course blog or wiki. They conduct their weekly tutoring of an ESL student through a combination of real-time text chat (e.g., at their virtual office at Tapped In [SRI, 2010], http://www .tappedin.org), real-time Internet telephony (such as Skype [Skype Technologies, 2010], http://www.skype.com) for speaking or pronunciation, or, for a writing class, in Google Docs ([Google, 2010a] http://docs.google.com) or a wiki (e.g., PBworks [2010], http://www.pbworks.com, which has free access for educators). The teachers ask permission of their students to record and use the transcript of their tutoring session for their class work. They select a part of the tutoring session to post to the class blog or wiki, with their comments (either text or audio/video) on the lesson and what was successful or what was not. (For suggestions on using Internet telephony for ESL tutoring, see Online Tutoring World's TEFL Guide to Teaching with Skype [2006], http://www.onlinetutoringworld.com/technology/teflskype.htm; and Stockwell, 2010.)

See also: Teacher Goal 4 Standard 1: E-mentoring;
Teacher Goal 4 Standard 2: CALL Professional Development

Goal 3: Language teachers apply technology in record keeping, feedback, and assessment.

Standard 1: Language teachers evaluate and implement relevant technology to aid in effective learner assessment.

Performance indicators

- Language teachers demonstrate familiarity with a variety of forms of assessment that employ technology.

- Language teachers employ appropriate record-keeping tools and techniques (e.g., software-based classroom management tools, electronic grade books, reports to stakeholders).

Performance indicators, expert level of technology

- Language teachers use computer-based diagnostic, formative, and summative testing where feasible.

- Language teachers use technology to illustrate learner progress (e.g., graphic representations of scores over time, revision history).

- Language teachers provide feedback through digital file exchange (e.g., review tools in writing; annotated comments in speaking).

Vocational English as a Second Language (VESL)
Teacher Goal 3 Standard 1 Vignette

Teacher profile: Teacher of adults, ages 18+, Developing/Low Advanced (Level 3, B1)

Context: VESL course for workers at a shipyard site: blended/hybrid class with face-to-face instruction and individual practice using computers and/or Internet

Focus: Workers practice job-related tasks and skills in a work-oriented curriculum focusing on safety, critical thinking, and problem solving.

Background

Shipyard workers take part in a face-to-face class convened in several different training rooms on the shipyard, including a docked ship, immediately following or preceding the workers' regular shift. This schedule allows them to conveniently access the class and maintain work and personal commitments while focusing on job-related tasks and skills, many of which involve computer use. The work-based curriculum is focused on safety, critical-thinking skills, and problem-solving tasks. Employees must complete certification in a variety of tests, so the teacher uses different kinds of assessments to accustom them to test-taking strategies and to familiarize them with the kinds of tests they will take. However, advanced grammar and writing are included to meet the specific requests of employees. The teacher creates quizzes appropriate to the weekly topics using a free quiz maker, such as Hot Potatoes ([Half-Baked Software, 2010] http://hotpot.uvic.ca) or SurveyMonkey ([2010] http://www.surveymonkey.com, free online), or on Quia ([2010] http://www.quia.com) if the sponsor is willing to pay. The computer lab is open for these additional activities on Saturdays, which is a day off for most workers. However, workers report that the additional work is one of their favorite activities. Based on employee preferences, the teacher designs further work in grammar, writing, and vocabulary related to job scenarios. (For examples of Quia tasks, see Shipyards VESL [Greenberg, 2010], http://www.quia.com/pages/igreenberg/page1.)

The teacher prepares short readings based on company safety documents, with comprehension questions that learners discuss in class. The teacher also assigns writing tasks similar to those they will encounter at work. Guest speakers are invited to address the class, and these include a blueprint reading specialist. Students take notes and ask questions of the speakers. The main points are written up later as part of a writing task. Students also work in small groups on problem-solving stories and grammar activities. Additional assignments include workplace ESL tasks using the word processor to write letters requesting OSHA information on tools and materials, notes asking for clarification of procedures, and performance reviews of coworkers on tasks related to safety. Students learn to use a computer word-processing program for writing tasks and a spreadsheet program to keep a record of the quizzes and activities they have completed.

The teacher is responsible for regularly preparing reports on employee progress to senior management. The teacher also keeps records of attendance, exercises and tests completed, and so on, in a digital grade book that will generate graphs and charts for each student. The teacher has workers keep all their written and oral work in electronic portfolios to help them understand their progress and see where further work is needed. At the end of the term, students are given the opportunity to revise some of the written or oral work in their portfolio and submit it with an explanation of what changes/improvements they have made.

Technology Tasks

Low-resource, low-access setting

With one computer for every three or four students and no Internet access, the instructor creates quizzes with desktop software and has teams work in groups on quizzes, writing tasks, and problem-solving activities during part of their class time while other students engage in communicative activities, such as dialogue practice and discussion of safety readings with comprehension activities. The instructor posts quizzes to a website so that students with computers at home may access them more conveniently. The instructor brings safety manuals and cardiopulmonary resuscitation (CPR) instructions to class so that students can summarize them and create short reports to give orally to their classmates to practice speaking. Workers use company protocols for formatting and citations.

Medium-resource, medium-access setting

With modest bandwidth for Internet access and a fully equipped computer lab with one computer for each pair of students, workers practice vocabulary and comprehension activities based on weekly safety readings using one of the online quiz programs suggested in the Background section. Student pairs sit together at a computer and take turns answering questions. Each receives the same score; students are thus encouraged to help their teammates study the required readings. Students also practice and record workplace dialogues and save the recorded speaking tasks as files in their e-portfolios. The teacher asks students to research online sites that describe safety equipment, CPR, fire safety procedures, and so on. Students write short reports on the information they have found and use the word processor's grammar and spell checkers to edit their own work. They present their reports orally to other students to practice speaking.

High-resource, high-access setting

With good bandwidth for Internet access and a computer lab with one workstation per student, students complete the previously described activities individually or in pairs or triads, as appropriate. Some students access the quizzes from their home computers.

See also: Learner Goal 1 Standard 4: Restaurant Employees

Based on a concept submitted by Ingrid Greenberg.

Online Integrated Skills (expert level)
Teacher Goal 3 Standard 1 Vignette

Teacher profile: EFL teacher of teenagers/adults, ages 17+, Expanding–Bridging/ High Advanced+ (Level 4–5, B1–C1)

Context: EFL integrated skills class in a blended or wholly online university environment

Focus: Students preparing to study or work in the United States learn about U.S. culture and prepare e-portfolios for evaluation of their language learning progress; videoconferencing (high-resource setting) enables deaf students to participate in the course.

Background

Through the use of a course management system (CMS) such as Moodle ([Moodle .org, 2010] http://www.moodle.org), students studying online gain exposure to authentic language materials, including audio and video news materials as well as contact with classmates, computer-based materials, and the language teacher. Interaction through a CMS allows for synchronous and asynchronous communication, and it provides the teacher with digital records of speech and writing that can be used to assess student progress over the course of the term. The course is built around theme- and project-based instructional principles and focuses on U.S. culture. Students devote time each week to reading and listening to web-based materials that inform them about different aspects of U.S. culture. The teacher posts short quizzes online through the CMS to ensure that students are keeping up with the readings and are ready to interact with their peers and discuss these concepts. Students produce individual and collaborative projects and explore English and thematic cultural concepts through the construction of language and content. (For more on using CMS tools, see Harrington, Staffo, & Wright, 2006.)

In small groups, students select a subtopic related to U.S. culture and collect artifacts to create a document that highlights features of this cultural characteristic. A starting point for their projects is a series of readings on cross-cultural differences and a discussion of events and conversations with native speakers that seemed odd to them at the time. Artifacts include text, images, videos, and audio. Documents can be constructed as a web page or wiki, word-processing document, movie, slideshow, or presentation, depending on the level of resources available. Individual students are assigned to their groups and have a specific role detailed for them within the group. Each group has its own discussion board within the CMS to share materials in draft form as they collaborate on their project. Eventually, the students share the completed materials with the other groups, allowing for further valuable language exchange during the presentation and structured feedback sessions organized by the teacher. A rubric (such as from Rubistar [ALTEC University of Kansas, 2008], http:// rubistar.4teachers.org/) helps students do self-evaluations and peer evaluations. The digital exchange of information provides the instructor with archived portfolios of student work that assist in record keeping, grading, and assessment. The instructor also uses CMS personal messaging and an online grade book to offer formative and summative feedback to students. After the final presentations of the projects, students evaluate their experiences in collaboration and with the technology.

Technology Tasks

Low-resource, low-access setting

With access to the Internet only through an Internet café or home computer, the teacher recommends sites where students can compile cultural information. Students in different locations and at different times access the CMS to upload their draft materials and eventually the final projects for others to view and assess asynchronously at their convenience. Students log on to the CMS regularly to share their research in group discussion forums, and the teacher helps them schedule appropriate online synchronous meeting times for their group using the chat room facility of the CMS. The teacher also sets aside class time for reports on the materials students have found.

Medium-resource, medium-access setting

With Internet access readily available in campus labs, students can easily access the CMS to upload their materials and final projects for others to view and assess asynchronously. Students also arrange times to discuss their ongoing projects in synchronous chats through the CMS chat room facility. Peer feedback provided through the class online discussion forum created by the teacher allows students to gain insight into their linguistic strengths and weaknesses as well as the effectiveness of the content and artifacts they have presented. The teacher holds virtual office hours with the CMS text chat tool to share formative feedback.

High-resource, high-access setting

With higher bandwidth for student Internet access and personal headsets and webcams for each student, learners use desktop videoconferencing (e.g., Dimdim [2010], http://www.dimdim.com/, or Skype.com [Skype Technologies, 2010], http://www.skype.com) to present their final projects synchronously, with other students and the instructor watching from their desktop computers. The videoconferencing tool also makes possible online learning for deaf students who need to use sign language for full participation.

See also: Learner Goal 2 Standard 1: Cross-cultural Communication; Learner Goal 2 Standard 1: Social Interactions; Learner Goal 2 Standard 2: Think-Pair-Share

Standard 2: Language teachers use technological resources to collect and analyze information in order to enhance language instruction and learning.

Performance indicators

- Language teachers demonstrate familiarity with research-based principles related to technology-enhanced assessment.

- Language teachers use technology-enhanced assessment results to plan instruction.

- Language teachers interpret computer-based test scores for stakeholders (e.g., TOEFL, other standardized tests).

- Language teachers elicit student feedback in order to improve teacher use of technology.

Performance indicators, expert level of technology

- Language teachers apply research findings related to technology-enhanced assessment.

- Language teachers collect student output for analysis (e.g., concordancer to analyze lexical complexity, chat logs).

- Language teachers use digital resources to document teaching for further analysis (e.g., digital recording of lectures and class interactions, digital logs of interactions).

Teacher profile: Reading teacher of adults, ages 19+, Expanding–Bridging/High Advanced+ (Level 4–5, B2–C1)

Context: IEP academic advanced reading–writing course

Focus: Teacher uses electronic tools to help academically oriented students find supplemental texts and to analyze a corpus of student writing to see if students are using appropriately sophisticated vocabulary.

Background

A reading teacher in a U.S. IEP wants to use interesting and different supplemental material with students but is concerned about the level of language used in authentic material downloaded from the Internet. Although a document can be scanned manually, comparing it against the teacher's general knowledge and the Academic Word List (Coxhead, 2007), this is very time consuming and not very accurate. The teacher also wants to monitor the level of vocabulary used by students in their writing, especially in high-intermediate and advanced levels. With readily available digital tools, the teacher can easily compare vocabulary and readability levels in electronic versions of the reading texts and students' writing. (For more on using concordancers with students, see Lamy & Klarskov Mortensen, 2010.)

Technology Tasks

Low-resource, low-access setting

With Internet access at home, the teacher is always looking for interesting copyright-free material to print out for use with students. The teacher has certain favorite sites used to look for topics, including BreakingNewsEnglish ([Banville, 2010] http://www.breakingnewsenglish.com). This site includes activities as well as readings, and the readings are often at a more basic and a more advanced level. The teacher also uses the search tool Twurdy ([2010] http://www.twurdy.com) to show the web pages related to a selected topic, color-coded by readability. Having found what seems like an appropriate reading, the teacher further assesses its readability by copying and pasting it into VocabProfiler ([Cobb, 2010b] http://www.lextutor.ca/vp) or a similar downloadable software program, such as Range (for Windows; [Heatley, 2009] http://www.victoria.ac.nz/lals/resources/range.aspx). VocabProfiler shows the percentage of words found in the first 1,000 most common words, the second 1,000 most common words, the Academic Word List (Coxhead, 2007), and off-list words (see Burell, 2008). Range will mark words that belong to different word lists, including the General Service List (Bauman, n.d.) and the Academic Word List (AWL). The teacher can see which words are in each category and decide whether to add an explanation or gloss for the less-common words. The teacher can also copy and paste the reading into Microsoft Word (2010b). Word's grammar checker will give a Flesch Reading

Ease score and Flesch-Kincaid Grade Level. (Openoffice.org also has a readability extension, but for Windows only; it uses a range of readability measures.) Since readability is based on native speaker standards, it is not always accurate for English language learners, but it can give a rough estimate.

The teacher can also see the level of language used by the students by pasting their papers into a word processor, using the word count feature to get the number of words and sentences, and employing VocabProfiler or Range to obtain information about their vocabulary use. The VocabProfiler output allows the teacher to quickly see what words, if any, students are using from the Academic Word List. The teacher copies and pastes the results from the word processor and the output table from VocabProfiler into a spreadsheet to easily track student progress.

Medium-resource, medium-access setting

In a one-computer classroom with Internet access and a computer projector, and students with relatively easy access to the Internet outside of class, the teacher wants a class of high-intermediate reading/writing students to help select additional readings related to the topics in their textbook. The teacher divides students into 10 groups and assigns each group one of the textbook topics. In class, using the projector, the teacher shows students how to use Twurdy ([2010] http://www.twurdy.com/) to search for the topic and create a subset of possible readings at the appropriate level. The teacher also shows them how to use the word and sentence count tools in the word processor, and how to use VocabProfiler. The teacher gives students a rubric to use, showing the target length of the reading in number of words, the target range in sentences, and the target percentages of words from the first 2,000 most common words and the Academic Word List (AWL). Students are expected to fill in the matrix with this information for each reading. Students outside of class divide up the list of readings, and each selects one or more to work on, first skimming the text to see if it looks interesting, then copying and pasting it into Word to get a word and sentence count. Next, they copy and paste it into VocabProfiler to get information about the vocabulary used. Students share their printouts with their group in class, describing what they have found, and the group picks which article(s) to read. The group can decide that a reading that seems to be too difficult may be interesting enough to include anyway. The teacher puts the selected readings into VocabProfiler, noting words from the AWL to target in class.

After students have read the selected texts and written their papers for each unit, or at a later stage when students have written papers on their assigned readings, the teacher will use VocabProfiler to look at student writing, seeing whether students did use the target vocabulary. The teacher tracks each student's vocabulary use by copying and pasting the output table from VocabProfiler into a spreadsheet for each student. The teacher also checks the number of words and sentences using the word count feature in the word processor, then adds this information to the spreadsheet as well. At the end of the term, teacher and students have a fairly complete picture of how reading and vocabulary levels have improved.

High-resource, high-access setting

With easy access to the Internet, a course wiki to share files and resources, and a course management system for grading and private file sharing, the teacher of an advanced reading/writing class does not use a specific textbook for the course. Instead, students read about controversial topics, discuss the topics, then write persuasive essays. The class as a whole decides which topics students will discuss at the beginning of the semester. The teacher assigns students to "for" and "against" teams. After showing students how to use the readability checker in their word processor and VocabProfiler, the teacher sends them to the Multnomah County Library Social Issues portal ([Multnomah County Library, 2010] http://www.multcolib .org/homework/sochc.html), Public Agenda ([2010] http://www.publicagenda.com /citizen), and an academic portal such as Intute ([2010] http://www.intute.ac.uk/) to search for articles. They fill in a matrix for their target reading, including the source (whether academic or popular interest), orientation to the topic (pro/con/balanced), target length of the reading in number of words, the target range in sentences, and the target percentages of words from the first 2,000 most common words and the Academic Word List (AWL). The teacher checks their matrices to make sure that readings are at an appropriate level of difficulty and to determine whether each reading is appropriately categorized in terms of orientation. The teacher then uses VocabProfiler to find target vocabulary to teach related to each topic—words that students will be expected to use in their writing. Once the readings are approved, students add the readings and their analysis of the readings to the appropriate area on the course wiki, which is set up so that only class members can view the content.

After students write their persuasive essays, they use a spreadsheet to record their word count and sentence count and the VocabProfiler output showing the number and percentage of words from the first 1,000 word list, second 1,000 word list, and AWL. They use a private shared area of the course wiki or course management system to send the essay and spreadsheet to the instructor, who in turn uses the same private area to send personal comments. Students add to the same spreadsheet throughout the semester so that they as well as the teacher can see what is happening with their writing. The teacher compiles student grade results each week into a private spreadsheet, where data from the word processor and VocabProfiler can be compared to see if there is a relationship between reading/vocabulary difficulty and student writing results. At the end of the semester, the instructor creates a chart from each student's individual spreadsheet to graphically display individual student results. The charts are attached to students' grade reports for the course.

Standard 3: Language teachers evaluate the effectiveness of specific student uses of technology to enhance teaching and learning.

Performance indicators

- Language teachers use appropriate procedures for evaluating student use of technology (e.g., rubrics, checklists, matrices—which may evaluate enjoyment).

- Language teachers elicit student feedback in order to improve student use of technology.

Performance indicators, expert level of technology

- Language teachers develop and share procedures for evaluating student use of technology.

- Language teachers examine student outcomes that result from use of technology (e.g., examining chat logs for more complex language).

Rubrics in English for Science (general and expert levels)
Teacher Goal 3 Standard 3 Vignette

Teacher profile: Teacher of adults, ages 19+, Expanding–Mastery/High Advanced+ (Level B2–C2)

Context: EFL English for Special Purposes (ESP) class in science at a university for science and technology

Focus: Students develop vocabulary and grammar for science using a variety of technologies that also provide digital skills for future employment and lifelong learning.

Background

A teacher in an English class for engineers seeks to help adult students develop their grammar and vocabulary for science. Because the students are familiar with technology for a variety of purposes, the teacher has them work on a number of creative projects that will be similar to the presentations and collaborative projects they will take part in as they enter the working world. The teacher uses rubrics to help students ascertain what skills they need to develop further, to ensure they have paid attention to all the steps needed for a successful creative project, to evaluate the technological tools they have used, and to ascertain their level of participation as members of the team. Students also participate in the development of the rubrics they use, which helps them clarify the assignment and the purpose of the tools they use.

Once the class has decided on the rubric categories, the teacher downloads the rubrics from the Internet or creates them at one of several sites, e.g., Rubistar ([ALTEC, 2008] http://rubistar.4teachers.org/), Rubrics and Rubric Makers ([Teachnology, 2010] http://www.teach-nology.com/web_tools/rubrics/; for K-12, but can be easily adapted), or PBL Checklists ([ALTEC, 2009] http://pblchecklist.4teachers.org/checklist .shtml). (For more about rubrics and a list of other rubric makers, see Goodrich, 1996/1997.) The teacher either prints out the rubrics or brings them to class on a portable memory device.

Technology Tasks

Low-resource, low-access setting

With one or more computers available in the classroom (and optionally a computer projector), and where the students also are able to work in a school computer lab or on a home computer, the teacher assigns a variety of writing tasks (description, narration, analysis) using widely available word-processing software such as Microsoft Word or Openoffice.org ([2010] free download at http://www.openoffice.org). In the course of each assignment, the teacher asks students to use the grammar checker function of the word-processing software and then to look up the items it calls out using a concordancer such as Simple Concordance Program ([Reed, 2010] free download at http://www.textworld.com/scp), loaded on the class computer. If the Internet is available, the online Compleat Lexical Tutor ([Cobb, 2010b] http://www .lextutor.ca) is also free, and students may also search in Google Scholar ([Google, 2010f] http://scholar.google.com) for documents with the same phrases or sentences. (For more on using concordances in the classroom, see Lamy & Klarskov Mortensen, 2010.) Students use at least two different methods of finding writing problems to offer a comparison. The teacher has students bring their toughest problematic or unsolvable sentences to class to be discussed by everyone using the projector. (Files may be carried to and from computers with portable memory devices, taking care to virus-check before using them in class.) The teacher then helps students create and complete a simple rubric, analyzing which program was of greatest use in resolving grammar and vocabulary questions (see Table 4.1). Students discuss their scoring of the different technologies and which tools they might use in their next assignment.

Medium-resource, medium-access setting

With access to the Internet and one computer for every four or five students, EFL science students in an ESP class are assigned a multimedia project to demonstrate aspects of the ecology of their country. Students work in small groups and take turns using the computers to research data, find appropriate images to represent their ideas, and create the slides in a presentation program. (Some students also place their slides on the Internet as a slide show at a photo site like Flickr [Yahoo.com, 2010a], http:// www.flickr.com, or in a wiki.) The teacher spends class time teaching students to appropriately cite all references for their project. Before beginning data collection, the teacher assists students in developing a rubric that will help them understand their task better and make clear how they are being evaluated for their creative collaboration. Categories might include those in Table 4.2; additional details are filled out by students during class discussion (for a related sample rubric, see Gromik, 2006, p. 121; Table 4.2 is based on an English for Science class at Kuwait University, taught by Buthaina Al-Othman, Spring 2004). The teacher reviews the rubric with the students periodically, assisting them in discovering how to strengthen weak areas. Students use the rubrics to score themselves and other teams/projects as part of their final evaluation scheme.

Table 4.1. Sample Rubric for Analyzing Technology Tools

Please rate each on a scale of 1 to 5	Grammar checker	Concordance	LexTutor online	Internet search of scholarly documents
Explanation was understandable				
Explanation was correct				
Sufficient discriminating examples were given				
Helped in deciding what word or construction to use				
TOTAL SCORE				

Table 4.2. Sample Rubric for a Collaborative Multimedia Project (Partially Completed)

Production aspects	1 Needs improvement	2 Satisfactory	3 Well done	4 Excellent
Planning	Storyboard is very basic or disorganized.	Storyboard has a clear structure but is very thin.		
Research	Skimpy use of resources; needs more evidence; several citations are missing or incorrect.		Covers most of the research areas, but some are incomplete; a few references are incorrect or missing.	
Product	Presentation is confusing or purpose is not sufficiently complex; has errors in grammar or spelling; unclear speech; slides missing.			
Presentation tool		Presentation tool is used appropriately.		Presentation tool is unobtrusive and makes the project much clearer than it would have been otherwise.
Teamwork	One of the team members did most of the work.			Team members all did extensive research and contributed equally in assembling the product.

High-resource, high-access setting

In a fully networked computer lab with text chat grouping software or an asynchronous discussion forum, or with live online text chat grouping (e.g., in TappedIn [SRI, 2010], http://www.tappedin.org), students are divided into discussion groups to talk about their next writing assignment. Text chat or forum grouping allows them to think about what they will say before writing, and it does not allow the loudest or most orally fluent student to dominate the discussion. Within a networked lab, the teacher "listens in" on the discussions, for example as a "guest," students are aware that they may be monitored silently. If a science teacher is available, he or she may take a turn in each of the groupings also. The teacher assigns a student leader of each discussion group whose task is to ensure that students stay focused on the discussion topic and respond to all the question prompts by the end of the allotted time in the lab. At the end of the session, the teacher automatically receives a transcript from each of the chat rooms or forum groups. The teacher uses the transcripts to analyze how students are using the language in this more impromptu setting. The teacher opens the transcripts in the word processor, makes comments on content related to the writing assignment, and suggests corrections where the vocabulary or syntax might be used in the writing assignment itself. Students also automatically receive transcripts from their group, and they save the transcripts in their own folders to use in practicing the corrected terms in their vocabulary blog, where they write a short paragraph using each term correctly. The teacher has students read each other's blogs at specific intervals. (An RSS [really simple syndication] feed will help remind them when new items have been written.) Students refer to the transcripts and blogs for help with corrections as they are writing their papers with a word processor. At the beginning of the semester, the teacher helps students develop a rubric to help analyze their contributions in the chats, blogging, peer editing workshops, and drafts of their papers. The teacher refers to the rubrics at regular intervals and helps with refinements over the course of the term. The rubrics are of particular importance for the teacher in analyzing individual students' contributions to group processes such as chats and editing workshops. (See Table 4.3.) Discussion of these rubrics throughout the term helps students determine how best to contribute to group interactions. Students include the rubrics in their e-portfolios.

See also: Learner Goal 3 Standard 4: Evaluating Web Sources

Table 4.3. Sample Checklist for Class Participation

	Seldom	Sometimes	Often	Almost every time
I speak in class . . .				
I participate in the online discussions or chats . . .				
I help my classmates with paper revisions . . .				
I suggest specific corrections . . .				
I tell my classmates about positive elements in their papers . . .				
I read my classmates' blogs . . .				
I make positive comments on their blogs . . .				
I am prepared for class work . . .				

Goal 4: Language teachers use technology to improve communication, collaboration, and efficiency.

Standard 1: Language teachers use communication technologies to maintain effective contact and collaboration with peers, students, administration, and other stakeholders.

Performance indicators

- Language teachers draw on resources (lesson plans and teaching ideas) for language teachers that are posted online.

- Language teachers implement lesson plans obtained from other teachers via the Internet.

- Teachers belong to online communities (e.g., mailing lists, blogs, wikis, podcasts) with other language teachers.

- Language teachers share their email address with students and peers.

Performance indicators, expert level of technology

- Language teachers maintain an electronic forum (e.g., web page, blog) to post information for students about the class.

- Language teachers view and comment on students' electronic work (e.g., electronic portfolios, project work, websites).

- Language teachers advise administration on the use of online technology to improve communication.

- Language teachers share instructional material digitally.

E-Mentoring
Teacher Goal 4 Standard 1 Vignette

Teacher profile: Teacher educators supervising pre- and in-service teachers, adults, ages 17+, native speakers or Bridging–Mastery (Level C2–C1)

Context: ESL elementary and secondary school pre- and in-service teachers interact with their mentors through an electronic community of practice

Focus: Teachers use technology for distance conferencing and web archiving of lesson plans and resources to help new interns and new teachers bridge the gap between theory and practice in their first years of teaching.

Background

Teacher educators of primary and secondary ESL teachers in a large university system send their pre-service trainees to internships in schools in a very large geographical area. Although the trainees have local supervisors in the classroom, distance makes it difficult for the interns' educators to discuss their progress and help with any problems. Some interns must drive several hours to attend a monthly seminar, and bad weather may prevent attendance. The director of the internship program has decided to use an online forum and email for asynchronous help and a chat site for a weekly synchronous, real-time chat in order to provide more immediate help and advice to new teachers. The chat allows time for interns to reflect on practices at their school and an opportunity to ask questions about their work, and it continues the practice of weekly reflective discussions formerly held during their initial training at the school of education. Supervising teachers and administrators in the schools are also invited to the chats to assist in bridging the gaps between pedagogical theory and classroom ESL practices. This e-mentoring is so successful that it is expanded to postgraduate teachers who are experiencing their first years of in-service teaching. Interns and new in-service teachers use dialogue journals or blogging to reflect on their activities, with comments by their university teachers, and an easily updated wiki provides avenues for linking to suggested readings, intern- and teacher-generated lesson plans, and other resources for pedagogy and language teaching. Both interns and in-service teachers are expected to write and respond regularly in the online forum. The teacher educators archive chat transcripts and recordings of discussions with their mentees at the resource website. (Based on an article by Dahlman and Tatinen, 2006; for more on communities of practice, see Hanson-Smith, 2006.)

Technology Tasks

Low-resource, low-access setting

With sporadic access to the Internet for interns and in-service teachers at their respective schools, the asynchronous forum, email, blogs, and website may be accessed through an Internet café on a regular basis or at a home computer. Teachers and their supervisors and school administrators set aside regular times for weekly text chat meetings at a free site, such as Tapped In ([SRI, 2010] http://www.tappedin.org). Teachers upload their lesson plans to the archive area of their Tapped In classroom or to a class wiki, where the other participants can comment on them.

Medium-resource, medium-access setting

With regular access to the Internet, either at home or through the school labs, interns and teachers participate more easily in forum discussions and send email questions or mobile texts to their supervisors or teacher educators for quick mentor responses. The weekly live text chat may be supplemented by audio if the technology is available, for example, with Yahoo Messenger ([Yahoo.com, 2010b] http://messenger.yahoo.com) or Google Phone ([Google, 2010e] http://mail.google.com >Call phone). Interns and in-service teachers contribute resources to the archive wiki and comment on them regularly.

High-resource, high-access setting

Where headsets and mobile phones are readily available, and the Internet connection is high speed and high capacity (broadband), live audio/video chats with a free Internet phone service (for example, Skype [Skype Technologies, 2010], http://www.skype.com/) or with audio/video applications such as Elluminate ([2010] http://www.elluminate.com/) or WiZiQ ([AuthorGEN, 2010] http://www.wiziq.com) allow frequent connections to mentors and supervisors and provide an appropriate setting for weekly reflective meetings. Participants videotape segments of their lessons with digital camera or mobile phone to discuss during their meetings. During the course of the weekly meeting, a web tour in the chat application allows the mentor teacher to skim through many of the pre- and in-service teachers' blogs and wiki contributions to review and discuss their progress and concerns. With web conferencing, pre-service teachers may elect to take the course entirely online.

See also: Teacher Goal 4 Standard 2: CALL Professional Development; Teacher Goal 2 Standard 4: Research in the Pedagogy of Technology

Standard 2: Language teachers regularly reflect on the intersection of professional practice and technological developments so that they can make informed decisions regarding the use of technology to support language learning and communication.

Performance indicators

- Language teachers take advantage of professional development related to technology integration (e.g., conferences, journals, mailing lists, communities of practice).

- Language teachers select technology resources that promote appropriate language use.

- Language teachers demonstrate awareness of multiple sources and perspectives that inform technology use.

- Language teachers discern which findings are most appropriate for their situation.

Performance indicators, expert level of technology

- Language teachers stay informed about how to use new technologies for instructional and professional purposes (e.g., podcasts for listening and speaking, blogs for writing and reading).

- Language teachers integrate technology in innovative ways.

- Language teachers engage in research (including classroom-based) and share the results.

- Language teachers advise decision-makers about appropriate technology resources and environments.

Teacher profile: Teacher trainer with background or degree in CALL pedagogy who works with EFL or ESL teachers, adults, ages 19+, Expanding–Mastery/High Advanced+ (Levels 4–5+, B2–C2)

Context: Online resource access and community of practice for continuous independent professional development-

Focus: Individual teacher conducts ongoing, individualized professional development in order to stay abreast of innovations in technology.

Background

To stay abreast of current developments in technology, in addition to subscriptions to technology journals, CALL teachers and teacher trainers join and regularly access an e-list or forum with a community of practitioners who discuss new technologies and pedagogical issues. Often this is the only way for expert educators to maintain contact with others who use and explore innovative technologies. They also follow one or more technology blogs and write regularly in their own technology-oriented blog or wiki, describing new experiments and discoveries and their relationship to classroom activities. Such writings provide self-knowledge and are also shared with the e-list community. To continually develop their skills, CALL educators regularly attend technology conferences and participate in free online presentations and workshops, such as TESOL's CALL Interest Section Electronic Village Online ([TESOL, 2010a] http://evosessions.pbworks.com/).

CALL teachers and teacher trainers develop their own website or wiki with links to appropriate instructional videos online, social networking sites, and other resources their teacher-students will use repeatedly, and they create instructional videos or screencasts as needed. (For more on CALL teacher preparation, see Kessler, 2006.)

Technology Tasks

Low resource, low-access setting

With one computer, low-bandwidth Internet access, and an optional digital camera or mobile phone, the CALL teacher/teacher trainer regularly accesses an email list or forum for technology-using teachers, writes regularly in a blog to analyze his or her own development as a technology user, and searches the Internet frequently for new tools to explore. Live text chats and synchronous online conferences (webinars) with other technology-using teachers are attended whenever possible. If available, a digital camera or mobile phone with camera capability allows the teacher to post pictures to websites and forums.

Medium-resource, medium-access setting

With one or more computers, good Internet access, headset, webcam, digital camera or video camera, and smart phone (e.g., an iPod or Android), the CALL teacher/teacher trainer can regularly attend live text, video, and audio chats, as well as synchronous online conferences (webinars) with other technology-using teachers. The educator also maintains regular contact with the community using instant messaging/chat (Yahoo Messenger [Yahoo, 2010b] at http://messenger.yahoo.com), Internet phone (Skype [Skype Technologies, 2010] at http://www.skype.com), and online conferencing (WiZiq.com [AuthorGEN, 2010] at http://www.wiziq.com and Elluminate.com [2010], at http://www.elluminate.com). The teacher follows online colleagues' blogs with RSS feeds. A digital camera/video camera or mobile phone with camera capability allows posting of pictures and video to websites and forums. The educator has access to both Mac and PC computers in order to experiment with tools and software for different types of computers.

High-resource, high-access setting

With one or more computers, high bandwidth Internet access, headset, webcam, digital camera or video camera, and smart phone, the CALL teacher/teacher educator sets up a presence in a virtual community, for example, Second Life ([Linden Research, 2010] http://www.secondlife.com), which can provide help for exploring new tools, locating projects, attending presentations, and examining educational virtual environments and games. The teacher explores new technologies for mobile learning, 3D copying, assistive devices for students with disabilities, and so on.

See also: Teacher Goal 4 Standard 1: E-mentoring

Standard 3: Language teachers apply technology to improve efficiency in preparing for class, grading, and maintaining records.

Performance indicators

- Language teachers use electronic resources to locate additional materials for lesson planning and classroom use.

- Language teachers demonstrate understanding of various methods of providing electronic feedback on student work (e.g., email, insert comments).

- Language teachers have a system to collect, organize, and retrieve material and student data.

Performance indicators, expert level of technology

- Language teachers maintain a resource that allows students to locate and retrieve material.

- Language teachers use electronic methods, as appropriate, for formative and summative assessment.

- Language teachers encourage students to use electronic methods to document their own progress.

Teacher profile: Experienced ESL classroom teacher of young learners, ages 11–12, Developing–Expanding/Low–High Advanced (Level 3–4, B1–B2)

Context: ESL middle school language arts class in the United States

Focus: An ESL teacher wants to improve grading and record-keeping methods for better formative and summative assessment of students.

Background

In a U.S. middle school, a sixth-grade group of Spanish-speaking students is taking an ESL language arts class. As part of a formative evaluation plan, their language teacher would like to ensure that each of the students is involved in ongoing self-assessment. Typically, the teacher creates a system in which students collect their work in folders (learner logs, drafts of essays with teacher and peer comments, vocabulary notebooks, double-entry journals, and self-reviews of essays) so that they can create end-of-semester portfolios to track their language growth. The teacher has subsequently found that the ESL students are often overwhelmed by the amount of paper that accumulates over time and therefore do not make the best use of their previous work. Because the school has recently acquired a CMS system (e.g., Moodle [Moodle.org, 2010], http://www.moodle.org) and placed it on their server, the teacher wants to use the technology to improve efficiency in grading and maintaining records for purposes of formative assessment. The instructor uses a variety of readily available CMS tools to help students understand their own progress during the year. When posting student grades or their work in the class CMS space, the teacher uses coded numbers to preserve students' privacy. (For more on assessment, see *Effective Assessment in a Digital Age* by the Higher Education Funding Council for England, 2010.)

Technology Tasks

Low-resource, low-access setting

With a single computer outside of class, but no in-class computers, the teacher learns how to use the school's CMS to maintain a grade book. The teacher posts students' coded grades on a weekly basis. Using a checklist to make weekly comments on each student's areas of language improvement and areas in need of improvement, the teacher keeps the comments organized into private areas or folders, accessible only to the individual student. The teacher also makes a compilation of these comments available to students at the end of the semester during one-on-one conferencing about their language progress. When student and teacher sit down together at the computer, the written comments provide a visual format that helps low-intermediate

ESL students follow the conversation. This process helps them self-assess their growth over time, and together the student and teacher set realistic language learning goals for the next semester.

Medium-resource, medium-access setting

With a networked computer lab available by reservation for one hour once a week, but also available after school, the teacher helps students see their growth in writing fluency by having them write for 30 minutes every other week using a variety of prompts (e.g., pictures, story starters, engaging questions). The students then use the word count tool built into the word-processing software to document the number of words they have written. Each student keeps a spreadsheet that tracks the number of words he or she writes across the semester. The spreadsheet allows for a visually appealing chart that shows a progress line of growth in the total number of words students can write in a 30-minute period.

To help students revise their essays, the teacher uses reviewing tools such as sidebar comments and change tracking with colors on students' essays (both functions built into the word processor). In the computer lab, students revise their essays based on the comments. The teacher maintains a class website or wiki within the CMS that allows centralization of the collection of the students' coded fluency spreadsheets and their reviewed essays.

High-resource, high-access setting

With a networked computer for each student available several times a week during class, as well as after school, the teacher maintains a class blog or discussion forum within the CMS so that students can locate course materials online for reference and collect all the course documents in one place. The students create electronic portfolios that document their language progress across the semester, in which they include the spreadsheets documenting word count in their free writing task. The portfolios ensure that students are using English in multiple genres (narrative and persuasive essays, book summaries, analyses, etc.) and in multiple modes (hyperlinked writing, multimedia projects, and audio files).

See also: Teacher Goal 3 Standard 3: Rubrics in English for Science

Chapter 5

The Relationship of the TESOL Technology Standards to Other Standards

This chapter compares the TESOL Technology Standards with technology standards developed by the International Society for Technology in Education (ISTE) and the United Nations Education, Scientific and Cultural Organization (UNESCO).

Organizations such as the International Society for Technology in Education (ISTE) and the United Nations Education, Scientific and Cultural Organization (UNESCO) have developed their own technology standards for educational settings: ISTE's National Educational Technology Standards (NETS) and UNESCO's Information and Communication Technologies Competency Standards for Teachers (ICT-CST). It is important to see the TESOL standards as not being in competition with these but rather complementing them. In fact, the previous versions of the ISTE NETS for students (ISTE, 1998) and for teachers (ISTE, 2000) strongly influenced the design of the TESOL Technology Standards. The ISTE NETS were revised while the TESOL standards were being developed, and the newer versions of ISTE NETS were released in 2007 for students and 2008 for teachers.

There are three major differences between the TESOL Technology Standards and the ISTE and UNESCO standards. First, the TESOL Technology Standards are specific to language learning while the ISTE and UNESCO standards are designed to cover all educational fields. Second, the TESOL standards apply to a considerable range of potential users: children and adults, ESL and EFL learners, all proficiency levels, situations with both high and low levels of technology resources, and a variety of educational settings. The ISTE and UNESCO standards seem most compatible with a more centralized institutional structure and assume development over a period of years. The ISTE student standards presuppose a relatively intact, age-appropriate level of communicative competence in the target language. They are not targeted at adults, nor at those whose objectives differ from those of general education. They are embedded in a developmental framework covering 13 years of an individual's life (kindergarten through 12th grade) and do not readily accommodate the distinction between those with high and low degrees of literacy (both traditional and digital) in their native cultures. Finally, the TESOL standards are more neutral to educational approach than most other standards. For example, they do not mandate the use of technology for the development of critical-thinking skills or creativity as both the ISTE and the UNESCO standards do, recognizing that those are objectives of specific curricula rather than the whole field of TESOL. The TESOL standards can accommodate the fact that English is taught and learned sometimes for purely instrumental purposes and sometimes for quite specific purposes. The effective use of technology can support these endeavors.

Concordance With the ISTE NETS

Like the TESOL standards, the ISTE NETS include separate listings for students and teachers, although ISTE additionally has a set of standards specifically targeted to administrators. Tables 5.1 and 5.2 provide a rough concordance between the TESOL Technology Standards and ISTE NETS drawn from the six ISTE NETS for students and teachers (indicated by numbers) and their associated performance indicators (indicated by letters). See http://www.iste.org/standards.aspx for the full set of the ISTE NETS (ISTE, 2000, 2007). Note that not all of the TESOL standards have obvious corollaries for the ISTE ones, and not all the ISTE standards link to ones for TESOL. Those listed here represent overlaps rather than exact equivalencies.

Table 5.1. Relationship Between TESOL Technology Standards for Language Learners and ISTE NETS for Students

TESOL Learner Standards	ISTE NETS for Students (2007)
GOAL 1: Language learners demonstrate foundational knowledge and skills in technology for a multilingual world.	6. Students demonstrate a sound understanding of technology concepts, systems, and operations.
STANDARD 1: Language learners demonstrate basic operational skills in using various technology tools and Internet browsers.	6a. Students understand and use technology systems. 6c. Students troubleshoot systems and applications.
STANDARD 2: Language learners are able to use available input and output devices (e.g., keyboard, mouse, printer, headset, microphone, media player, electronic whiteboard).	6a. Students understand and use technology systems. 6c. Students troubleshoot systems and applications.
STANDARD 3: Language learners exercise appropriate caution when using online sources and when engaging in electronic communication.	5a. Students advocate and practice safe, legal, and responsible use of information technologies.
STANDARD 4: Language learners demonstrate basic competence as users of technology.	6b. Students select and use applications effectively and productively.

(Continued on p. 131)

Table 5.1 (continued). Relationship Between TESOL Technology Standards for Language Learners and ISTE NETS for Students

TESOL Learner Standards	ISTE NETS for Students (2007)
GOAL 2: Language learners use technology in socially and culturally appropriate, legal, and ethical ways.	5. Students understand human, cultural, and societal issues related to technology and practice legal and ethical behavior.
STANDARD 1: Language learners understand that communication conventions differ across cultures, communities, and contexts.	2c. Students develop cultural understanding and global awareness by engaging with learners of other cultures.
STANDARD 2: Language learners demonstrate respect for others in their use of private and public information.	5a. Students advocate and practice safe, legal, and responsible use of information technologies. 3 b. Students locate, organize, evaluate, and ethically use information from a variety of sources and media.
GOAL 3: Language learners effectively use and critically evaluate technology-based tools as aids in the development of their language learning competence as part of formal instruction and for further learning.	3. Students apply digital tools to gather, evaluate, and use information.
STANDARD 1: Language learners effectively use and evaluate available technology-based productivity tools.	3. Students apply digital tools to gather, evaluate, and use information.
STANDARD 2: Language learners appropriately use and evaluate available technology-based language skill-building tools.	—
STANDARD 3: Language learners appropriately use and evaluate available technology-based tools for communication and collaboration.	2. Students use digital media and environments to communicate and work collaboratively, including at a distance, to support individual learning and contribute to the learning of others.
STANDARD 4: Language learners use and evaluate available technology-based research tools appropriately.	3. Students apply digital tools to gather, evaluate, and use information.
STANDARD 5: Language learners recognize the value of technology to support autonomy, lifelong learning, creativity, metacognition, collaboration, personal pursuits, and productivity.	5b. Students exhibit a positive attitude toward using technology that supports collaboration, learning, and productivity. 5c. Students demonstrate personal responsibility for lifelong learning. 5d. Students exhibit leadership for digital citizenship. 6d. Students transfer current knowledge to learning of new technologies.

Table 5.2. Relationship Between TESOL Technology Standards for Language Teachers and ISTE NETS for Teachers

TESOL Teacher Standards	ISTE NETS for Teachers (2008)
GOAL 1: Language teachers acquire and maintain foundational knowledge and skills in technology for professional purposes.	3a. Teachers demonstrate fluency in technology systems and the transfer of current knowledge to new technologies and situations.
STANDARD 1: Language teachers demonstrate knowledge and skills in basic technological concepts and operational competence, meeting or exceeding TESOL technology standards for students in whatever situation they teach.	—
STANDARD 2: Language teachers demonstrate an understanding of a wide range of technology supports for language learning and options for using them in a given setting.	3a. Teachers demonstrate fluency in technology systems and the transfer of current knowledge to new technologies and situations.
STANDARD 3: Language teachers actively strive to expand their skill and knowledge base to evaluate, adopt, and adapt emerging technologies throughout their careers.	5c. Teachers evaluate and reflect on current research and professional practice on a regular basis to make effective use of existing and emerging digital tools and resources in support of student learning.
STANDARD 4: Language teachers use technology in socially and culturally appropriate, legal, and ethical ways.	4a. Teachers advocate, model, and teach safe legal and ethical use of digital information and technology, including respect for copyright, intellectual property, and the appropriate documentation of sources. 4c. Teachers promote and model digital etiquette and responsible social interactions related to the use of technology and information.
GOAL 2: Language teachers integrate pedagogical knowledge and skills with technology to enhance language teaching and learning.	2. Teachers design, develop, and evaluate authentic learning experiences and assessments incorporating contemporary tools and resources to maximize content learning in context and to develop the knowledge, skills, and attitudes identified in the NETS-S.
STANDARD 1: Language teachers identify and evaluate technological resources and environments for suitability to their teaching context.	2. Teachers design, develop, and evaluate authentic learning experiences and assessments incorporating contemporary tools and resources to maximize content learning in context and to develop the knowledge, skills, and attitudes identified in the NETS-S.
STANDARD 2: Language teachers coherently integrate technology into their pedagogical approaches.	2a. Teachers design or adapt relevant learning experiences that incorporate digital tools and resources to promote student learning and creativity.

(Continued on p. 133)

Table 5.2 (continued). Relationship Between TESOL Technology Standards for Language Teachers and ISTE NETS for Teachers

TESOL Teacher Standards	ISTE NETS for Teachers (2008)
STANDARD 3: Language teachers design and manage language learning activities and tasks using technology appropriately to meet curricular goals and objectives.	2a. Teachers design or adapt relevant learning experiences that incorporate digital tools and resources to promote student learning and creativity.
STANDARD 4: Language teachers use relevant research findings to inform the planning of language learning activities and tasks that involve technology.	5c. Teachers evaluate and reflect on current research and professional practice on a regular basis to make effective use of existing and emerging digital tools and resources in support of student learning.
GOAL 3: Language teachers apply technology in record keeping, feedback, and assessment.	2. Teachers design, develop, and evaluate authentic learning experiences and assessments incorporating contemporary tools and resources to maximize content learning in context and to develop the knowledge, skills, and attitudes identified in the NETS-S.
STANDARD 1: Language teachers evaluate and implement relevant technology to aid in effective learner assessment.	2d. Teachers provide learners with multiple and varied formative and summative assessments aligned with content and technology standards and use resulting data to inform learning and teaching.
STANDARD 2: Language teachers use technological resources to collect and analyze information in order to enhance language instruction and learning.	—
STANDARD 3: Language teachers evaluate the effectiveness of specific student uses of technology to enhance teaching and learning.	—
GOAL 4: Language teachers use technology to improve communication, collaboration, and efficiency.	3b Teachers collaborate with students, peers, parents, and community members using digital tools and resources to support student success and innovation.
STANDARD 1: Language teachers use communication technologies to maintain effective contact and collaboration with peers, students, administration, and other stakeholders.	3b. Teachers collaborate with students, peers, parents, and community members using digital tools and resources to support student success and innovation. 3c. Teachers communicate relevant information and ideas effectively to students, parents, and peers using a variety of digital-age media and formats. 5a. Teachers participate in local and global learning communities to explore creative applications of technology to improve student learning.

(Continued on p. 134)

Table 5.2 (continued). Relationship Between TESOL Technology Standards for Language Teachers and ISTE NETS for Teachers

TESOL Teacher Standards	ISTE NETS for Teachers (2008)
STANDARD 2: Language teachers regularly reflect on the intersection of professional practice and technological developments so that they can make informed decisions regarding the use of technology to support language learning and communication.	5c. Teachers evaluate and reflect on current research and professional practice on a regular basis to make effective use of existing and emerging digital tools and resources in support of student learning.
STANDARD 3: Language teachers apply technology to improve efficiency in preparing for class, grading, and maintaining records.	—

Concordance With UNESCO Standards

In a set of three core documents (UNESCO 2008a, 2008b, 2008c), UNESCO has laid out a framework for Information and Communication Technologies Competency Standards for Teachers (ICT-CST). According to the foreword, "Schools and classrooms, both real and virtual, must have teachers who are equipped with technology resources and skills and who can effectively teach the necessary subject matter content while incorporating technology concepts and skills" (UNESCO, 2008c, p. 1). However, unlike the TESOL Technology Standards for Language Teachers, the ICT-CSTs focus heavily on teachers' use of technology to "play an essential role in producing technology capable students" (UNESCO, 2008c, p. 1), despite the fact that the documents do not provide explicit standards for the students themselves analogous to either the TESOL Technology Standards for Language Learners or ISTE NETS for students.

A further distinction between the UNESCO ICT-CST and the TESOL and ISTE standards is in their basic structure. The UNESCO ICT-CST standards are divided among three overlapping approaches that are seen as a developmental continuum. The first approach, technology literacy, sets the foundation for ICT competency. The second approach, knowledge deepening, involves the application of knowledge in complex problem solving and tasks, as well as an educational movement from traditional classrooms to collaborative learning. The third approach, knowledge creation, involves development of 21st-century skills, self-management, and learning organizations. Each of these approaches includes six dimensions: policy and vision, curriculum and assessment, pedagogy, ICT, organization and administration, and teacher professional development. However, these dimensions reach well beyond the classroom. For example, the policy and vision statement for the technology literacy approach begins as follows: "The policy goal of this approach is to prepare learners, citizens, and a workforce that is capable of taking up new technologies so as to support social development and improve economic productivity" (UNESCO, 2008a, p. 10).

Table 5.3. Overview of the Relationship Between TESOL Technology Standards for Language Teachers and UNESCO ICT-CST

Technology Literacy	Knowledge Deepening	Knowledge Creation
Policy and vision: technology literacy (I.A.)	Policy and vision: knowledge deepening	Policy and vision: knowledge creation
Curriculum and assessment: basic knowledge (I.B.)	Curriculum and assessment: knowledge application	Curriculum and assessment: 21st-century skills
Pedagogy: integrate technology (I.C.)	Pedagogy: complex problem solving	Pedagogy: self-management
ICT: basic tools (I.D.)	ICT: complex tools (II.D.)	ICT: pervasive tools (III.D.)
Organization and administration: standard classroom (I.E.)	Organization and administration: collaborative groups	Organization and administration: learning organizations
Teacher professional development: digital literacy (I.F.)	Teacher professional development: manage and guide (II.F.)	Teacher professional development: teacher as model learner (III.F.)

Of the three UNESCO documents (2008a, 2008b, 2008c), the one that most closely connects to the TESOL Technology Standards for Language Teachers is the Implementation Guidelines (UNESCO 2008b), and it is with those guidelines that we attempt a rough concordance. The objective is to clarify where the TESOL and UNESCO standards appear to overlap and where they appear to differ so that teachers, teacher educators, administrators, and policy makers attempting to reconcile the two will have a clearer idea of their interrelationship.

As suggested above, the concordance of the TESOL Technology Standards for Language Teachers with UNESCO ICT-CST is less clear than with ISTE NETS for teachers. The shaded parts of Table 5.3 show the areas of greatest overlap: all six components of the technology literacy approach, and ICT and professional development components of the other two approaches. Those cells are numbered in parentheses according to the system used within UNESCO (2008c). Note that technology competence also plays a role in several of the nonshaded cells, but to a lesser extent, and in many cases the directives provided in those categories relate to the teacher's role in developing a technologically proficient citizenry.

The concordance is listed in Table 5.4. The numbers in the UNESCO column correspond to the categories in Table 5.3 and are the same ones used in UNESCO's *ICT Competency Standards for Teachers: Implementation Guidelines* (2008c).

Table 5.4. Concordance Between TESOL Technology Standards for Language Teachers and UNESCO ICT-CST

TESOL Teacher Standards	UNESCO ICT-CST (2008c)
	Teachers should be able to:
GOAL 1: Language teachers acquire and maintain foundational knowledge and skills in technology for professional purposes.	—
STANDARD 1: Language teachers demonstrate knowledge and skills in basic technological concepts and operational competence, meeting or exceeding TESOL technology standards for students in whatever situation they teach.	I.D.1. Describe and demonstrate the use of common hardware technologies. I.D.2. Describe and demonstrate the basic tasks and uses of word processors, such as text entry, editing text, formatting text, and printing. I.D.3. Describe and demonstrate the purpose and basic function of presentation software and other digital resources. I.D.4. Describe and demonstrate the purpose and basic function of graphic software and use a graphic software package to create a simple graphic display. (Note: The list continues through I.D.8., covering using the Internet and web, searching, using email, and using tutorial software.)
STANDARD 2: Language teachers demonstrate an understanding of a wide range of technology supports for language learning and options for using them in a given setting.	I.D.9. Locate off-the-shelf educational software packages and web resources and evaluate them for their accuracy and alignment with the curriculum standards and match them with the needs of individual students. II.D.1. Operate various open-ended software packages appropriate to their subject matter area, such as visualization, data analysis, role play simulations, and online references.
STANDARD 3: Language teachers actively strive to expand their skill and knowledge base to evaluate, adopt, and adapt emerging technologies throughout their careers.	I.F.2. Use ICT resources to support their own acquisition of subject matter and pedagogical knowledge. II.F.1. Use ICT to access and share resources to support their activities and their own professional development. II.F.2. Use ICT to access outside experts and learning communities to support their activities and their own professional development. II.F.3. Use ICT to search for, manage, analyze, integrate, and evaluate information that can be used to support their professional development. III.F.1. Continually evaluate and reflect on professional practice to engage in ongoing innovation and improvement.
STANDARD 4: Language teachers use technology in socially and culturally appropriate, legal, and ethical ways.	1.E.3. Identify the appropriate and inappropriate social arrangements to use with various technologies.

(Continued on p. 137)

Table 5.4 (continued). Concordance Between TESOL Technology Standards for Language Teachers and UNESCO ICT-CST

TESOL Teacher Standards	UNESCO ICT-CST (2008c)
GOAL 2: Language teachers integrate pedagogical knowledge and skills with technology to enhance language teaching and learning.	—
STANDARD 1: Language teachers identify and evaluate technological resources and environments for suitability to their teaching context.	I.B.1. Match specific curriculum standards to particular software packages and computer applications and describe how these standards are supported by these applications. I.D.9 Locate off-the-shelf educational software packages and web resources and evaluate them for their accuracy and alignment with the curriculum standards and match them with the needs of individual students. II.D.2. Evaluate the accuracy and usefulness of web resources in support of project-based learning in the subject area.
STANDARD 2: Language teachers coherently integrate technology into their pedagogical approaches.	I.C.3. Use presentational software and digital resources to support instruction. II.D.1. Operate various open-ended software packages appropriate to their subject matter area, such as visualization, data analysis, role play simulations, and online references. III.D.1. Describe the function and purpose of ICT production tools and resources (multimedia recording and production equipment, editing tools, publication software, web design tools) and use them to support students' innovation and knowledge creation. III.D.2. Describe the function and purpose of virtual environments and knowledge building environments (KBEs) and use them to support increased knowledge and understanding of subject matter and the development of online and face-to-face learning communities.
STANDARD 3: Language teachers design and manage language learning activities and tasks using technology appropriately to meet curricular goals and objectives.	I.B.1. Match specific curriculum standards to particular software packages and computer applications and describe how these standards are supported by these applications. I.C.2. Incorporate appropriate ICT activities into lesson plans so as to support students' acquisition of school subject matter and knowledge. I.E.2. Manage the use of supplemental ICT resources with individuals and small groups of students in the regular classroom so as not to disrupt other instructional activities in the class. II.D.3. Use an authoring environment or tools to design online materials.

(Continued on p. 138)

Table 5.4 (continued). Concordance Between TESOL Technology Standards for Language Teachers and UNESCO ICT-CST

TESOL Teacher Standards	UNESCO ICT-CST (2008c)
STANDARD 4: Language teachers use relevant research findings to inform the planning of language learning activities and tasks that involve technology.	—
GOAL 3: Language teachers apply technology in record keeping, feedback, and assessment.	—
STANDARD 1: Language teachers evaluate and implement relevant technology to aid in effective learner assessment.	II.D.4. Use a network and appropriate software to manage, monitor, and assess progress of various student projects.
STANDARD 2: Language teachers use technological resources to collect and analyze information in order to enhance language instruction and learning.	II.D.4. Use a network and appropriate software to manage, monitor, and assess progress of various student projects.
STANDARD 3: Language teachers evaluate the effectiveness of specific student uses of technology to enhance teaching and learning.	II.D.4. Use a network and appropriate software to manage, monitor, and assess progress of various student projects.
GOAL 4: Language teachers use technology to improve communication, collaboration, and efficiency.	—
STANDARD 1: Language teachers use communication technologies to maintain effective contact and collaboration with peers, students, administration, and other stakeholders.	I.D.7. Create an email account and use it for a sustained series of email correspondence. I.D.11. Use common communication and collaboration technologies, such as text messaging, videoconferencing, and web-based collaboration and social environments. II.D.5. Use ICT to communicate and collaborate with students, peers, parents, and the larger community in order to nurture student learning. II.F.1. Use ICT to access and share resources to support their activities and their own professional development. III.F.2. Use ICT resources to participate in professional communities and share and discuss best teaching practices.

(Continued on p. 139)

Table 5.4 (continued). Concordance Between TESOL Technology Standards for Language Teachers and UNESCO ICT-CST

TESOL Teacher Standards	UNESCO ICT-CST (2008c)	
STANDARD 2: Language teachers regularly reflect on the intersection of professional practice and technological developments so that they can make informed decisions regarding the use of technology to support language learning and communication.	I.F.2.	Use ICT resources to support their own acquisition of subject matter and pedagogical knowledge.
	II.F.2.	Use ICT to access outside experts and learning communities to support their activities and their own professional development.
	III.F.1.	Continually evaluate and reflect on professional practice to engage in ongoing innovation and improvement.
STANDARD 3: Language teachers apply technology to improve efficiency in preparing for class, grading, and maintaining records.	I.D.8.	Use networked record-keeping software to take attendance, submit grades, and maintain student records.
	I.F.1.	Use ICT resources to enhance their productivity.

Conclusion

This chapter has focused on the ISTE NETS and UNESCO ICT-CST because they are widely recognized internationally. In fact, the previous version of the ISTE NETS provided an important base for considerations that were incorporated into the TESOL Technology Standards. There are and will continue to be other organizational entities—governmental, institutional, and professional—providing standards or other formal guidelines delineating the expectations of teachers and students with regard to technology competence for language learning purposes.

Regardless of what other requirements come into play, the TESOL Technology Standards arguably provide the clearest and most consistent link to date between technology and the specific considerations relevant to the tasks and processes of second language learning. Given that teachers and students may be subject to standards from multiple sources, it is critical at an institutional level to be aware of potential conflicts or contradictions among them so that the expectations are clear. It is hoped that the concordances provided here will provide a model for individuals and administrators with a need to reconcile any other standards with the TESOL Technology Standards so that students and teachers may be provided with a coherent and reasonable set of targets to demonstrate their competency.

PART 3

Integration

Part 3 focuses on specific groups of users of the technology standards: teacher educators, administrators, and fully online teachers. Separate chapters address each of these groups. In addition, checklists are provided for those who want to assess themselves and their programs based on the performance indicators for each of the standards. A separate checklist for administrators is also included, which focuses on how the standards are integrated into an English language program.

Chapter 6

Implications and Recommendations for Teacher Educators

This chapter addresses why the standards are important for teacher educators and teacher trainers. It also suggests ways to incorporate the standards into teacher education programs.

The use of digital technology in language teaching is growing, yet it is clear that many teachers are completing professional certificate and degree programs that include little if any formal instruction in using technology for teaching (Hubbard, 2008; Kessler, 2006). Given the potential for new teachers to be in the field for 40 years or more, it is critical that such a practice not continue.

Kessler (2007) notes that a high percentage of graduates from Master of Arts in TESOL (MA TESOL) programs were dissatisfied with the preparation they received for using technology in language teaching. All those who responded to the survey underlying his study were active on professional email lists and therefore somewhat technically inclined. This implies that the problem is likely to be even worse than reported.

With the increasing centrality of technology in many language learning settings, it is not clear why the topic is treated so haphazardly in many teacher education programs. One likely explanation, though, is the lack of sufficient interest, training, and experience among the teacher educators themselves. The problem is one of inertia: there is a tendency for courses or programs that appear successful in meeting their goals to continue to conduct their teacher training in the same way that has worked for them in the past. One purpose of the TESOL Technology Standards is to motivate programs of all sorts that train English language teachers to overcome that inertia by

- recognizing that they have an obligation to prepare teacher candidates adequately in technology proficiency for their field and

- upgrading their own staff of teacher educators if needed, either by providing them with additional knowledge and skill (training the trainers—Rickard, Blin, & Appel, 2006) or by making technology proficiency a high priority in their new hires.

The more institutional problems in teacher education programs are caused by a lack of three things: an understanding of the role of technology, a will to change, and the necessary expertise. In addition, there are barriers in the teacher candidates themselves. These include teacher resistance, technophobia (Robb, 2006), lack of teacher readiness, and a naïve view that technology skills and knowledge from personal use will be sufficient for language teaching. The last point is an extension of Prensky (2001). Prensky's claim that the rising generation is digitally "native" may be interpreted to mean that technology training is not needed for young teacher candidates, at least in countries where technology is pervasive. A large-scale study of language students at a U.S. university by Winke & Goertler (2008) offers convincing evidence that this is not the case for learners. It seems reasonable to extend their conclusions to language teachers. By emphasizing the TESOL Technology Standards as *standards*, rather than as an optional add-on as has so often been the case with technology training, educators can provide motivation to teachers who might otherwise be reluctant to immerse themselves in the digital stream.

In addition to the issue of teacher preparation programs, there is the question of how to help those who have completed their professional preparation and are now engaged in practice. Teacher educators can be involved in formal in-service training initiatives (e.g., Rickard et al., 2006) as well as informal ones, such as conference workshops. In some ways, this issue is a larger one than that of teacher preparation programs. The scale of the problem is due to the sheer number of practicing teachers with an inadequate understanding of how to use technology appropriately to support their teaching. It is hoped that the standards will serve as a strong incentive for professional organizations, teacher education departments, and individual English language programs to begin assessing and educating in-service teachers to meet the targets specified in the performance indicators.

Theoretical Grounding and Frameworks

Some of the established concepts in teacher education are particularly relevant for technology training. This section provides a brief overview of three of these along with a summary of a general framework for language teacher technology education. Specifically, we will look at situated learning, reflective learning, and project-based learning. While conceptually distinct, these three approaches can be and often are coherently integrated.

Situated learning

A common concern with teachers who receive instruction in technology is that they are unable to connect what they learn to their classroom setting. This is particularly the case when the instruction is in a generic instructional technology course rather than one specifically for language teaching. One way to make this connection is through *situated learning* (Lave & Wenger, 1991), where the context of the classroom is taken into account during the teacher's educational process. In this way the connections between the skills and knowledge being taught and their eventual realization is made clear. Using technology in a situated way can allow teachers with nascent CALL awareness to develop competence within specific contexts (Kessler & Plakans, 2008). Egbert (2006) shows how this can be put into practice through an online learning course in CALL and through the use of cases. Egbert's cases are somewhat similar to the vignettes that appear in this book.

Reflective learning

Reflectivity is a common theme throughout much of the literature on technology and teacher education. This can appear in any of a number of ways—reflective reports, class discussions, online discussion boards, and portfolios with annotated work. Slaouti & Motteram (2006) focus on the transformative nature of reflective learning in a CALL course. They note how the reflective process leads to reconstruction of knowledge from their course, personalization of the material, and the experience. Reflective learning is particularly appropriate for in-service education. Practicing teachers have the potential to make immediate connections between what they learn in a technology-focused course or workshop and how they may be able to use that information in a class they are currently teaching.

Project-based learning

Technology in language teaching and learning has both a knowledge base and a skill base, as can be seen in the standards themselves and especially in the performance indicators. Using projects as a basis for learning can provide a much richer and more lasting impression of the requisite knowledge and skills than a traditional lecture/ discussion model. Even in a hands-on setting such as a lab-based course, a project provides a coherent context to aid in retention. Further, if the project has practical value for the instructor beyond the course, it is likely to have a positive impact on motivation. Debski (2006) provides an example of project-based learning in a CALL course at the University of Melbourne. Students there developed a website to prepare visitors from Japan for their cultural experience in Australia. Debski draws its theoretical underpinning from the constructionist theory of Papert (1980) (a product-based variant of constructivism). Chao (2006) discusses using a WebQuest as the central project.

In addition to the three preceding concepts, it is important to consider technology training for language learning from the perspective of the roles the participants in the course may be playing. This is captured in a framework for CALL education proposed by Hubbard and Levy (2006b). The framework distinguishes technical and pedagogical domains for both knowledge and skills (alternatively, declarative and procedural knowledge) across two dimensions. The first of these, institutional roles, refers to one's actual or perceived position within an organization. It distinguishes pre-service and in-service teachers but also adds the advanced practice categories of *specialist* and *professional*. The former is defined in terms of having deep knowledge and an elaborated skill set within one or more areas. The latter refers to an individual whose professional career is to a significant degree defined in terms of broad and deep expertise in technology and language learning (see Hubbard,

2009b, for a discussion of educating CALL specialists). These categories of specialist and professional are captured to some degree in the performance indicators for the "expert level" provided in the standards. Although institutional roles are relatively static at least in the short term, functional roles vary constantly, even within the space of a single classroom session. The four functional roles in this framework are practitioner, developer, researcher, and trainer. These four roles come into play even at the level of the classroom teacher. A classroom teacher may be expected to teach using technology (practitioner), create or adapt technology-based tasks or activities (developer), review student performance and revise practice accordingly (researcher, especially action researcher), and teach students the necessary technical and strategic skills to use the technology effectively on their own (trainer).

The following section will discuss several alternative models for educating language teachers about technology that can be used individually or in combination in order to meet the performance indicators of the TESOL Technology Standards. Whatever model or combination is selected, consideration should be given to incorporating aspects of situatedness, reflection, and project-based learning. Attention should be paid also to addressing the range of functional and in some cases institutional roles that the participants may be expected to play in the future.

Methodology and Models

A number of possible models are available to draw from when embarking on either creating a new course or revising a current one. The key is to ensure that the participants meet or exceed the standards for the educational environment in which the course is embedded as well as that in which the participants may ultimately be teaching. From the perspective of the standards, the goal is the same:

- to provide teachers with a wide range of knowledge regarding their options;

- to give them experience in choosing among those options, making effective use of technology in English language instruction and learning tasks and activities; and

- to learn how to support students when appropriate in meeting the learner standards.

The models discussed here include breadth first, depth first, using technology to teach technology, collaborative learning, communities of practice, and self-directed learning (see Hubbard, 2008; Kessler, in press). While all of these are possible in a pre-service setting, the last three are particularly well-suited to the practical limitations of many in-service teachers, for whom extended formal education opportunities may be limited. The section concludes with advice for educators on supporting ongoing professional development.

Breadth first

One common approach can be referred to as "breadth first." This is typical of a survey course for technology in language learning and is the type supported by most introductory textbooks in the field (see the Resources section). An advantage of breadth first is that teacher candidates are exposed to a wide range of options they might otherwise be unfamiliar with. In principle, teacher candidates can then select among the options in an informed manner. A potential disadvantage is that teacher candidates may spend time learning about technologies and activities that are not immediately relevant to them and thus may be easily forgotten once the course has ended.

Depth first

An alternative to breadth first is a depth-first approach. Here, teachers learn about a much narrower range of options but have the opportunity to explore them in greater detail. An example of a depth-first course can be found in Chao (2006). Chao describes a class centered on building a WebQuest, a learning task in which students search online for content in the target language that is connected with meeting a goal or solving a problem. During this class, teachers learned a variety of technology skills associated with creating the WebQuest and accompanying lessons. The depth-first approach may be particularly useful for shorter, in-service training or when dealing with teachers whose technology skills are limited. The depth-first approach may provide a strong introduction to the use of technology in English language teaching. However, it will be necessary to complement such a course with additional training to meet many of the performance indicators in the teacher standards.

Using technology to teach technology

Using technology to teach about the use of technology is an effective way of building teacher confidence, either during a dedicated technology course or as an accompaniment to some other course. This practice allows teachers with emerging abilities to experience the use of the technology firsthand as they discuss its potential in the language classroom. This is of necessity the case with online teacher training courses. In online courses, Teacher Goal 4 Standard 1 regarding communication technologies is an integral part of the course structure. When teachers receive some or all of their instruction through technology, they experience what it is like to learn rather than simply teach with technology. This exposure makes them more comfortable with using the devices and infrastructure. Using technology in the course also provides teacher educators with the opportunity to ensure that candidates meet the learner standards on their way to mastering the teacher standards. The TESOL Online Certificate Program similarly uses an online setting to help teachers make the transition from the classroom to online teaching. For those contemplating a move from classroom to online teacher education, Bauer-Ramazani (2006) describes some of the challenges involved in moving a technology for language teaching course online. These include scheduling, differing levels of technology proficiency among the students, resource limitations, and additional expenditures of time on the part of both instructor and students.

Collaborative learning

Collaborative learning represents another option around which to structure all or part of a course. The value of collaborative learning is well established for language learners, but it is also a valuable approach for technology education for teachers. Working collaboratively has the potential to improve motivation, especially in teachers who have limited experience with technology or lack confidence in using it in their teaching. As noted in Debski (2006), it is also the case that teams working collaboratively on a technology project can learn from the expertise of individual members in specific areas. Arnold, Ducate, and Lomicka (2007) present an example of collaborative learning in an online setting involving three graduate classes at two universities.

Communities of practice

So far the discussion has focused on approaches that can take place within formal structures. However, a further role of teacher educators in supporting learning and maintaining the technology standards is to provide teachers with the tools for continuing their development after the course is over. Following the theme of collaborative learning, one such approach is through communities of practice (Wenger, 1998). In this case, communities of practice (CoPs) are groups of individuals who share information and support and learn from one another as they develop their professional competence in using technology for language teaching. In fact, Arnold et al. (2007) suggest that their collaborative approach included many of the characteristics ascribed to CoPs, though missing a couple of key ones: voluntary participation and longevity. Hanson-Smith (2006) provides an overview of CoPs for teachers using and learning about technology for their language courses. Among other groups, she mentions Webheads in Action, a group that describes itself as a "worldwide, cross-cultural, and vibrant online community of educators with an open enrollment for anyone who wants to join" (2010; http://www.webheadsinaction.org /about: para. 1).

Self-directed learning

In addition to CoPs, teacher educators can provide experiences and resources that will enable teachers to continue with self-directed learning after the course is over. The need to prepare teachers for ongoing learning is implied in Goal 1 Standard 3, *Language teachers actively strive to expand their skill and knowledge base to evaluate, adopt, and adapt emerging technologies throughout their careers.*

With regard to more formal continuing in-service education, there are other stakeholders beyond individual teacher educators and ESOL teacher education programs. The role of program administrators and other management and policy personnel is spelled out in Chapter 7 of this volume. However, professional organizations have a role to play as well. The impact of the standards will be enhanced to the degree that such organizations encourage workshops and classes to index their content to the standards. A good place to start would be with TESOL's own initiatives, such as the Online Teaching Certificate Program and the six-week preconference Electronic Village Online courses.

Integrating the Standards Into Teacher Education

The preceding sections in this chapter have provided a rationale for the importance of teacher education in technology for language instruction and learning, discussed some of the theoretical grounding and frameworks, and offered a range of methods and models. This section discusses some of the issues involved in integrating the standards into pre-service and in-service teacher education programs. The first task for both the learner and teacher standards focuses on technical knowledge and skills, areas covered by Goal 1 Standard 1. Although some teachers enter a teacher education program or other professional course relatively strong in this area, many do not. Further, there are likely to be gaps in knowledge and skills similar to those found by Winke & Goertler (2008) for foreign language students.

As reported in Hubbard (2008), the majority of MA TESOL programs in the United States and Canada did not offer dedicated technology training courses. Many of the programs that did have technology training courses left them as electives. This suggests that the technology training, if it occurred at all, often took place during the latter part of the program—after required course work had been completed. Hegelheimer (2006) reports on an alternative, a curriculum-wide approach in a master's program. This model is based on the notion that beginning with a required technology course offers graduate students a common foundation that can be exploited by instructors in succeeding classes. In his course, students work on advanced search and computer-based presentational skills; learn to use course management tools, quiz generation programs, and screen-capturing applications; create a professional home page; use spreadsheets for descriptive statistics; and understand language corpora and concordancing programs. Such a foundation in the early stages could have positive consequences for teacher education program outcomes. Regardless of how and when technology expertise is provided during a pre-service program, the core of Goal 1 should be attained: *Language teachers acquire and maintain foundational knowledge and skills in technology for professional purposes.* The infrastructure for meeting this goal is more of a challenge for in-service settings. Still, in-service teacher educators can address this target and make significant progress, especially with the support of administrators.

Beyond Goal 1, the remainder of the teacher standards should be addressed in a pre-service program in ways that (a) persuade teacher candidates of the value of various technology applications, activities, and tasks for language teaching and learning; and (b) demonstrate to them that technology will be a significant aspect of their teaching throughout their careers.

In the first case, that means it is incumbent upon the teacher education program to show that the use of technology *in certain circumstances* makes language learning "better." Hubbard (2009a) claims that assessing improvements in language learning when using technology from the learner's perspective involves the following dimensions:

- learning efficiency: learners are able to pick up language knowledge or skills faster or with less effort;

- learning effectiveness: learners retain language knowledge or skills longer, make deeper associations, and/or learn more of what they need;

- access: learners can get materials or experience interactions that would otherwise be difficult or impossible to get or do;

- convenience: learners can study and practice with equal effectiveness across a wider range of times and places;

- motivation: learners enjoy the language learning process more and thus engage more fully;

- institutional efficiency: learners require less teacher time or fewer or less expensive resources. (pp. 1–2)

Although making such assessments convincingly is often not feasible, the literature on computer-assisted language learning includes empirical research in these areas to support teacher decision-making (see Chapter 2 of this volume). Introducing teacher candidates to such research and to sources for obtaining additional findings is in line with Goal 2 Standard 4: *Language teachers use relevant research findings to inform the planning of language learning activities and tasks that involve technology.*

The second point is the notion that technology use for language teaching and learning will continue and almost certainly expand and change radically during the ensuing decades of a newly minted professional teacher's career. This means that teacher education programs not only need to teach to the goals and standards relevant to current technology options, they must provide teachers with the tools and experiences to enable continuing professional growth. Goal 1 Standard 3 addresses this explicitly with respect to the technologies: *Language teachers actively strive to expand their skill and knowledge base to evaluate, adopt, and adapt emerging technologies throughout their careers.* This same philosophy indirectly permeates the remaining three goals. Teacher education programs have a responsibility to create a culture of lifelong learning that will help their candidates weather not only the rapid shifts in technology but also the likely pedagogical changes that will occur in their future, including new pedagogies that may incorporate technology as a central actor in their theoretical underpinnings. The bleak alternative is a potential fossilization of technology use and pedagogical practice in teachers, frozen in the time frame of their formal teacher training.

Teacher standards are not the only concern of teacher educators: Learner standards as well should be addressed. The place of the learner standards in teacher education programs is likely to be highly variable due to the wide range of settings in which teacher candidates may ultimately find themselves. However, in addition to fulfilling the teacher standards themselves, many teachers will also have some degree of responsibility in ensuring that their students meet some or all of the learner standards. This responsibility will vary significantly depending on the institutional setting, the objectives of the course the teacher will be leading, and the technology preparation of the students. These may be unknowable for many teacher candidates in pre-service programs. Therefore, some consideration should be given to preparing teacher candidates for flexibility in the trainer role with respect to the learner standards. An option here is to have teachers individually or in small groups learn specific technology applications for language learning in line with Teacher Goal 2, for example, and then instruct their classmates in how to use them. In this way the teachers can rehearse the trainer role in a systematic way prior to working with their language students. To accommodate this need, not only should teacher educators be responsible for knowing all the teacher standards in order to prepare teachers effectively, but they should also be familiar with the learner standards and how both sets of standards would likely impact various learning environments.

Finally, at the administrative level within language teacher education programs, thought must be given to how the overall curriculum will accommodate the technology standards. Besides determining which model or models to use (breadth first, depth first, etc.), there is a question of whether to incorporate dedicated technology courses, to integrate technology more seamlessly throughout the program, or to use a combination of the two. As technology works its way into all areas of education, it seems unlikely that a stand-alone course with no further thought given to technology integration will be a useful long-term solution. On the other hand, providing the appropriate depth to meet Goal 1 will be challenging if the responsibility is distributed throughout a range of courses and instructors.

At the time of this writing there is no formal way of externally certifying compliance with the TESOL Technology Standards. However, it would arguably be to the benefit of both the teacher education program and the graduating teacher candidates if some form of documentation could be provided. One approach would be to create a concordance table across required and elective courses that showed where specific standards were being addressed. Another would be to assist teachers in creating a structured electronic portfolio containing course work and projects (both individual and collaborative) that could be cross-referenced to specific standards and performance indicators. The program assessment component of Chapter 9 in this volume will be helpful in that effort. As the standards become established, more formal mechanisms may be made available for demonstrating that teachers have met them.

Conclusion

This chapter has provided an overview of issues and options in educating language teachers in using technology effectively in their classrooms. It has emphasized the responsibility of both teacher educators and the programs in which they may be housed to incorporate the TESOL Technology Standards into their offerings in a systematic way. Regardless of whether one is reviewing an individual course or an entire program, a reasonable place to start would be to use the standards as a tool for evaluating current offerings. Is there a course or courses in which particular standards are being addressed? If so, which of the performance indicators are built into assessments for those courses? What strengths and gaps does this evaluation illuminate, and how could the gaps be addressed? Finally, what kinds of educational options can be set up to accommodate the large number of currently practicing ESOL teachers who either have no technology training or whose training may need refreshing? Although the challenges facing teacher educators and programs seeking to integrate the technology standards into their curricula may be significant, avoiding those challenges is no longer an option.

Resources

There have been at least two edited volumes specifically on the topic of technology and language teacher education (Hubbard & Levy, 2006b; Kassen, Lavine, Murphy-Judy & Peters, 2007) as well as special issues of the journals *Language Learning & Technology* (2002) and *Innovation in Language Learning and Teaching* (2009).

Additionally, teacher educators can benefit from a number of useful books that serve as either classroom texts or valuable references to technology and language learning (e.g., Beatty, 2003; Blake, 2008; Butler-Pascoe & Wiburg, 2003; de Szendeffy, 2005; Ducate & Arnold, 2006; Egbert, 2005; Egbert & Hanson-Smith, 2007; Fotos & Browne, 2004; Hanson-Smith & Rilling, 2007; Levy & Stockwell, 2006).

Teacher educators more centrally involved with technology should be aware of the professional organizations dedicated to this field. These include the Computer-Assisted Language Learning (CALL) and Video and Digital Media (VDM) interest sections of TESOL (http://www.tesol.org), the Computer-Assisted Language Instruction Consortium (CALICO; http://www.calico.org), the International Association of Language Learning Technologies (http://www.iallt.org), the European Association for Computer-Assisted Language Learning (http://www.eurocall-languages.org), the Pacific Association for Computer-Assisted Language Learning (http://www.paccall.org), and the Asia Pacific Association for Computer-Assisted Language Learning (http://www.apacall.org).

Chapter 7

Administrators and the Technology Standards

This chapter explains how the standards affect administrators of English language programs and programs that include English language learners and teachers. The vignettes give examples of administrators taking action to meet all seven of the goals in the learner and teacher standards.

The TESOL Technology Standards offer guidance for administrators in many aspects of decision-making about technology use in their programs. The TESOL standards have a unique focus on language teaching and learning. This differs from other technology-focused standards, e.g., the ISTE National Educational Technology Standards and the UNESCO Information and Communication Technologies Competency Standards for Teachers (see Chapter 5 for a detailed comparison). The standards for language learners provide a baseline for expectations about what students should be able to do with technology while they are learning language in the program. These expectations for learners have strong implications for decision-making about classroom facilities, designing and implementing curriculum, and teaching practice. The standards for language teachers set a baseline for expectations that can be used in hiring and that should be used in professional development. The standards provide elements for administrators to consider when they are designing and assessing facilities and curriculum and evaluating teaching practices. The standards for language teachers also allow administrators to recognize teachers with higher levels of technological ability ("expert" level) and compensate them accordingly.

Suggestions from the technology standards are echoed in Witbeck and Healey's (n.d.) "Technology and the Language Program Administrator." For effective decision making about instructional use of technology, Witbeck and Healey suggest that administrators must

- Have a basic understanding of technological language-learning tools and the ways in which each tool can support (or subvert!) different pedagogical models.

- Listen and respond to what teachers say about their classroom needs and which tools are needed.

- Provide funding for ongoing technical support.

- Ensure that adequate budget and staff effort are devoted to maintaining and regularly upgrading facilities. (p. 253)

Effective use of technology in instruction requires ongoing professional development for teachers, as well, according to Witbeck and Healey. They point out that

> institutions need to protect their instructional technology investments by funding initial and ongoing training so that teachers can make effective use of the technology available to them. A teacher skilled in the use of instructional technology can take advantage of free or inexpensive resources and use them well. An unskilled teacher will need help even to reach a basic level of competence, and students will likely be far from satisfied. (p. 265)

Administrators who meet the basic standards for teachers (Goal 1 in technology standards for language teachers, in particular) will be better able to make appropriate decisions about funding for technology and about overall technology use in their institutions. Teachers should participate actively in decision-making about technology purchases and curricular use (Goal 2 Standard 1 in the standards for language teachers). When teachers help decide what technology to buy, they are more likely to use it. This is especially important with expensive or complex technology tools.

Technical support is an essential component of technology use. It is reflected directly in Goal 1 Standard 4 of the technology standards for language learners, Goal 2 Standard 2 of the standards for language teachers, and indirectly anywhere that technology use is mentioned. Changes are occurring rapidly in hardware, software, and other digital tools and material. Threats from viruses and other malware are ongoing risks. The changes and threats mean that a technology-enhanced activity that worked in class or the lab yesterday may not work today. Teachers do need to have basic troubleshooting skills in order to handle routine problems, typically ones that are resolved by restarting a computer. However, good technical support can be proactive in warding off technology failures before they occur and in dealing with them on the spot, in class or in the lab. Teachers and students who cannot trust technology, at least at some level, are unlikely to use it.

The learner standards and the teacher standards have curricular implications for administrators as well. Students require not only basic computer skills but also an ability to use technology-based productivity, skill-building, and communication and collaboration tools. These skills, especially with communication and collaboration, should be integrated into the curriculum. Training for students in how to be more independent in learning with technology should also be part of the curriculum. This implies that learners are not simply left on their own to puzzle out what to use and how to use it in a computer lab. Another consequence is that learners should have some choices about what to learn and instruction in making good choices. Also essential for students is an awareness of Internet safety precautions.

Where possible, administrators should provide technology tools for teachers to use in preparing for class, grading, record keeping, and learner assessment. At a minimum, this will include access to the Internet and to productivity software, such as a word processor and grade book. Wherever feasible, administrators should provide secure digital storage space for teachers and for student work and a mechanism for teachers and students to communicate and share information and material with each other. Teachers will also need legal access to the material they use, which means that administrators should put guidelines and procedures in place to discourage piracy and protect student privacy. Teachers will need access to information and research, and administrators should encourage teachers to conduct their own research, as well.

The standards repeatedly emphasize the importance of professional development for teachers. Professional development is at the heart of Goal 1 of the teacher standards, especially Standard 3, and is implied in many of the other goals and standards. Technology changes rapidly, so even someone who is hired with technical skills can quickly become out of date without ongoing professional development. Especially in settings with little money for professional development, it can be cost-effective to use a training of trainers model: encouraging and appropriately compensating one or more of the teachers to provide in-house training for his or her colleagues. It is also very important for administrators to reward teachers who do use technology appropriately, meeting all the basic or expert-level standards. With a system of recognition and rewards in place, teachers will see that administrators take technology use in teaching seriously. When administrators are fully supportive of technology use, teachers are more likely to respond accordingly.

The standards deliberately do not make recommendations for use of specific hardware and software. The mandate is for appropriate use of "available" technology. As a result, the standards can be applied equally in high-resource settings and in low-resource settings, though exactly what is "available" will be different. In high-resource settings, technology should be more extensively used in teaching and learning. Administrators in every setting should work with teachers, learners, and other stakeholders to meet the highest expectations of appropriate use of technology. The emphasis is on quality, not quantity.

The standards do assume that almost all teachers and most learners will have access to computers and the Internet to some degree. Access may be at home, in an Internet café, or at work. Even if students cannot use technology directly due to restricted access to computers and the Internet, teachers can generally find a way to access and download useful information and material to bring into the classroom. Free and low-cost resources are available for online file storage and sharing. (Google Docs [Google, 2010a] is an example.) Free email accounts and free websites or wikis are also available. Increasingly, educational content can be delivered and language learners can interact with teachers and other learners on mobile phones and other portable devices. Given the historical precedents with technology, it can be expected that more technology tools will be available over time in all settings, which provides another reason for ongoing professional development for teachers.

Sample Vignette for Administrators

The following vignette helps to exemplify how administrators can implement the TESOL Technology Standards in low-resource, low-access environments; medium-resource, medium-access environments; and high-resource, high-access environments.

Decision Making:
Adding Technology Resources

Background

The administrator's institution is discussing adding technology resources to enhance teaching and learning. Having additional technology resources in the school would also address the demands of parents, sponsors, and students who feel that technology must be part of the learning process. The administrator examines the TESOL Technology Standards for guidance as to how to proceed. Teacher Goal 1, *Language teachers acquire and maintain foundational knowledge and skills in technology for professional purposes,* emphasizes the need to ensure that teachers have the necessary skills in order to implement whatever technology resources are added.

Before embarking on a technology-related change, the administrator asks teachers to fill out a CALL questionnaire regarding:

- their current skill level with technology,

- their access to computers and the Internet at home,

- how much they have used technology in teaching, and

- their areas of interest in learning more about using technology in teaching.

The responses allow the administrator to determine who among those already on staff might be at expert level as described in the technology standards. The administrator also seeks faculty advice about who on staff might be a good lead technology teacher to provide teacher training workshops, demonstrate appropriate pedagogical resources for language learning, advise on design of a lab, and so forth.

Interested teachers form part of a CALL committee, reviewing and sharing information about the one-computer classroom (e.g., Burkhart, 1999; Gaer, n.d.), computer labs and self-access centers (e.g., Healey, 2009; Self-access, 2002), and use of mobile technologies (e.g., Chinnery, 2006). All teachers are encouraged to participate in learning communities related to technology in language teaching, such as Webheads in Action ([2010] http://webheadsinaction.org/), IATEFL Learning Technologies Special Interest Group ([2010] http://groups.yahoo.com/group /LearningTechnologiesSIG/), LearnCentral ([Elluminate, 2010] webcasts, http:// www.learncentral.org/), MERLOT (Multimedia Educational Resource for Learning and Online Teaching [California State University, 2010], http://www.merlot.org /merlot/index.htm), and the TESOL CALL Interest Section ([2010b] http://www .call-is.org/info/).

Technology Tasks

Low-resource, low-access setting

This environment has very few resources: one computer and a data projector for checkout, but little else available. The administrator encourages teachers to learn how to use free and low-cost resources to enhance the one-computer classroom (meeting Goal 2, *Language teachers integrate pedagogical knowledge and skills with technology to enhance language teaching and learning*). One of the teachers already has more skills with technology, so she is designated the leader of this effort and is given a stipend for technology work (see Teacher Goal 1 Standard 1 Vignette: New Technology Course for Teachers). The administrator provides the lead technology teacher with funding for professional development. This pays for an online course to start, then attending a conference.

Other teachers receive a small stipend for attending a series of short evening and weekend workshops presented by the lead teacher to colleagues. The workshops give basic information about how to use a one-computer classroom and about online resources that would be appropriate with the school curriculum, including material that the teachers can print out to bring to their classes and material to use in a one-computer classroom. The administrator includes attendance at these workshops as part of the teachers' yearly professional development plans. Teachers are expected to use this information in their classes. The administrator asks for reports from each teacher describing what they have done with the materials as part of the teachers' annual evaluations.

The administrator equips the teachers' room with several computers with Internet connections so that teachers have a safe place to practice what they are learning. The computers are also equipped with easy-to-use grade book software or with access to an online grade book program (e.g., SnapGrades [2010], http://snapgrades.com) to help meet Goal 3, *Language teachers apply technology in record keeping, feedback, and assessment.* Connecting with a wider community of practice through the Internet helps teachers meet Goal 4, *Language teachers use technology to improve communication, collaboration, and efficiency.* At the same time as professional development is ongoing for teachers, the administrator seeks out grants that would pay for projectors and Internet connections in every classroom.

Medium-resource, medium-access setting

This environment has modest resources available: a small computer lab with Internet access, two computers and projectors to check out, and Internet access in several classrooms. The administrator looks at the results of the CALL questionnaire to determine where the areas of expertise are among the teachers. One teacher is designated as the lead technology teacher and given a stipend for technology work. Using the results of the CALL questionnaire, the lead teacher organizes study groups among the teachers to build pedagogical and technical expertise in their areas of interest. He provides resources and guides the initial meetings of the groups. He encourages teachers to try what they are learning after each session to meet Goal 2, *Language teachers integrate pedagogical knowledge and skills with technology to enhance language teaching and learning.*

In order to meet Goal 3, *Language teachers apply technology in record keeping, feedback, and assessment*, the administrator has a course management system (CMS), such as the free Moodle ([Moodle.org, 2010] http://moodle.org) or Sakai ([Sakai Foundation, 2010] http://sakaiproject.org), or the commercial Blackboard ([2010] http://blackboard.com) set up on the school's server. The CMS allows teachers to record their grades and provide students with online access to their grades. Teachers are expected to use the CMS. The administrator makes sure that there are enough computers available in the teacher resource room so that teachers who do not have access at home can use the equipment at school.

Email is used for school communication, part of meeting Goal 4, *Language teachers use technology to improve communication, collaboration, and efficiency*. In order to meet this collaborative goal, the administrator makes sure that teachers can share their resources with each other on the school server. For student privacy and security, teachers are reminded to use password protection and other security messages in handling confidential information electronically. (See Teacher Goal 1 Standard 4 Vignette: Compliance with Privacy Regulations.)

The administrator provides funding for the lead technology teacher to attend an international conference. The lead technology teacher and several others who have been active in using technology in their classes receive funding to attend a regional conference. Teachers are expected to use the information from the conference and other training in their classes. The administrator asks for reports from each teacher about how they have used technology in their teaching as part of the teachers' annual evaluations.

High-resource, high-access setting
The school has access to a web server and file server (intranet). The school also has a networked set of 25 netbooks and a computer with a projector or with an interactive whiteboard in most classrooms. (See Davies, Walker, Rendall, & Hewer, 2010; and Dallas ISD, n.d., for more on interactive whiteboards.) The administrator is interested in expanding the technology infrastructure at the school and increasing the use of technology for language teaching. In order to ensure effective implementation, the administrator reviews the results of the CALL questionnaire. She uses the results to create a CALL committee, a group of teachers interested in technology who will work closely with the school's technical support staff. The administrator requests the committee to gather information about possible improvements to the technology infrastructure and equipment. The committee is expected to discuss the options with all the teachers and build consensus.

As a result of the committee's work, the administrator decides to upgrade the school server, add wireless Internet connectivity throughout the school, purchase a class set of networked laptops (netbooks), and add a data projector or an interactive whiteboard in most classrooms. Teachers reserve the use of the class set of netbooks online. Teachers with an interest in working with the interactive whiteboards are scheduled to use those rooms. The school server offers web space for each class, so teachers can set up class web pages that are kept secure. All the teachers take part in ongoing workshops about how to use the class set of laptops, the interactive whiteboards, class web pages, and a one-computer classroom to achieve their course goals (meeting Goal 2, *Language teachers integrate pedagogical knowledge and skills with technology to enhance language teaching and learning*).

The administrator addresses Goal 3, *Language teachers apply technology in record keeping, feedback, and assessment*, by setting up a course management system (CMS) on the school server. The CMS allows teachers to record their grades and provide students with online access to their grades. All teachers have email accounts and use email for communicating with their students, parents, administrators, and each other. The teachers also share resources with each other on the school server. The use of the CMS, email, and shared resources helps meet Goal 4, *Language teachers use technology to improve communication, collaboration, and efficiency.*

The administrator encourages teachers to submit proposals to conferences about their use of technology and provides funding for teachers who have a proposal accepted. At least one member of the CALL committee and one technical support staff person are funded to attend a major international conference together. The administrator will use the new ideas that both the teacher and the tech support person see as useful. Improved use of technology is a part of the school's five-year plan. The administrator uses reports from each teacher about what they have done with technology as part of the teachers' annual evaluations.

Conclusion

This chapter has addressed considerations for administrators in applying the technology standards in their programs. A key objective in the technology standards for language learners is to have access to technology for students. At a minimum, access should be at the level of technology that is readily available. Successful use of technology requires technical support for students when they need it. Technical support also ensures that classroom equipment is in good working order. Administrators should address the curricular implications for learners, as well: that courses employ available technology as appropriate, and that students become more skilled users of the technology that is available.

To meet the TESOL Technology Standards for Language Teachers, administrators need to hire teachers with the requisite level of technological competence or provide training to bring teachers to that level of skill. Although having technical support available for teachers is necessary, it is not enough to ensure that technology will be used effectively. Ongoing professional development is essential. In order to perform at the highest levels, teachers will also need access to resources: productivity tools, classroom material, and information and research about best practices. Teachers need access to the Internet and a mechanism to collaborate with their colleagues and share information with students, parents, administrators, and other stakeholders. Setting up mechanisms and resources that enable teachers to share information about technology use with each other is helpful and relatively low-cost. Teachers who are at an "expert" skill level and who use their skills to help their students and their colleagues should be compensated appropriately.

The standards recommend that administrators enable teachers to be part of decision-making about technology purchases and use. Administrators should also encourage teachers to design and manage how they use technology in their teaching. Including assessment of student use of technology in classroom assessment processes helps ensure accountability.

Administrators will find the Program Assessment Rubric in Chapter 9 of this volume useful in setting targets and assessing whether these targets have been met.

Resources

Background Information

Burkhart, L. J. (1999). *Strategies and applications for the one-computer classroom.* Retrieved from http://www.lburkhart.com/elem/strat.htm

Chinnery, G .M. (2006). *Going to the MALL: Mobile assisted language learning.* Retrieved from http://llt.msu.edu/vol10num1/emerging/default.html

Gaer, S. (n.d.) *ESL activities for the one computer classroom.* Retrieved from http://www.susangaer.com/sgaer/onecomputer/

Healey, D. (2010). *Creating a computer lab/learning center.* Retrieved from http://www.eltexpert.com/complab/index.html

TE Editor (2002). *Self-access: A framework for diversity.* Retrieved from http://www.teachingenglish.org.uk/think/articles/self-access-a-framework-diversity

Tools

Blackboard. (2010). *Blackboard.* Retrieved from http://blackboard.com. Commercial course management system.

Google. (2010g). Google Sites. Retrieved from http://sites.google.com Free wiki/shared website

Moodle.org. (2010). Moodle. Retrieved from http://moodle.org. Open source (non-commercial) course management system.

Sakai Foundation. (2010). Sakai. Retrieved from http://sakaiproject.org/. Non-commercial course management system.

SnapGrades. (2010). SnapGrades. Retrieved from http://snapgrades.com. Online gradebook

WordPress (2010). WordPress. Retrieved from http://wordpress.com. Class blog/website

Learning Communities

California State University. (2010). *MERLOT (Multimedia Educational Resource for Learning and Online Teaching). California State University.* Retrieved from http://www.merlot.org/merlot/index.htm Resources and learning communities to join

Elluminate. (2010). LearnCentral. Retrieved from http://www.learncentral.org/ Free webcasts on education topics

IATEFL Learning Technologies Special Interest Group (2010). Retrieved from http://groups.yahoo.com/group/LearningTechnologiesSIG/ Membership-based organization

TESOL CALL Interest Section (2010b). http://www.call-is.org/info/ Membership-based organization

Webheads in Action. (2010) http://webheadsinaction.org/ Learning community

Chapter 8

Online Teaching and Learning With the Technology Standards

This chapter focuses on ways to apply the standards to online teaching. It indicates the implications of each standard for those involved in online teaching, learning, and administration.

This chapter focuses on issues in fully online courses. However, the information also applies to hybrid courses that include both online and face-to-face components. Fundamentally, good online teaching is good teaching. The TESOL Technology Standards apply to all teaching settings, including online environments. That said, certain elements take on added importance in fully online environments. These include creating an effective technology infrastructure, setting the learning environment appropriately, managing time, and establishing teacher and learner presence.

Technology Infrastructure

In an online course, technology is the infrastructure. Teachers need to fully understand the electronic learning environment and to have a basic level of skill with the tools that they use regularly, such as a course management system or videoconferencing tool. Learners need to have access to explicit instruction in how to use the course tools. This generally includes information in a variety of formats (text, graphics, video). Both teachers and learners need regular, skilled technical support that is available through multiple routes (California State University, Chico, 2009). It does not help a learner to have a tech support website when the Internet is not working; a phone number or other offline means of contact has to be available as well.

Teachers in an online course need to be well aware that a technical problem for the learner can prevent his or her participation in the course. The learner's frustration grows with each day that the course or a needed component is not available. Learners may be working in isolation rather than as part of a cohort, which feeds the frustration when something does not work. As much as possible, teachers need to be responsive to problems that prevent learners from participating fully in the course (Fish & Wickersham, 2009). These problems can include software upgrades that prevent a course element from functioning on a learner's computer, a missing browser plug-in, a file-naming convention that does not work on all types of computers, different versions of word-processing software, and times when the Internet is not available. Blocked websites are a problem in some countries where the government has taken offense or wishes to make a political statement by preventing access to certain websites. (See Helft & Wines, 2010, on Google and China, for example.) Quick responses and flexibility in the face of these obstacles are a must, especially when online learners are in distant settings.

Internet safety is a very large consideration in online courses. Learners and teachers need to be on the alert for viruses and other harmful programs (malware) on their computers that could be passed to others through shared files. When email addresses appear on a website or other publicly visible place online, they may become the target of false and fraudulent email messages (spam). Young learners are particularly vulnerable to online predators. Special caution needs to be taken to protect the personal information and photos of young learners online.

One very positive element in online courses is access to adaptive technology, including assistive devices for those with physical disabilities. Screen readers that translate text to speech, speech recognition software, the ability to increase the size of print, and alternative input devices—these and more are available to online learners. For best results, websites and other online information should be created in accordance with the Principles of Universal Design: "the design of products and environments to be usable by all people, to the greatest extent possible, without the need for adaptation or specialized design" ([Center for Universal Design, 2010, para. 1] http://www.ncsu.edu/www/ncsu/design/sod5/cud/about_ud/udprinciples text.htm). Websites and materials created appropriately can readily be used with assistive devices as needed.

Learning Environment

A positive learning environment has a number of attributes. Students feel safe to express their ideas in a positive environment, and they feel supported by their classmates, or colleagues, and the teacher. In addition, students are aware of what they are supposed to do, when, and how. Most online environments cannot get by on the force of the teacher's personality. In many fully online courses, the teacher is not present much of the time that learning is going on. Learners are expected to be getting as much if not more from their collaborations with each other in discussions and on tasks.

For optimum learning, the online environment should be one that supports interaction and collaboration among learners, creating a learning community (Karayan & Crowe, 1997; Garrison, Anderson, & Archer, 2000). Interaction often takes place through asynchronous online discussion and may also include synchronous tools such as chat, interactive whiteboards, audioconferencing, or videoconferencing. The learning environment should include a method to share resources for lessons (following appropriate copyright laws) and to collect and share student work. Collaboration can be enabled by file-sharing. Sharing can be enabled through individual email, file-sharing websites (e.g., Google Sites [Google, 2010g] at http:// sites.google.com), or a school's file server. The course designer may be working with a standard course management system such as Moodle, Sakai, or Blackboard. The instructor may also include different stand-alone elements to enable asynchronous and synchronous discussion and file- and resource-sharing (Educause, 2010).

Teachers need to be aware of how students are using the environment and work actively to promote appropriate use. They should offer opportunities for students to apply different learning strategies, in terms of media, format, and collaboration (Illinois Online Network, 2010; San Juan College, 2008). The teacher sets the stage, provides resources, models interaction, and moves interactions in the learning environment forward in a positive way. In order to be effective, teachers in online learning environments need to be supported with ongoing training, adequate time for preparation and participation, appropriate class size, and appropriate remuneration (Colwell & Jenks, 2004). A class of 50–75 students, whether online or face-to-face, will not have the same learning outcomes as a class of 15–20. A change in platform does not create a change in the work. Fifty essays in electronic format take as long to read and grade as 50 essays on paper.

Time

Many adult students are involved in online courses because they need to juggle conflicting demands of study, work, and family. They need a clear timeline so that other aspects of their lives can be scheduled appropriately to the extent possible. Planning ahead is essential in order to provide deadlines that can be met and that learners can count on (Shi, Bonk, & Magjuka, 2006; Fish & Wickersham, 2009). The teacher in a face-to-face class can take a quick look around the classroom to see who is ready to move on from one activity to the next. The quick look is not an option in an asynchronous online class. Some flexibility is possible, but it needs to be built into course descriptions and expectations. Ideally, the teacher will poll students before changing the schedule to make sure the revisions will work for everyone.

Synchronous, real-time activities (e.g., chat, collaborative whiteboards, and interactive presentations) are readily available options in settings with geographically similar learners. World Clock ([Time and Date, 2010a] http://www.timeanddate.com) and especially World Clock Meeting Planner ([Time and Date, 2010b] http://www.timeand date.com/worldclock/meeting.html) can be very helpful in setting times that will work with geographically dispersed learners. Text chat is generally available even to learners in areas with poor Internet access. Other synchronous tools, however, may be out of the reach of learners outside of areas with high-speed Internet connections. Any synchronous activity requires advance notice and planning so that all learners have an equal opportunity to participate.

Teacher and Learner Presence

An area of ongoing research in online education is that of *presence*, typically described as social presence, teaching presence, and cognitive presence. Presence is at the heart of creating a community of inquiry, which is one direction to take in creating a learning environment. The three presences are described extensively in Garrison, Anderson, and Archer (2000). A diagram showing the interaction of the three presences to create the online educational experience is shown in Figure 8.1.

The teacher's role is to set up structures and processes for a successful learning environment. This includes selecting content, setting the climate, and encouraging appropriate discourse (Cini & Vilic, 2004). Learners and teachers work together to create *social presence* in the course, where learners feel comfortable with their interactions with others. Including a place to share photos, a purely social discussion thread, and other nonacademic options can enhance social presence and the willingness to learn. In a face-to-face class, this would be seen as lowering the affective filter (Krashen, 1981, and many others).

Cognitive presence refers to the teaching and learning components in a course or a community of inquiry. Socializing motivates and intensifies the educational experience and creates the context in which students learn best. However, content also needs to be available for learning to take place. If there is little or no exposure to meaningful language data, language learning is unlikely to happen. The teacher, usually also the course designer, is central to providing cognitive presence in an online course.

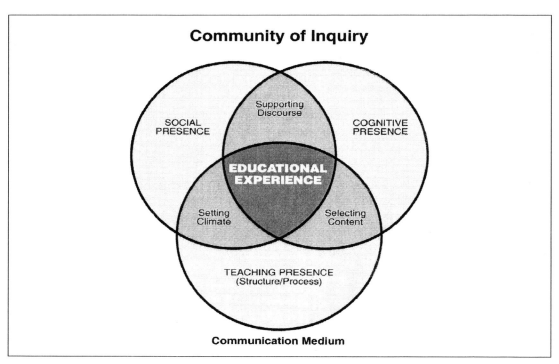

Figure 8.1. Community of Inquiry Model
(Reprinted by permission from Garrison, Anderson, & Archer, 2000, p. 88)

Teaching presence is the visibility of the teacher in the community. The teacher is one part of the community. It is relatively easy to replicate a teacher-dominated class online, where the teacher initiates, responds to, critiques, and grades all activity. Such a teacher-dominated class offers little chance to develop student autonomy for self-sustaining, lifelong learning. The teacher-centered class also does not enable adequate socializing to prepare students for team-based workplaces. On the other hand, students learn better when they feel they have adequate feedback from instructors on their work in the course (Fish & Wickersham, 2009).

Tables 8.1 and 8.2 examine each of the TESOL Technology Standards (Table 8.1, for language learners, and Table 8.2, for language teachers) to describe some of their implications for online teaching and learning.

Table 8.1. Implications for Online Learning in the Standards for Language Learners

Goal and Standard	Text of the Standard	Implication
Goal 1	**Language learners demonstrate foundational knowledge and skills in technology for a multilingual world.**	
Standard 1	Language learners demonstrate basic operational skills in using various technology tools and Internet browsers. *Performance indicators* mention learner capability with available digital devices, Internet browsers, and email.	Successful online teaching requires that learners be familiar with course tools. Teaching online may require providing additional instruction so that learners are able to use the course tools effectively.
Standard 2	Language learners are able to use available input and output devices (e.g., keyboard, mouse, printer, headset, microphone, media player, electronic whiteboard).	Learners need explicit instruction in order to use required course tools in an online environment (e.g., microphone, headset, webcam).
Standard 3	Language learners exercise appropriate caution when using online sources and when engaging in electronic communication.	Internet safety must be part of any online course.
Standard 4	Language learners demonstrate basic competence as users of technology. *Performance indicators* mention learner capability with finding help as needed.	Learners need clear information about where and how to find technical support in an online course. They need multiple routes to technical help, including approaches that do not require Internet access (e.g., via mobile phone).

(Continued on p. 168)

Table 8.1 (continued). Implications for Online Learning in the Standards for Language Learners

Goal and Standard	Text of the Standard	Implication
Goal 2	**Language learners use technology in socially and culturally appropriate, legal, and ethical ways.**	
Standard 1	Language learners understand that communication conventions differ across cultures, communities, and contexts.	Information about cross-cultural communication must be explicit in an online course.
Standard 2	Language learners demonstrate respect for others in their use of private and public information.	Respect for others and how to show it needs to be made explicit in an online course, especially if learners are new to online course work. There are consequences for misuse of information, and learners need to be aware of what the consequences are.
Goal 3	**Language learners effectively use and critically evaluate technology-based tools as aids in the development of their language learning competence as part of formal instruction and for further learning.**	
Standard 1	Language learners effectively use and evaluate available technology-based productivity tools. *Performance indicators* include student use of productivity tools such as word processors, presentation software, web design software, and electronic dictionaries; students work individually and collaboratively.	Online learners need to know how to integrate productivity tools into their online work (e.g., by cutting and pasting from a word processor into a discussion forum or by attaching files to messages).
Standard 2	Language learners appropriately use and evaluate available technology-based language skill-building tools. *Performance indicators* include use of appropriate vocabulary during collaborative work, appropriate use of skill-building tools, and student evaluation of the tools they use in meeting their own language learning goals.	Ongoing formative learner feedback is a good idea in an online course, because teachers are not able to see learners in order to assess their satisfaction with the tools they are using.
Standard 3	Language learners appropriately use and evaluate available technology-based tools for communication and collaboration.	Good online learning generally includes collaborative work; learners need to have expectations about appropriate communication made explicit, such as with rubrics for online discussion posts.

(Continued on p. 169)

Table 8.1 (continued). Implications for Online Learning in the Standards for Language Learners

Goal and Standard	Text of the Standard	Implication
Standard 4	Language learners use and evaluate available technology-based research tools appropriately. *Performance indicators* include finding information, evaluating online information, and documenting information appropriately.	Online learners should be instructed in effective use of web searching, evaluating online resources, and documenting sources. Teachers should model appropriate documentation for learners.
Standard 5	Language learners recognize the value of technology to support autonomy, lifelong learning, creativity, metacognition, collaboration, personal pursuits, and productivity. *Performance indicators* include learner ability to set learning goals and objectives that use technology and to select and use technology for independent language learning, to monitor their progress, to express themselves, and to work more effectively.	Online work generally requires learners to be more autonomous, using good time management skills. These skills learned as part of an online course can build competence for lifelong learning.

Table 8.2. Implications for Online Teaching in the Standards for Language Teachers

Goal and Standard	Text of the Standard	Implication
Goal 1	**Language teachers acquire and maintain foundational knowledge and skills in technology for professional purposes.**	
Standard 1	Language teachers demonstrate knowledge and skills in basic technological concepts and operational competence, meeting or exceeding TESOL Technology Standards for students in whatever situation they teach. *Performance indicators* include the ability to perform basic functions with digital devices; prepare material for students using basic technological tools, such as a word processor and presentation software; and use appropriate caution when using online sources and communicating online.	More technical competence is generally required in an online course than in a face-to-face course with occasional use of technology. Teachers should be able to respond to basic technical questions, including frequently asked questions about hardware and course tools, and recognize which questions need to be forwarded to technical support staff.

(Continued on p. 170)

Table 8.2 (continued). Implications for Online Teaching in the Standards for Language Teachers

Goal and Standard	Text of the Standard	Implication
Standard 2	Language teachers demonstrate an understanding of a wide range of technology supports for language learning and options for using them in a given setting. *Performance indicators* include the ability to identify appropriate technology, evaluate options, share information with colleagues, use online technology as available, and locate and adapt digital resources.	Online teachers should be aware of the options available in their course management system (or their alternatives to a course management system) so that they can use the most appropriate options.
Standard 3	Language teachers actively strive to expand their skill and knowledge base to evaluate, adopt, and adapt emerging technologies throughout their careers.	Online teaching is a developing field, so there are many emerging technologies to be aware of. The teacher should be engaging in continuous professional development, both informally and in courses or workshops.
Standard 4	Language teachers use technology in socially and culturally appropriate, legal, and ethical ways. *Performance indicators* include showing sensitivity to differences in cross-cultural communication, acting as a model for legal and ethical use of technology, and protecting student privacy.	This is especially appropriate in an online learning environment. Teachers should be aware of what constitutes fair use when posting material online, for example, and behave appropriately. Teachers need to be vigilant in protecting learner privacy in online courses (e.g., using BCC as appropriate to address email to everyone in the group).

(Continued on p. 171)

Table 8.2 (continued). Implications for Online Teaching in the Standards for Language Teachers

Goal and Standard	Text of the Standard	Implication
Goal 2	**Language teachers integrate pedagogical knowledge and skills with technology to enhance language teaching and learning.**	
Standard 1	Language teachers identify and evaluate technological resources and environments for suitability to their teaching context.	Connectivity may be an issue in online courses. If students have less connectivity, the teacher needs to adapt the material used (e.g., video may not be usable in low-bandwidth areas).
Standard 2	Language teachers coherently integrate technology into their pedagogical approaches. *Performance indicators* include embedding technology into teaching and engaging in regular professional development. *Expert-level performance indicators* include the ability to work around limitations and to support peers in their professional development.	An online course is an example of technology embedded into teaching. Online teaching is an emerging field, so ongoing professional development is necessary to stay abreast of current pedagogy.
Standard 3	Language teachers design and manage language learning activities and tasks using technology appropriately to meet curricular goals and objectives. *Performance indicators* include making appropriate technology choices and helping students use technology appropriately and critically. *Expert-level performance indicators* include the ability to adapt activities, create an appropriate technology environment, and have more than one approach to achieve objectives.	Transferring a face-to-face course to an online format is more than just providing material in electronic form. Online teachers determine which electronic media and approaches are most appropriate to meet curricular goals. Teachers raise learners' awareness of the advantages and drawbacks to using technology. Teachers use strategies to encourage community online (e.g., posting learner photos as appropriate, setting up small groups and learning partners, expecting learners to comment on each other's posts).
Standard 4	Language teachers use relevant research findings to inform the planning of language learning activities and tasks that involve technology. *Expert-level performance indicators* include identifying gaps in research, helping others learn about research into technology use, and producing and disseminating their own research.	Online learning is a developing field, which means that there are many needs and opportunities for research.

(Continued on p. 172)

Table 8.2 (continued). Implications for Online Teaching in the Standards for Language Teachers

Goal and Standard	Text of the Standard	Implication
Goal 3	**Language teachers apply technology in record keeping, feedback, and assessment.**	
Standard 1	Language teachers evaluate and implement relevant technology to aid in effective learner assessment. *Performance indicators* include familiarity with different forms of assessment and use of appropriate record-keeping tools. *Expert-level performance indicators* include using computer-based testing where available and providing technology-enhanced feedback to learners.	Online formative assessment can take many forms. Online summative assessment issues include test security, which may require use of local proctors.
Standard 2	Language teachers use technological resources to collect and analyze information in order to enhance language instruction and learning. *Performance indicators* include the use of technology-enhanced assessment results in instruction. *Expert-level performance indicators* include applying research findings to technology-enhanced assessment and using technology to analyze student output and to document teaching for further analysis.	Online courses generally provide a wealth of data about student behavior online. Because the learners are not physically present, the teacher needs to be able to make sense of data collected from learners' online work.
Standard 3	Language teachers evaluate the effectiveness of specific student uses of technology to enhance teaching and learning. *Expert-level performance indicators* include developing and sharing procedures for evaluating student use of technology.	Evaluation of students' use of technology should be ongoing in an online course.

(Continued on p. 173)

Conclusion

This chapter has examined the implications of the TESOL Technology Standards for online teaching and learning. The technology standards are particularly applicable to online courses because technology is a routine part of teaching and learning in such settings. With hybrid (partially online and partially face-to-face) courses, technology needs to be blended effectively in order to produce high-quality learning. Online teaching is more than transferring a face-to-face course into digital mode. Online educators need to be aware of the effects of having technology as the infrastructure for a course, the centrality of establishing a productive learning environment, and

Table 8.2 (continued). Implications for Online Teaching in the Standards for Language Teachers

Goal and Standard	Text of the Standard	Implication
Goal 4	**Language teachers use technology to improve communication, collaboration, and efficiency.**	
Standard 1	Language teachers use communication technologies to maintain effective contact and collaboration with peers, students, administration, and other stakeholders. *Performance indicators* include effective use of online teaching resources and collaboration with colleagues. *Expert-level performance indicators* include setting up methods to communicate with students, having students create and submit work electronically, advising administrators about digital communication methods, and digitally sharing material.	Effective communication with students is at the heart of good online teaching.
Standard 2	Language teachers regularly reflect on the intersection of professional practice and technological developments so that they can make informed decisions regarding the use of technology to support language learning and communication. *Expert-level performance indicators* include making innovative use of technology, engaging in research, and sharing the results of their research.	Online teaching and learning is a developing area, so ongoing professional development is necessary. In addition, course management systems are frequently updated, requiring teachers to familiarize themselves with new features and changes in their accustomed uses.
Standard 3	Language teachers apply technology to improve efficiency in preparing for class, grading, and maintaining records. *Expert-level performance indicators* include maintaining a resource that allows students to locate and retrieve material, using electronic methods to assess students' learning, and teaching students to use electronic methods to document their own progress.	Online teaching routinely uses technology for course management, archived learning objects, assessment, and student self-evaluation.

the need for teacher responsiveness and attention to timing. It takes time and energy to create an effective learning environment (Colwell & Jenks, 2004). *Presence* is an ongoing topic for research, exploring the intersection of teaching, social, and cognitive presence on learning outcomes. As an emerging field, online education requires appropriate compensation and ongoing teacher development so that teachers and learners can make best use of a rapidly changing medium of instruction.

Resources

Center for Research on Learning and Teaching. (2010). *Teaching strategies: Online teaching*. Retrieved from http://www.crlt.umich.edu/tstrategies/tsot.php Links to research on and guidelines for effective teaching online.

Language Learning & Technology. (2010). Retrieved from http://llt.msu.edu/default.html. Refereed electronic journal of research in technology and second language learning.

San Juan College. (2008). *Research on best practices*. Retrieved from http://www.sanjuancollege.edu /pages/2825.asp. Links to research on and guidelines for effective teaching online.

Chapter 9

Checklists for Self-Assessment and Program Assessment

"Can-do" checklists are provided for both the learner standards and the teacher standards. The program assessment rubric is a way to examine compliance at the institutional or program level.

This chapter is designed for those who want to evaluate themselves and their programs against the TESOL Technology Standards. Teachers should use the Technology Standards for Language Teachers Rubric to look at their own skills and use the Technology Standards for Language Learners Rubric to assess how well they are enabling their students' use of technology. Having read Chapter 6, Implications and Recommendations for Teacher Educators, teacher educators will want to ensure that their graduates are able to meet all elements in the Technology Standards for Language Teachers Rubric. Administrators will wish to look at the Program Assessment Rubric, as well as the Technology Standards for Language Learners Rubric, the Technology Standards for Language Teachers Rubric, and the guidelines in Chapter 7, Administrators and the Technology Standards.

Technology Standards for Language Learners Rubric

LEARNER GOAL 1: *Language learners demonstrate foundational knowledge and skills in technology for a multilingual world.*

GOAL 1 STANDARD 1: Language learners demonstrate basic operational skills in using various technology tools and Internet browsers.

	Very well	Adequately	Not so well	Not at all	N/A
I can perform basic functions on digital devices present in my learning environment: desktop computer, mobile/laptop computer, electronic whiteboard, mobile phone, MP3/video player, and other relevant devices.					
I can turn digital devices on and off and restart them as needed.					—
I can open, close, and resize software windows.					—
I can save, edit, and organize files and folders.					—
I can copy, cut, and paste elements within a document.					—
I can recognize file types (e.g., *docx, pdf, ppt*).					—
I can launch and exit various software applications.					—
I can log in and out of shared devices.					
I can perform basic browser functions.					—
I can recognize and use hyperlinks.					—
I can navigate forward and back.					—
I can type in an address.					—
I can use bookmarks and favorites.					—
I can recognize the format of a URL (e.g. *.edu, .com, .gov, .org*).					—
I can check security settings.					

(Continued on p. 177)

GOAL 1 STANDARD 1 (continued): Language learners demonstrate basic operational skills in using various technology tools and Internet browsers.

	Very well	Adequately	Not so well	Not at all	N/A
I can open a new window without losing an existing one.					
I recognize that an email address typically has the format *username@ xxxxx.xxx*, such as *publications@ tesol.org*.					
I can do basic troubleshooting when a device is not working properly.					—
I can check that the device is plugged in securely and the power is on.					—
I can restart the computer.					—
I can use the help option.					—
I can use the Task Manager and end nonresponding tasks (Windows) or Apple-option-esc (Macintosh).					
I recognize when I am and am not online.					—
I can use accessibility options as needed.					
I can enlarge a document or text in a browser (zoom in).					
I can use a Braille keyboard.					
I can use text to speech options.					
I can change the speed of mouse clicks or adjust controls on other input devices.					

GOAL 1 STANDARD 2: Language learners are able to use available input and output devices (e.g., keyboard, mouse, printer, headset, microphone, media player, electronic whiteboard).

	Very well	Adequately	Not so well	Not at all	N/A
I understand the layout of a standard English keyboard.					
I can change the keyboard layout between different languages when I need to.					
I know where available media, devices, and other peripherals go.					
I can put a CD into its slot or into a CD drive.					
I can put memory sticks (USBs) into the correct ports.					
I can put headsets into correct ports (either USB or separate microphone and audio outlets).					
I can operate available peripherals (e.g., printers and scanners).					
I can switch available peripherals on and off.					
I can operate the software controls and settings for the peripheral on my computer.					
I can operate classroom technologies and personal technologies.					
I can operate a data projector.					
I can operate an interactive whiteboard.					
I can operate a video camera.					
I can operate a mobile phone.					
I can operate other technologies available to me (e.g., clickers).					

GOAL 1 STANDARD 3: Language learners exercise appropriate caution when using online sources and when engaging in electronic communication.

	Very well	Adequately	Not so well	Not at all	N/A
I am cautious when opening attachments and clicking on links in email messages.					
I can check who sent the email (a person I know or an unknown person).					
I do not trust that the information in the *From* line is correct.					
I have security software running on my computer and other devices, and I keep it current (e.g., antivirus and firewall software).					
I can check whether there is antivirus software on my computer and whether it is current.					
I can renew antivirus and firewall software on my computer and other devices.					
(FOR YOUNG/UNDERAGE STUDENTS) I do not provide personal contact information to anyone unless directed by my parents or teacher.					
I never provide my photograph to anyone, and I do not upload it online unless directed by my parents or teacher.					
I never give my personal address, phone number, school name, or school address to anyone unless directed by my parents or teacher.					
I never post my daily and weekly activities and whereabouts online unless directed by my parents or teacher.					
(FOR OLDER STUDENTS) I exercise caution in providing personal contact information.					
I choose carefully and decide cautiously when it is OK to share or upload personal photographs, my home address, or my phone number.					

(Continued on p. 180)

GOAL 1 STANDARD 3 (continued): Language learners exercise appropriate caution when using online sources and when engaging in electronic communication.

	Very well	Adequately	Not so well	Not at all	N/A
I choose carefully and decide cautiously when it is OK to give my work address and other whereabouts.					
I exercise caution in computer-mediated communication (CMC).					
I log out when I have finished my conversation or when a conversation makes me feel uncomfortable.					
I do not leave my email account or other personal information in a public chatroom, CMC area, or on a public computer.					
I understand that any information or work placed online can become part of a permanent record.					
I upload work (text, audio, or video) that shows the very best of my efforts.					
I do not upload work (text, audio, or video) that can discredit me or anyone else.					
I can identify false and potentially malicious information online.					
I can check the origin of the website that offers the information.					
I can check whether references or links are made to respectable/ well-known people, institutions, companies, or Internet sites.					
I can search to see if the information appears or is referenced on other Internet sites.					

GOAL 1 STANDARD 4: Language learners demonstrate basic competence as users of technology.

	Very well	Adequately	Not so well	Not at all	N/A
I can perform basic troubleshooting operations.					
I can check whether the power is on, whether the monitor is turned on, and whether the volume is turned on.					
I can restart the computer safely.					
I can check if the digital device has been plugged into the correct place.					
I can search for a file.					
I can use the digital device's search options.					
I can organize file folders so that information to find the file will be made available to me (e.g., date created, date modified).					
I can access and use the help menu (where available).					
I can ask for technical help when appropriate.					
I can identify who to call if technical help is needed (e.g., teacher, school or lab technician, online help desk).					
(FOR UNDERAGE STUDENTS) I can call an adult when I find offensive or inappropriate material.					
I can turn off the monitor or digital device if I feel uncomfortable by what is appearing on the screen.					

LEARNER GOAL 2: *Language learners use technology in socially and culturally appropriate, legal, and ethical ways.*

GOAL 2 STANDARD 1: Language learners understand that communication conventions differ across cultures, communities, and contexts.

	Very well	Adequately	Not so well	Not at all	N/A
I can identify similarities and differences in local and global communication.					
I understand multiple ways that computer-mediated communication (CMC) can be interpreted and misinterpreted.					
I can use the appropriate register in my communication.					
I can take turns and respect the expected length and content of my messages.					
I can tell the difference between literal and rhetorical meanings in messages.					
I can show sensitivity to my use of communication conventions, according to the context.					
I do not use all capital letters in my messages.					
I can use turn-taking cues and wait for lag time in synchronous communication.					
I can check spelling before sending a message.					
I can conform to current social conventions when using technology in communication (e.g., social conventions in the classroom may restrict cell phone use).					
I can identify cultural variables at play in interpreting and responding to a message.					

GOAL 2 STANDARD 2: Language learners demonstrate respect for others in their use of private and public information.

	Very well	Adequately	Not so well	Not at all	N/A
I can demonstrate my understanding that public information in one community may be considered private in other communities.					
I can demonstrate my understanding that images may carry different connotations in different communities (e.g., pigs as symbols of prosperity vs. unclean animals).					
I ask whether an image is acceptable rather than assuming that images carry the same meaning for me as for my partners from other communities.					
I use communications and digital media tools ethically and responsibly.					
I do not secretly videotape others or share videos sent to me without the permission of the individuals in the video (who may not be the same as those who sent the video).					
I do not forward email messages or use BCC (blind copying of a message to a third person) inappropriately.					
I practice legal, responsible, and ethical use of technology systems, information, and software.					
I do not make or distribute illegal copies.					
I document the sources that I use.					
I can understand and respond appropriately to different communication styles online.					

LEARNER GOAL 3: *Language learners effectively use and critically evaluate technology-based tools as aids in the development of their language learning competence as part of formal instruction and for further learning.*

GOAL 3 STANDARD 1: Language learners effectively use and evaluate available technology-based productivity tools.

	Very well	Adequately	Not so well	Not at all	N/A
I can use technology-based productivity tools as aids in production.					
I can use a word processor for classroom, academic, or professional work, and the associated applications such as a spell-checker and thesaurus.					
I can use presentation software for classroom, academic, or professional work.					
I can use templates for preparing presentations, newsletters, reports, and other standard documents.					
I can use tools for brainstorming and creating different graphic organizers.					
I can use technology-based productivity tools as aids in comprehension (e.g., translators, electronic dictionaries).					
I can use translation software to give me a rough idea, and I know that the translation is probably not very accurate.					
I understand the limits of an electronic dictionary in giving me the exact meaning and usage of a translated word.					
I can use technology-based productivity tools with others and on my own in order to enhance my language learning ability.					
I can use peer-editing features in my word processor, such as inserting comments and tracking changes.					
I can apply criteria to evaluate how well I am using particular technology tools for specific language learning tasks.					

GOAL 3 STANDARD 2: Language learners appropriately use and evaluate available technology-based language skill-building tools.

	Very well	Adequately	Not so well	Not at all	N/A
I can use appropriate vocabulary and pragmatics/body language during collaborative work that uses technology.					
I know when to ask for help in order to achieve my language learning goals when using technology.					
I can decide when to use skill-building software, such as for vocabulary, grammar, and pronunciation practice.					
I can read instructions, use help features, and assess whether or not the software is helping me achieve my skill-building goals.					
I can decide when to use devices such as MP3 recorders to enhance specific skill areas.					
I can evaluate Internet resources to use in order to enhance my language learning (e.g., web-based listening exercises, online sentence jumbles).					
I can match my learning style and study strategies to different Internet resources.					
I can tell the difference between Internet resources that are helpful to my learning and ones that are just fun.					

GOAL 3 STANDARD 3: Language learners appropriately use and evaluate available technology-based tools for communication and collaboration.

	Very well	Adequately	Not so well	Not at all	N/A
I can communicate in appropriate ways with those from other cultures and communities using digital tools.					
I can actively encourage others to participate in conversations that use technology-based tools for language learning (e.g., simulations, mobile phones, other communication tools).					
I can use criteria to determine which technology tools work best to collaborate with others for specific types of language learning.					
I can use the comment function in the word processor.					
I can use a wiki, interactive whiteboard, or other tools for improving communication as available.					
I can evaluate how I use particular digital resources to communicate ideas effectively to peers or a wider audience.					
I can use blogs, podcasts, or movie-making tools as available and appropriate.					
I can use the technology that is available either on my own or with others to create content that I can share online or offline.					

GOAL 3 STANDARD 4: Language learners use and evaluate available technology-based research tools appropriately.

	Very well	Adequately	Not so well	Not at all	N/A
I can use technology to find and collect information from a variety of sources.					
I use strategies to evaluate online information.					
I can document source material appropriately.					
I can decide which technology tools to use to organize information from research.					
I can sort information in a word processor, spreadsheet, or database.					
I can create charts and graphs in a spreadsheet to organize information visually.					
Where available, I can use statistical software appropriately.					
Where available, I can use bibliographic tools to store and organize references.					

GOAL 3 STANDARD 5: Language learners recognize the value of technology to support autonomy, lifelong learning, creativity, metacognition, collaboration, personal pursuits, and productivity.

	Very well	Adequately	Not so well	Not at all	N/A
I can choose the most appropriate available technology for independent language learning and can explain why I chose it.					
I can set language learning goals and objectives that employ technology, with a teacher's support or on my own.					
I can use technology to monitor my progress, with a teacher's support or on my own.					
I can use record-keeping functions where available in software or online to monitor how well I am doing.					
I can create an electronic portfolio of my work to demonstrate my progress.					
I can express my creativity using technology.					
I can use technology to create works of art.					
I can use technology to showcase my interests and expertise.					
I can explain why technology is important for personal and professional communication.					
I can explain why technology is important for having access to authentic material that supports my language learning.					
I can use technology to work in English more effectively.					
I can use an electronic dictionary when it is more efficient, such as when working online.					
I can use a spelling- and grammar-checker appropriately.					

Technology Standards for Language Teachers Rubric

TEACHER GOAL 1: *Language teachers acquire and maintain foundational knowledge and skills in technology for professional purposes.*

GOAL 1 STANDARD 1: Language teachers demonstrate knowledge and skills in basic technological concepts and operational competence, meeting or exceeding TESOL technology standards for students in whatever situation they teach.

	Very well	Adequately	Not so well	Not at all	N/A
I can perform basic functions with available digital devices in order to accomplish instructional and organizational goals.					
I can turn devices on and off.					
I can open, close, and resize software windows.					
I can save, edit, and organize files and folders and recognize file times (to see which files are newer).					
I can copy, cut, and paste elements within a document.					
I can launch and exit software applications.					
I can prepare instructional materials for students using basic technology tools.					
I can use word-processing software, presentation software, and software that creates Internet resources.					
I exercise appropriate caution when using online sources and when engaging in electronic communication.					
I realize that online communication is not private.					
I am cautious about what I post online.					

GOAL 1 STANDARD 2: Language teachers demonstrate an understanding of a wide range of technology supports for language learning and options for using them in a given setting.

	Very well	Adequately	Not so well	Not at all	N/A
I can identify appropriate technologies to support a range of instructional objectives.					
I can use evaluation tools to analyze the appropriateness of specific technology options.					
I share information about available technology with colleagues.					
I can use online technology as available to deliver instructional or support material.					
I can locate and adapt a variety of digital resources as appropriate for my learners.					

GOAL 1 STANDARD 3: Language teachers actively strive to expand their skill and knowledge base to evaluate, adopt, and adapt emerging technologies throughout their careers.

	Very well	Adequately	Not so well	Not at all	N/A
I can use technology tools to expand on a conventional activity.					
I keep up with information through a variety of sources (e.g., books, journals, mailing lists, conventions).					
I read professional books and journals and belong to mailing lists that keep me abreast of current trends in technology.					
I attend conferences when possible, either online or in person.					
I participate in a relevant community of practice.					
I explore the possibilities inherent in emerging technologies with a critical eye.					

GOAL 1 STANDARD 4: Language teachers use technology in socially and culturally appropriate, legal, and ethical ways.

	Very well	Adequately	Not so well	Not at all	N/A
I demonstrate sensitivity to the similarities and differences in communication conventions across cultures, communities, and contexts.					
I show an awareness of my role as a model, demonstrating respect for others in my use of public and private information.					
I respect student ownership of their own work.					
I do not share student work inappropriately or require students to post their work publicly if they would prefer not to do so.					
I show awareness and understanding when approaching culturally sensitive topics and offer students alternatives.					
I conform to local legal requirements regarding the privacy of students' personal information, accessibility, fair use, and copyright.					
I follow local guidelines regarding use of human subjects for research.					
I demonstrate awareness that electronic communication is not secure and private, and that in some localities, email may be subject to "open records" laws.					
I seek help in identifying and implementing solutions related to legal requirements.					
I protect student privacy.					
I do not put student email addresses, biodata, or photos online inappropriately.					
I fully inform students about public sharing of blogs and websites.					
I use password-protected sites when possible.					

TEACHER GOAL 2: *Language teachers integrate pedagogical knowledge and skills with technology to enhance language teaching and learning.*

GOAL 2 STANDARD 1: Language teachers identify and evaluate technological resources and environments for suitability to their teaching context.

	Very well	Adequately	Not so well	Not at all	N/A
I can identify the technological resources available and the limitations of the current teaching environment.					
I am aware of the hardware resources available both outside and inside my institution (e.g., computer lab used for math classes at school, Internet cafés available to students, use of my own laptop in class).					
I know about different communication technologies available to me, both provided by the school and freely available online.					
I know what digital material is available online, including both free and paid resources.					
I am aware of courseware, including course management systems, available to me.					
I understand that there may be infrastructure and financial limits to what I have available in my current teaching environment.					
I can identify appropriate technology environments to meet specific learning/teaching goals.					
I consider possibilities other than the ones that I am currently using, especially in terms of what students can use outside of class.					
I consider the pluses and minuses of using a lab versus a one-computer classroom.					

(Continued on p. 193)

GOAL 2 STANDARD 1 (continued): Language teachers identify and evaluate technological resources and environments for suitability to their teaching context.

	Very well	Adequately	Not so well	Not at all	N/A
I think about ways students can use technology in pairs, groups, and on their own.					
I can evaluate technology environments for alignment with the goals of my class.					
I can evaluate technological resources for alignment with the needs and abilities of my students.					
I ask students what technology-related resources they have used and which ones they would like to learn about.					

GOAL 2 STANDARD 2: Language teachers coherently integrate technology into their pedagogical approaches.

	Very well	Adequately	Not so well	Not at all	N/A
I demonstrate understanding of my own teaching style					
I review my personal pedagogical approach in order to use technology to support my current teaching style.					
I demonstrate my understanding of the potential and limitations in technology.					
I embed technology into my teaching rather than making it an add-on.					
I make sure that the technology I use is what the task requires.					
I engage regularly in professional development related to technology use.					
I regularly think about and evaluate my use of technology in teaching.					
I routinely examine whether a technology addition has added value to student learning (and if not, I change or eliminate it).					

Goal 2 Standard 2: Expert Level

	Very well	Adequately	Not so well	Not at all	N/A
I work around the limitations in available technology to achieve my instructional goals.					
I can find multiple ways and different technologies to use in order to achieve a goal.					
I support my peers in their professional development with technology.					

GOAL 2 STANDARD 3: Language teachers design and manage language learning activities and tasks using technology appropriately to meet curricular goals and objectives.

	Very well	Adequately	Not so well	Not at all	N/A
I demonstrate my familiarity with a variety of technology-based options.					
I choose a technology environment that is aligned with the goals of my class.					
I choose technology that is aligned with the needs and abilities of my students.					
I choose skill-building software at the appropriate language level and use it in ways that meet my students' language needs.					
I choose whether to have students use productivity tools with menus in the target language or in their home language, where available, depending on their abilities and goals.					
I use content tools with my students that will benefit their learning outside of language class.					
I am aware of my students' level of digital competence.					
I ensure that students understand how to use the technology to meet instructional goals.					
I teach students how to evaluate online resources.					
I clearly explain the pedagogical purpose of the technologies I use and that I ask students to use.					
I enable students to think critically about their use of technology in an age-appropriate manner.					
Where age-appropriate, I have students discuss the advantages and disadvantages of their uses of technology.					

(Continued on p. 196)

Goal 2 Standard 3: Expert Level

	Very well	Adequately	Not so well	Not at all	N/A
I adapt technology-based activities and tasks to align with the goals of my class and with the needs and abilities of my students.					
I create an appropriate technology environment to meet specific teaching and learning goals.					
I understand the underlying structure of the technology that I use.					
I draw on a wide range of functions in technological resources.					
I identify more than one approach to achieve an objective.					
I have at least one and generally more than one backup plan in case different elements of my technology-enhanced lesson are not working.					
I am aware of technology resources that students can use outside of school.					

GOAL 2 STANDARD 4: Language teachers use relevant research findings to inform the planning of language learning activities and tasks that involve technology.

	Very well	Adequately	Not so well	Not at all	N/A
I am familiar with suggestions from research related to classroom practice using technology.					
I use a variety of avenues for getting information about research related to technology use.					
I am part of a community of practice, either face-to-face or online.					
I read research about technology use online.					
I attend face-to-face or online conferences when possible.					
I understand that technology changes over time, so older research may not be applicable to current settings.					
I am aware of multiple research sources and perspectives that inform technology use.					
I can discern which findings about technology use are most appropriate for my situation.					
I share relevant research findings about technology use with others.					
I identify the context and limitations of research about technology use and do not apply findings inappropriately.					
I can see the underlying principles in specific studies to determine whether the findings might apply to current settings.					

(Continued on p. 198)

Goal 2 Standard 4: Expert Level

	Very well	Adequately	Not so well	Not at all	N/A
I use relevant research findings related to technology use for language learning.					
I identify gaps in current research about technology use.					
I help others recognize the context and limitations of research about technology use.					
I produce and disseminate research related to technology use.					

TEACHER GOAL 3: *Language teachers apply technology in record keeping, feedback, and assessment.*

GOAL 3 STANDARD 1: Language teachers evaluate and implement relevant technology to aid in effective learner assessment.

	Very well	Adequately	Not so well	Not at all	N/A
I demonstrate my familiarity with a variety of forms of assessment that use technology.					
I use appropriate record-keeping tools and techniques.					
I use software- or Internet-based classroom management tools.					
I use electronic grade books, where appropriate.					
I can use electronic tools to create reports about student achievement for students, parents, and administrators.					

Goal 3 Standard 1: Expert Level

	Very well	Adequately	Not so well	Not at all	N/A
I use computer-based diagnostic, formative, and summative testing where feasible.					
I use technology to illustrate learner progress.					
I can create graphic representations of learner scores over time.					
I have students create e-portfolios that document their change over time.					
I provide feedback through digital file exchange.					
I use word-processing tools to comment and track changes on written work.					
I add voice annotations to audio work.					

GOAL 3 STANDARD 2: Language teachers use technological resources to collect and analyze information in order to enhance language instruction and learning.

	Very well	Adequately	Not so well	Not at all	N/A
I demonstrate familiarity with research-based principles related to technology-enhanced assessment.					
I use technology-enhanced assessment results to plan instruction.					
I interpret computer-based test scores for stakeholders (e.g., I explain what the results of TOEFL and other standardized tests mean).					
I elicit student feedback in order to improve teacher use of technology.					

Goal 3 Standard 2: Expert Level

	Very well	Adequately	Not so well	Not at all	N/A
I apply research findings related to technology-enhanced assessment.					
I collect student output for analysis.					
I use a concordancer or other lexical tools to analyze the lexical complexity of student work and to document change over time.					
I assess students' language output through chat logs and postings in online discussions over time.					
I keep multiple versions of student work to compare.					
I use digital resources to document my teaching for further analysis.					
I create and analyze digital recordings of my lectures and class interactions.					
I keep and analyze digital logs of written interactions with students.					
I regularly ask students for feedback on my teaching via electronic surveys.					

GOAL 3 STANDARD 3: Language teachers evaluate the effectiveness of specific student uses of technology to enhance teaching and learning.

	Very well	Adequately	Not so well	Not at all	N/A
I elicit student feedback in order to improve my students' use of technology.					
I use appropriate procedures for evaluating student use of technology.					
I use rubrics where appropriate to evaluate student use of technology.					
I use checklists and matrices to evaluate student work with technology.					
I survey students about their enjoyment of technology-based activities.					

Goal 3 Standard 3: Expert Level

	Very well	Adequately	Not so well	Not at all	N/A
I develop and share procedures for evaluating student use of technology.					
I examine student outcomes that result from use of technology (e.g., I examine chat logs for more complex language).					

TEACHER GOAL 4: *Language teachers use technology to improve communication, collaboration, and efficiency.*

GOAL 4 STANDARD 1: Language teachers use communication technologies to maintain effective contact and collaboration with peers, students, administration, and other stakeholders.

	Very well	Adequately	Not so well	Not at all	N/A
I can draw on resources (lesson plans and teaching ideas) for language teachers that are posted online.					
I can implement lesson plans obtained from other teachers via the Internet.					
I belong to one or more online communities.					
I belong to a mailing list with other teachers, either in my school or outside it.					
I read teaching-related blogs regularly.					
I listen to teaching-related podcasts.					
I have access to teaching-related file-sharing sites, such as wikis.					
I share my email address with students and peers.					

Goal 4 Standard 1: Expert Level

	Very well	Adequately	Not so well	Not at all	N/A
I maintain an electronic forum to post information for students about the class.					
I have course-related websites or blogs that I update regularly.					
I view and comment on students' electronic work.					
I assign and grade electronic work by students on projects.					
I have students create and update an electronic portfolio.					
I comment on websites that students create for class.					
I advise administration on the use of online technology to improve communication.					
I share instructional material digitally.					
I use the school's file-sharing site, where available, or I use an online file-sharing site.					

GOAL 4 STANDARD 2: Language teachers regularly reflect on the intersection of professional practice and technological developments so that they can make informed decisions regarding the use of technology to support language learning and communication.

	Very well	Adequately	Not so well	Not at all	N/A
I can take advantage of professional development related to technology integration (e.g., conferences, journals, mailing lists, communities of practice).					
I can select technology resources that promote appropriate language use.					
I can demonstrate awareness of multiple sources and perspectives that inform technology use.					
I can discern which research findings are most appropriate for my situation.					

Goal 4 Standard 2: Expert Level

	Very well	Adequately	Not so well	Not at all	N/A
I stay informed about how to use new technologies for instructional and professional purposes.					
I learn about and try new technologies as they become available and determine whether or not they would be appropriate in my teaching.					
I can use blogs for reading/ writing and podcasts for listening/ speaking.					
I integrate technology in innovative ways.					
I engage in research (including classroom-based) and share the results.					
I advise decision-makers about appropriate technology resources and environments.					

GOAL 4 STANDARD 3: Language teachers apply technology to improve efficiency in preparing for class, grading, and maintaining records.

	Very well	Adequately	Not so well	Not at all	N/A
I can use electronic resources to locate additional materials for lesson planning and classroom use.					
I understand various methods of providing electronic feedback on student work (e.g., email, insert comments).					
I have a system to collect, organize, and retrieve material and student data.					

Goal 4 Standard 3: Expert Level

	Very well	Adequately	Not so well	Not at all	N/A
I maintain a resource that allows students to locate and retrieve material.					
I use electronic methods, as appropriate, for formative and summative assessment.					
I encourage students to use electronic methods to document their own progress.					

Program Assessment Rubric

The Program Assessment Rubric consists of elements from the technology standards for language learners and the technology standards for language teachers. The primary audience for this rubric consists of administrators and stakeholders. As a result, it does not use the "can-do" formulation that the learner and teacher self-assessments use but rather refers to learners, teachers, expert teachers, online teachers, and administrators as appropriate.

Technology Standards for Language Learners

LEARNER GOAL 1: *Language learners demonstrate foundational knowledge and skills in technology for a multilingual world.*

	Very much so	Adequately	Not so much	Not at all	N/A
Goal 1 Standard 1: Language learners demonstrate basic operational skills in using various technology tools and Internet browsers.					
Learners have access to a range of technology in their learning to the extent possible in the local context.					
Students are expected to use technology in their learning, in class and as out-of-class assignments as feasible.					
Fully online students receive additional instruction as needed to use the course tools effectively.					
Goal 1 Standard 2: Language learners are able to use available input and output devices (e.g., keyboard, mouse, printer, headset, microphone, media player, electronic whiteboard).					
Basic computer skills are part of the curriculum so that learners can demonstrate basic operations skills with available digital devices, browsers, email, and input and output devices.					
Fully online students receive explicit instruction in order to use digital devices required in the course (e.g., microphone, headset, webcam).					

(Continued on p. 207)

LEARNER GOAL 1 (continued): *Language learners demonstrate foundational knowledge and skills in technology for a multilingual world.*

	Very much so	Adequately	Not so much	Not at all	N/A
Goal 1 Standard 3: Language learners exercise appropriate caution when using online sources and when engaging in electronic communication.					
The curriculum includes information about Internet safety, and learners are exposed to safe practices in their classes where technology is used.					
The curriculum includes methods for determining the validity of online sources and for understanding that not all online sources are trustworthy.					
Fully online learners have repeated exposure to guidelines for online safety.					
Goal 1 Standard 4: Language learners demonstrate basic competence as users of technology.					
Teachers are aware of basic troubleshooting techniques and share this information with students so that they know how to check for common problems when the device or software is not working correctly.					
Learners have access to technical support, preferably professional, for the technologies that they use.					
Fully online learners have access to help in a variety of ways, including ones that are not dependent on Internet access (e.g., via mobile phone).					

LEARNER GOAL 2: *Language learners use technology in socially and culturally appropriate, legal, and ethical ways.*

	Very much so	Adequately	Not so much	Not at all	N/A
Goal 2 Standard 1: Language learners understand that communication conventions differ across cultures, communities, and contexts.					
Students receive instruction in cultural literacy and netiquette (appropriate behavior online) before they engage in cross-cultural online interactions.					
Students recognize that different registers are appropriate in different communication settings (more formal language for academic work, less formal language such as that typical of texting with friends).					
Fully online learners receive explicit instruction about appropriate online communication with teachers, staff, and peers.					
Goal 2 Standard 2: Language learners demonstrate respect for others in their use of private and public information.					
Administrators formulate institutional rules related to privacy and respect for copyright.					
Disciplinary structures are in place and are used when these institutional rules are broken.					
Fully online learners are given the rules at or before the beginning of an online course, with an opportunity to get more information as needed.					

TESOL Technology Standards: Description, Implementation, Integration

LEARNER GOAL 3: *Language learners effectively use and critically evaluate technology-based tools as aids in the development of their language learning competence as part of formal instruction and for further learning.*

	Very much so	Adequately	Not so much	Not at all	N/A
Goal 3 Standard 1: Language learners effectively use and evaluate available technology-based productivity tools (e.g., word processors, presentation software, web design software, and electronic dictionaries).					
In order to ensure that students learn how to use productivity tools effectively and understand when and where to use them, use of such tools is integrated into the curriculum.					
Fully online learners know how to integrate productivity tools in their online work (e.g., by cutting and pasting from a word processor into a discussion forum or attaching files to messages).					
Collaborative work with technology is integrated into the curriculum.					
Goal 3 Standard 2: Language learners appropriately use and evaluate available technology-based language skill-building tools.					
Students learn appropriate use of language skill-building tools and are encouraged to think critically about their use of the tools.					
Students have assistance to figure out what to use and why when working on their own in a computer lab or online.					
Ongoing formative learner feedback is used with fully online students in order to assess their satisfaction with the tools they are using.					
Goal 3 Standard 3: Language learners appropriately use and evaluate available technology-based tools for communication and collaboration.					
Using collaboration and communication tools (e.g., comments in the word processor, discussion forums, blogs, wikis, mobile phones, and other available communication technologies) is part of the curriculum in order to ensure that students can make appropriate use of the tools and understand when and why to use different tools.					

(Continued on p. 210)

LEARNER GOAL 3 (continued): *Language learners effectively use and critically evaluate technology-based tools as aids in the development of their language learning competence as part of formal instruction and for further learning.*

	Very much so	Adequately	Not so much	Not at all	N/A
Goal 3 Standard 4: Language learners use and evaluate available technology-based research tools appropriately.					
Using research tools is part of the curriculum, and students think critically about when and why to use different tools.					
Learners are taught how to find, evaluate, and document information appropriately.					
Goal 3 Standard 5: Language learners recognize the value of technology to support autonomy, lifelong learning, creativity, metacognition, collaboration, personal pursuits, and productivity.					
In order to develop autonomy when learning with technology, students can make some choices about their learning with technology. The curriculum and teaching approach are designed to enable learner autonomy, at least to some degree.					
Learners are encouraged to use technology to express themselves (e.g., with graphics programs, audio recording, and movie making).					
Fully online learners receive guidance with time management skills in order to be effective as autonomous learners.					

TESOL Technology Standards: Description, Implementation, Integration

Technology Standards for Language Teachers

TEACHER GOAL 1: *Language teachers acquire and maintain foundational knowledge and skills in technology for professional purposes.*

	Very much so	Adequately	Not so much	Not at all	N/A
Goal 1 Standard 1: Language teachers demonstrate knowledge and skills in basic technological concepts and operational competence, meeting or exceeding TESOL technology standards for students in whatever situation they teach.					
Administrators ensure that teachers are either hired with the requisite level of technological competence or provided with training to bring them to that level of skill. Just having technical support available for teachers in their classes is not enough.					
Teachers are able to perform basic functions with digital devices; prepare material for students using basic technological tools, such as a word processor and presentation software; and use appropriate caution when using online sources and communicating online.					
Online teachers are able to respond to basic technical questions, including frequently asked questions about hardware and course tools, and recognize which questions need to be forwarded to technical support staff.					
Goal 1 Standard 2: Language teachers demonstrate an understanding of a wide range of technology supports for language learning and options for using them in a given setting.					
Teachers are able to identify appropriate technology, evaluate options, use online technology as available, and locate and adapt digital resources. Training is provided to ensure that teachers stay current in their ability.					
Online teachers are aware of the options in their course management system (or in their alternatives to a course management system) so that they can use the most appropriate options.					

(Continued on p. 212)

TEACHER GOAL 1 (continued): *Language teachers acquire and maintain foundational knowledge and skills in technology for professional purposes.*

	Very much so	Adequately	Not so much	Not at all	N/A
Teachers are able to share information about use of technology with each other. This may mean in-house workshops, a file-sharing system, or an internal email mailing list.					
Goal 1 Standard 3: Language teachers actively strive to expand their skill and knowledge base to evaluate, adopt, and adapt emerging technologies throughout their careers.					
Teachers have opportunities for ongoing professional development and technology training. This should be subsidized to the greatest degree possible.					
Online teaching is a developing field, so there are many emerging technologies to be aware of. Teachers engage in continuous professional development, both informally and in courses or workshops.					
Goal 1 Standard 4: Language teachers use technology in socially and culturally appropriate, legal, and ethical ways.					
Teachers have legal access to the material they need.					
Administrators put guidelines and procedures in place to discourage piracy and protect student privacy.					
Administrators provide opportunities for teacher development related to legal and ethical use of electronic information and media.					
Online teachers are aware of what is and is not fair use in their online environment and behave appropriately.					
Online teachers are vigilant in protecting learner privacy in online courses (e.g., using BCC as appropriate to address email to everyone in the group).					

TEACHER GOAL 2: *Language teachers integrate pedagogical knowledge and skills with technology to enhance language teaching and learning.*

	Very much so	Adequately	Not so much	Not at all	N/A
Goal 2 Standard 1: Language teachers identify and evaluate technological resources and environments for suitability to their teaching context.					
Teachers are part of decision-making about technology purchases and use.					
If students in online courses have poor connectivity, the teacher adapts the material used (e.g., video may not be usable in low-bandwidth areas).					
Goal 2 Standard 2: Language teachers coherently integrate technology into their pedagogical approaches.					
Teachers have the technical support and training that they need to use available technology in their teaching.					
Online teachers regularly engage in professional development to stay abreast of the changes in the field.					
Administrators recognize and compensate expert-level teachers who support or train their peers in technology use.					
Goal 2 Standard 3: Language teachers design and manage language learning activities and tasks using technology appropriately to meet curricular goals and objectives.					
Administrators enable teachers to design and manage how they use available technology in their teaching; the curriculum allows flexibility.					
Teachers train learners in appropriate and critical use of technology for language learning.					
Expert-level teachers adapt activities, create an appropriate technology environment, and can change as needed in response to problems.					
Online teachers determine which electronic media and approaches are most appropriate to meet curricular goals, adapting tasks and material for best use in an online environment.					

(Continued on p. 214)

TEACHER GOAL 2 (continued): *Language teachers integrate pedagogical knowledge and skills with technology to enhance language teaching and learning.*

	Very much so	Adequately	Not so much	Not at all	N/A
Online teachers use strategies to encourage community in a fully online environment (e.g., posting learner photos as appropriate, setting up small groups and learning partners, expecting learners to comment on each other's posts).					

Goal 2 Standard 4: Language teachers use relevant research findings to inform the planning of language learning activities and tasks that involve technology.

	Very much so	Adequately	Not so much	Not at all	N/A
Teachers have access to information and research on teaching with technology.					
Administrators encourage teachers to conduct their own research on technology use, including classroom-based research.					
Expert-level teachers identify gaps in research, help others learn about research, and do their own research on technology use in language teaching and learning. This is especially true for online teachers.					

TEACHER GOAL 3: *Language teachers apply technology in record keeping, feedback, and assessment.*

	Very much so	Adequately	Not so much	Not at all	N/A
Goal 3 Standard 1: Language teachers evaluate and implement relevant technology to aid in effective learner assessment.					
Teachers have technology tools to assist in learner assessment, such as classroom management tools and electronic grade books, where possible.					
Teachers are familiar with different forms of assessment and record-keeping tools.					
Online summative assessment, especially in high-stakes testing, may require the use of local proctors in order to ensure test security.					
Expert-level teachers use computer-based testing when available and technology-enhanced feedback for their learners.					
Goal 3 Standard 2: Language teachers use technological resources to collect and analyze information in order to enhance language instruction and learning.					
Where possible, teachers have technology-based assessment tools and receive adequate training to use them.					
Teachers use technology-enhanced assessment results in their teaching.					
Online courses provide a wealth of data about student behavior online. Teachers can determine how to collect data and make sense of the data that is collected.					
Expert-level teachers use technology to analyze student output and document teaching for further analysis.					
Goal 3 Standard 3: Language teachers evaluate the effectiveness of specific student uses of technology to enhance teaching and learning.					
Technology is used in teaching and learning, and assessment of student use of technology is part of classroom assessment processes.					
Expert-level teachers are encouraged to develop and share procedures for evaluating student use of technology.					

TEACHER GOAL 4: *Language teachers use technology to improve communication, collaboration, and efficiency.*

	Very much so	Adequately	Not so much	Not at all	N/A
Goal 4 Standard 1: Language teachers use communication technologies to maintain effective contact and collaboration with peers, students, administration, and other stakeholders.					
Teachers and students have ways to interact with each other electronically. This may mean establishing an in-house email system or providing a way of disseminating email addresses among teachers and students.					
Teachers interact with students electronically and share material with each other electronically.					
Teachers have a secure space to share digital material and training in doing so.					
Expert-level teachers set up methods to communicate with students, have their students create and submit work electronically, advise administrators about digital communication methods, and digitally share material.					
Goal 4 Standard 2: Language teachers regularly reflect on the intersection of professional practice and technological developments so that they can make informed decisions regarding the use of technology to support language learning and communication.					
Teachers reflect on their use of technology in teaching and change what they do as needed. This is especially true for online teaching.					
Teachers using course management systems are familiar with features added as part of updates and prepared to change what they do as needed in response to new possibilities.					
Expert-level teachers use technology in innovative ways, do research on how they are using technology, and share the results with others.					
Administrators encourage teachers to present their research at professional conferences.					

(Continued on p. 217)

TESOL Technology Standards: Description, Implementation, Integration

TEACHER GOAL 4 (continued): *Language teachers use technology to improve communication, collaboration, and efficiency.*

	Very much so	Adequately	Not so much	Not at all	N/A
Goal 4 Standard 3: Language teachers apply technology to improve efficiency in preparing for class, grading, and maintaining records.					
Administrators provide technology tools for teachers to use in preparing for class, grading, and record keeping. These will generally include access to the Internet and to productivity software, such as a word processor and grade book.					
Teachers use technology tools in preparing for class, grading, and record keeping.					
Expert-level teachers provide a digital space for students to locate and retrieve material.					
Expert-level teachers use electronic methods for assessing student learning and teach students to use electronic methods to document their own progress.					
Administrators provide secure digital space for teachers and students to store student work. Secure space is particularly necessary with online courses.					

PART 4
Supporting Matter

Part 4 consists of a variety of supporting information for the book. It includes the full references for all the citations in the book and for the websites mentioned; a glossary of terms used; and three appendices, which provide a short version of the technology standards themselves, proficiency level descriptors for English language learners, and tables of the language and technology skills described in the vignettes for each standard. An About the Authors and Contributors section and an Index complete Part 4.

References

By Author

Abrams, Z. (2006). From theory to practice: Intracultural CMC in the L2 classroom. In L. Ducate & N. Arnold (Eds.), *Calling on CALL: From theory and research to new directions in foreign language teaching* (pp. 181–209). San Marcos, TX: CALICO.

Academy of American Poets. (2010). *Poets.org.* Retrieved from http://www.poets.org

Adobe. (2010). *Photoshop Express.* Retrieved from http://www.photoshop.com

ALTEC, University of Kansas (2008). *Rubistar.* Retrieved from http://rubistar4teachers.org.

ALTEC, University of Kansas. (2009). *PBL checklists.* Retrieved from http://pblchecklist .4teachers.org/checklist.shtml

Apple Computer. (2006). *Using iPod as a tour guide.* Retrieved from http://developer.apple .com/hardwaredrivers/ipod/iPodNoteReaderGuide.pdf

Apple Computer. (2009). *iMovie.* Retrieved from http://www.apple.com/ilife/imovie

Arnold, N., Ducate, L., & Lomicka, L. (2007). Virtual communities of practice in teacher education. In M. Kassen, R. Lavine, K. Murphy-Judy, & M. Peters (Eds.), *Preparing and developing technology-proficient L2 teachers* (pp. 103–132). San Marcos, TX: CALICO.

A to Z Teacher Stuff. (2010). *A to z teacher stuff.* Retrieved from http://www.atozteacherstuff .com

Audacity Development Team. (2010). *Audacity.* Retrieved from http://audacity.sourceforge.net

AuthorGEN. (2010). *WiZiQ.* Retrieved from http://www.wiziq.com

Banville, S. (2010). *BreakingNewsEnglish.* Retrieved from http://www.breakingnewsenglish.com

Barrett, T. (2007). *28 interesting ways to use audio in your classroom.* Retrieved from https://docs .google.com/present/edit?id=0AclS3lrlFkCIZGhuMnZjdjVfNDQwaHAzbXFxZnI&hl=en

Barrette, C. (2001). Students preparedness and training for CALL. *CALICO Journal, 19*(1), 5–36.

Bauer-Ramazani, C. (2006). Training CALL teachers online. In P. Hubbard & M. Levy (Eds.), *Teacher education in CALL* (pp. 183–200). Amsterdam: John Benjamins.

Bauman, J. (n.d.) *About the General Service List.* Retrieved from http://jbauman.com/aboutgsl .html

Bax, S. (2003). CALL—Past, present, and future. *System, 31*(1), 13–28.

Beasley, R. E., & Chuang, Y. (2008). Web-based music study: The effects of listening repetition, song likeability, and song understandability on EFL learning perceptions and outcomes. *TESL-EJ, 12*(2), n.p. Retrieved from http://www.tesl-ej.org/wordpress/issues/volume12/ej46/ej46a3

Beatty, K. (2003). *Teaching and researching computer-assisted language learning.* London: Longman.

Belz, J. A. (2003). Linguistic perspectives on the development of intercultural competence in telecollaboration. *Language Learning and Technology, 7*(2), 68–99.

Blackboard. (2010). *Blackboard.* Retrieved from http://blackboard.com

Blake, R. (2008). *Brave new digital classroom: Technology and foreign language learning.* Washington, DC: Georgetown University Press.

Bloch, J. (2008). *Technologies in the second language composition classroom.* Ann Arbor: The University of Michigan Press.

Board of Education, San Diego County. (2007). *Academic vocabulary journal.* Retrieved from http://kms.sdcoe.net/getvocal/89.html

Borras, I., & Lafayette, R. C. (1994). Effect of multimedia courseware subtitling on the speaking performance of college students of French. *The Modern Language Journal, 78,* 61–75.

Boss, S., & Krauss, J. (2007). *Reinventing project-based learning: Your field guide to real-world projects in the digital age.* Eugene, OR: ISTE.

Boston Public Library. (n.d.). *Netiquette for kids.* Retrieved from http://www.bpl.org/kids/netiquette.htm

Boyer, T. (2010). *HowJSay.* Retrieved from http://www.howjsay.com

BrammertsRuhr-Universität Bochum. (2005). *Tandem Server Bochum.* Retrieved from http://www.slf.ruhr-uni-bochum.de/index.html

Brandl, K. (2002). Integrating Internet-based reading materials into the foreign language curriculum: From teacher to student-centered approaches. *Language Learning & Technology, 6*(3).

Burell, C. (2008). *Wordle with teeth: U of Quebec's Vocab Profiler.* Retrieved from http://beyond-school.org/2008/07/15/vocabulary-profiler

Burkhart, L. (1999). *Strategies and applications for the one-computer classroom.* Retrieved from http://www.lburkhart.com/elem/strat.htm

Burston, J. (2003). Software selection: A primer on sources and evaluation. *CALICO Journal, 21*(1). Retrieved from https://www.calico.org/a-280-Software%20Selection%20A%20Primer%20on%20Sources%20and%20Evaluation.html

Butler-Pascoe, M.E., & Wiburg, K. (2003). *Technology and teaching English language learners.* Boston: Allyn & Bacon.

California State University. (2010). *MERLOT (Multimedia Educational Resource for Learning and Online Teaching).* Retrieved from http://www.merlot.org/merlot/index.htm

California State University, Chico. (2009). *Rubric for online instruction.* Retrieved from http://www.csuchico.edu/tlp/resources/rubric/rubric.pdf

Celce-Murcia, M., Brinton, D., & Goodwin, J. (1996). *Teaching pronunciation: Reference for teachers of English to speakers of other languages.* Cambridge: Cambridge University Press.

Center for Universal Design. (2010). *The principles of universal design.* Retrieved from http://www.ncsu.edu/www/ncsu/design/sod5/cud/about_ud/udprinciplestext.htm

Chambers, A. (2005). Integrating corpus consultation in language studies. *Language Learning & Technology, 9*(2), 111–125.

Chao, C. C. (2006). How WebQuests send technology to the background: Scaffolding EFL teacher professional development in CALL. In P. Hubbard & M. Levy (Eds.), *Teacher education in CALL* (pp. 221–234). Amsterdam: John Benjamins.

Chapelle, C. A. (2003). *English language learning and technology: Lectures on teaching and research in the age of information and communication.* Amsterdam: John Benjamins.

Chapelle, C. A., & Hegelheimer, V. (2004). The English language teacher in the 21st century. In S. Fotos & C. Browne (Eds.), *New perspectives in CALL for second language classrooms* (pp. 299–316). Mahwah, NJ: Erlbaum.

Chapelle, C. A., & Jamieson, J. (2008). *Tips for teaching with CALL: Practical approaches to computer assisted language learning.* White Plains, NY: Pearson Longman.

Chinnery, G. (2006). Going to the MALL: Mobile Assisted Language Learning. *Language Learning & Technology, 10*(1), 9–16.

Chun, D. M. (2006). CALL technologies for L2 reading. In L. Ducate & N. Arnold (Eds.), *Calling on CALL: From theory and research to new directions in foreign language teaching.* CALICO Monograph series, Vol. 5 (pp. 69–98). San Marcos, TX: CALICO.

Cini, M. A., & Vilic, B. (2004). *Faculty guidelines for online teaching.* Retrieved from http://www.scribd.com/doc/8696942/Faculty-Guidelines-Rider

Clerkin, P. (2010). *Archiseek: Online architecture resources.* Retrieved from http://www.archiseek.com

Cobb, T. (2007). Computing the vocabulary demands of L2 reading. *Language Learning & Technology, 11*, 38–63.

Cobb. T. (2010a). *Compleat lexical tutor.* Retrieved from http://www.lextutor.ca

Cobb, T. (2010b). *VocabProfiler.* Retrieved from http://www.lextutor.ca/vp

Colwell, J. L., & Jenks, C. F. (2004). *The upper limit: The issues for faculty in setting class size in online courses.* Retrieved from http://www.ipfw.edu/tohe/Papers/Nov%2010/015__the%20upper%20limit.pdf

Compton, L. K. L. (2009). Preparing language teachers to teach language online: A look at skills, roles, and responsibilities. *Computer Assisted Language Learning, 22*, 73–99.

Council of Europe. (2009). *Through the wild web woods.* Retrieved from http://www.wildwebwoods.org

Council of Europe. (2010). *European language portfolio.* Retrieved from http://www.coe.int/T/DG4/Portfolio/?L=E&M=/main_pages/levels.html

Coxhead, A. (2007). *Academic word list.* Retrieved from http://www.victoria.ac.nz/lals/resources/academicwordlist/default.aspx

Cuban, L. (2001). *Oversold and underused: Computers in classrooms.* Cambridge, MA: Harvard University Press.

Dahlman, A., & Tatinen, S. (2006). Virtual basegroup: E-mentoring in a reflective electronic support network. In E. Hanson-Smith & S. Rilling (Eds.), *Learning languages through technology*, pp. 221–232. Alexandria, VA: TESOL.

Dallas ISD. (n.d.). *Ways to use interactive whiteboards in the classroom*. Retrieved from http://www.dallasisd.org/inside_disd/depts/radicalthinking/wb_class.pdf

Davies, G., Walker, R., Rendall, H., & Hewer, S. (2010) Introduction to Computer Assisted Language Learning (CALL): Whole-class teaching and interactive whiteboards. In G. Davies (Ed.), *Information and communications technology for language teachers (ICT4LT)*. Retrieved from http://www.ict4lt.org/en/en_mod1-4.htm#iwbs

Davis, C., Ferenz, K., & Gray, L. (2010). *Web search lesson plan: Believe it or not*. Retrieved from https://docs.google.com/View?id=dfvwdtqp_1c8x6bmd8

Davis, R. (2010). *Randall's ESL cyber listening lab*. Retrieved from http://www.esl-lab.com

Davison, C. (Ed). (2005). *Innovation and information technology in language education*. Hong Kong: Hong Kong University Press.

Debski, R. (2006). Theory and practice in teaching project-oriented CALL. In P. Hubbard & M. Levy (Eds.), *Teacher education in CALL* (pp. 99–116). Amsterdam: John Benjamins.

De Szendeffy, J. (2005). *A practical guide to using computers in language teaching*. Ann Arbor, MI: University of Michigan Press.

Dimdim. (2010). *Dimdim*. Retrieved from http://www.dimdim.com

Discovery Education. (2008). *Puzzlemaker*. Retrieved from http://puzzlemaker.discovery education.com

DLTK's Sites. (2010). *Educational activities for children*. Retrieved from http://www.dltk-teach .com

Dodge, B. (2007). *WebQuest.Org*. Retrieved from http://webquest.org/index.php

Ducate, L., & Arnold, N. (Eds). (2006). *Calling on CALL: From theory and research to new directions in foreign language teaching*. San Marcos, TX: CALICO.

easyDNS Technologies. (2010). *easyWhois*. Retrieved from http://www.easywhois.com

Educational Testing Service. (2010). TOEFL (Test of English as a Foreign Language). Princeton, NJ: Educational Testing Service. Information at http://www.ets.org/toefl

Educause. (2010). *7 things you should know about LMS alternatives*. Retrieved from http://www .educause.edu/Resources/7ThingsYouShouldKnowAboutLMSAl/207429

EduTools. (2010). *EduTools course management system comparisons—Reborn*. Retrieved from http://www.edutools.info/static.jsp?pj=4&page=HOME

Egbert, J. (2005). *CALL essentials*. Arlington, VA: TESOL.

Egbert, J. (2006). Learning in context: Situating language teacher learning in CALL. In P. Hubbard & M. Levy (Eds.), *Teacher education in CALL* (pp. 167–182). Amsterdam: John Benjamins.

Egbert, J., & Hanson-Smith, E. (Eds.) (2007). *CALL environments: Research, practice and critical issues* (2nd ed.). Alexandria, VA: TESOL.

Egbert, J., Hanson-Smith, E., & Chao, C. C. (2007). Introduction: Foundations for teaching and learning. In J. Egbert & E. Hanson-Smith (Eds.), *CALL environments: Research, practice, and critical issues* (2nd ed., pp. 1–18). Alexandria, VA: TESOL.

Egbert, J., & Petrie, G. M. (Eds.) (2005). *CALL research perspectives*. Mahwah, NJ: Lawrence Erlbaum.

Elia, A. (2006). Language learning in tandem via Skype. *The Reading Matrix, 6*(3), pp. 269–280. Retrieved from http://www.readingmatrix.com/articles/elia/article.pdf

Ellis, R. (1999). *Learning a second language through interaction*. Amsterdam: John Benjamins.

Elluminate. (2010). *LearnCentral*. Retrieved from http://www.learncentral.org

Elluminate.com. (2010). *Elluminate*. Retrieved from http://www.elluminate.com

EnchantedLearning.com. (2010). *Enchanted learning*. Retrieved from http://www.enchanted learning.com/Home.html

EnglishClub.com. (2010). *EnglishClub*. Retrieved from http://www.englishclub.com/esl-exams /ets-toefl-practice-speaking.htm

ESLflashcards.com. (2010). *ESL flashcards*. Retrieved from http://www.eslflashcards.com

European Commission. (2001). *The eLearning action plan: Designing tomorrow's education*. Brussels: Author.

Facebook. (2010). *Facebook*. Retrieved from http://www.facebook.com

Feldman, K., & Kinsella, K. (2005). *Narrowing the language gap: The case for explicit vocabulary instruction*. Retrieved from http://teacher.scholastic.com/products/authors/pdfs /Narrowing_the_Gap.pdf

FERPA resources. (n.d.). *National forum on education statistics*. Retrieved from http://nces .ed.gov/forum/ferpa_links.asp

Fiori, M. (2005). The development of grammatical competence through synchronous computer-mediated communication. *CALICO Journal, 22*(3), 567-602.

Fischer, R. (2007). How do we know what students are actually doing? Monitoring students' behavior in CALL. *Computer Assisted Language Learning, 20(5)*, 409–422.

Fish, W.W., & Wickersham, L.E. (2009). Best practices for online instructors: Reminders. *The Quarterly Review of Distance Education, 10* (3), pp. 279–284.

Fotos, S., & Browne, C. (Eds). (2004). *New perspectives on CALL for second language classrooms*. Mahwah, NJ: Lawrence Erlbaum.

Freemind Development Team. (2010). *Freemind*. [Computer software] Available at http:// freemind.sourceforge.net

Gaer, S. (2007). E-mail and web projects. In E. Hanson-Smith & J. Egbert (Eds.), *CALL environments: Research, practice, and critical issues* (2nd ed., pp. 71–88). Alexandria, VA: TESOL.

Gaer, S. (n.d.). *ESL activities for the one computer classroom*. Retrieved from http://www .susangaer.com/sgaer/onecomputer

Garrison, D. R., Anderson, T., & Archer, W. (2000). Critical inquiry in a text-based environment: Computer conferencing in higher education. *The Internet and Higher Education, 2*(2–3), 87–105. Retrieved from http://communitiesofinquiry.com/files /Critical_Inquiry_model.pdf

Gimp Team. (2010). *Gimp*. [Computer software] Available at http://www.gimp.org

González, D. (2008). Using synchronous communication collaboratively in ESP. In E. Hanson-Smith & S. Rilling (Eds.), *Learning languages through technology* (pp. 11–24). Alexandria, VA: TESOL.

Goodrich, H. (1996/1997). Understanding rubrics. *Educational Leadership, 54*(4), 14–17. Retrieved from http://www.ascd.org/publications/educational-leadership/dec96/vol54 /num04/Understanding-Rubrics.aspx. [Report with additional resources at http://www .middleweb.com/rubricsHG.html]

Google. (2010a). *Google docs.* Retrieved from http://docs.google.com

Google. (2010b). *Google earth.* Retrieved from http://earth.google.com

Google. (2010c). *Google for educators: Geo education home.* Retrieved from http://www.google .com/educators/geo.html

Google. (2010d). *Google for educators: Google web search: Classroom lessons and resources.* Retrieved from http://www.google.com/educators/p_websearch.html

Google. (2010e). *Google phone.* Retrieved from http://gmail.com/ >Call phone

Google. (2010f). *Google scholar.* Retrieved from http://scholar.google.com

Google. (2010g). *Google sites.* Retrieved from http://sites.google.com

Google. (2010h). *Picasa.* Retrieved from http://picasaweb.google.com

Greaves, C. (2011) *XWord interactive crossword puzzles.* Retrieved from http://vlc.polyu.edu.hk /XWord/xword.htm

Greenberg, I. (2010). *Shipyards VESL.* Retrieved from http://www.quia.com/pages/igreenberg /page1

Grgurović, M., & Chapelle, C. (2007). Effectiveness of CALL: A meta-analysis and research synthesis. Paper presented at CALICO 2007, San Marcos, Texas.

Grgurović, M., & Hegelheimer, V. (2007). Help options and multimedia listening: Students' use of subtitles and the transcript. *Language Learning & Technology, 11*(1), 45–66.

Gromik, N. (2006). Meaningful tasks with video in the ESOL classroom. In E. Hanson-Smith & S. Rilling (Eds.), *Learning languages through technology.* Alexandria, VA: TESOL.

Gu, P. G. (2003). Vocabulary learning in a second language: Person, task, context and strategies. *TESL-EJ, 7* (2). Retrieved from http://www.tesl-ej.org/wordpress/issues/ volume7/ej26/ej26a4

Half-Baked Software. (2010). *Hot Potatoes* (Ver. 6). [Computer software]. Available from http://hotpot.uvic.ca

Haft, S. (Producer), & Weir, P. (Director). (1989). *Dead Poets Society* [Motion picture]. United States: Touchstone Pictures.

Hanson-Smith, E. (2006). Communities of practice for pre- and in-service teacher education. In P. Hubbard & M. Levy (Eds.), *Teacher education in CALL* (pp. 301–315). Amsterdam: John Benjamins.

Hanson-Smith, E. (2007). Tasks for collaborative learning. In E. Hanson-Smith & J. Egbert (Eds.), *CALL environments: Research, practice, and critical issues* (2nd ed., pp. 194–209). Alexandria, VA: TESOL.

Hanson-Smith, E. (2009). Tools for teaching language and literature online. In I. Lancashire (Ed.), *Teaching literature and language online*, pp. 53–68. New York: The Modern Language Association of America.

Hanson-Smith, E., & Rilling, S. (Eds.) (2007). *Learning languages through technology*. Alexandria, VA: TESOL.

Harrington, T., Staffo, M., & Wright, V. H. (2006). Faculty uses of and attitudes toward a course management system in improving instruction. *Journal of Interactive Online Learning, 5*(2), 178–190.

Healey, D. (2007). Theory and research: Autonomy and language learning. In J. Egbert & E. Hanson-Smith (Eds.), *CALL environments: Research, practice, and critical issues* (2nd ed., pp. 277–289). Alexandria, VA: TESOL.

Healey, D. (2009). *Creating a computer lab/learning center*. Retrieved from http://www.eltexpert .com/complab/index.html

Heatley, A., & Nation, P. (1994). *Range*. [Computer software]. Available from http://www .victoria.ac.nz/lals/resources/range.aspx

Hedge, T. (2005). *Writing*. Oxford: Oxford University Press.

Hegelheimer, V. (2006). When the technology course is required. In P. Hubbard & M. Levy (Eds.), *Teacher education in CALL* (pp. 117–133). Amsterdam: John Benjamins.

Helft, M., & Wines, M. (2010). Google faces fallout as China reacts to site shift. *New York Times*, March 23. Retrieved from http://www.nytimes.com/2010/03/24/technology/24google .html

Herring, D. (2008). *Google Earth education community*. Retrieved from http://edweb.tusd.k12. az.us/dherring/ge/googleearth.htm

Higher Education Funding Council for England. (HEFCE). (2010). *Effective assessment in a digital age: A guide to technology-enhanced assessment and feedback*. Retrieved from http:// www.jisc.ac.uk/media/documents/programmes/elearning/digiassass_eada.pdf

Hincks, R., & Edlund, J. (2009). Promoting increased pitch variation in oral presentations with transient visual feedback. *Language Learning and Technology, 13*(3), 32–50.

Hinkel, E., & Fotos, S. (2002). *New perspectives on grammar teaching in second language classrooms*. Mahwah, NJ: Erlbaum.

Hopelink Education. (2009). *Tips for using technology*. Retrieved from http://www.eastside literacy.org/tutorsupport/Tech/TechTips.htm

Huang, H. T., & Liou, H. C. (2007). Vocabulary learning in an automated graded reading program. *Language Learning & Technology, 11*, 64–82.

Hubbard, P. (2004). Learner training for effective use of CALL. In S. Fotos & C. Browne (Eds.), *New perspectives on CALL for second language classrooms* (pp. 45–68). Mahwah, NJ: Lawrence Erlbaum.

Hubbard, P. (2005). *Survey of unanswered questions site*. Retrieved from http://www.stanford .edu/~efs/callsurvey

Hubbard, P. (2008). CALL and the future of language teacher education. *CALICO Journal, 25*(2), 175–188.

Hubbard, P. (2009a). General introduction. In P. Hubbard (Ed.), *Computer assisted language learning: Critical concepts in linguistics: Vol. 1. Foundations of CALL* (pp. 1–20). New York: Routledge. Retrieved from http://www.stanford.edu/~efs/callcc

Hubbard, P. (2009b). Educating the CALL specialist. *Innovation in Language Learning and Teaching, 3*(1), 3–15.

Hubbard, P., & Levy, M. (2006a). The scope of CALL education. In P. Hubbard & M. Levy (Eds.), *Teacher education in CALL* (pp. 3–21). Amsterdam: John Benjamins.

Hubbard, P., & Levy, M. (2006b). *Teacher education in CALL.* Amsterdam: John Benjamins.

IATEFL Learning Technologies Special Interest Group. (2010). Retrieved from http://groups.yahoo .com/group/LearningTechnologiesSIG

ICT4LT Project. (2009). *ICT4LT CALL software and website evaluation forms.* Retrieved from http://www.ict4lt.org/en/evalform.doc

iEARN (International Education and Resource Network). (2011). *Collaboration Centre.* Retrieved from http://www.iearn.org

Illinois Online Network. (2010). *Instructional strategies for online courses.* Retrieved from http:// www.ion.illinois.edu/resources/tutorials/pedagogy/instructionalstrategies.asp

IMDb.com. (2010). *The Internet movie database.* Retrieved from http://www.imdb.com

Innovation in Language Learning and Teaching, 3(1). (2009). New York: Routledge.

Inspiration Software. (2008). Kidspiration, Ver. 3. Information retrieved from http://www .inspiration.com/Kidspiration

Internet Archive. (2010). *WayBackMachine.* Retrieved from http://www.archive.org

Intute Consortium. (2010). *Intute.* Retrieved from http://www.intute.ac.uk

Ioannou-Georgiou, S., & Michaelides, P. (2001). MOOtivating English language learners in pastures new. Gateway to the Future. St. Louis, Missouri. (35th TESOL Conference)

ISTE. (1998). *National educational technology standards for students.* Eugene, OR: Author.

ISTE. (2000). *National educational technology standards for teachers.* Eugene, OR: Author.

ISTE. (2007). *National educational technology standards for students* (2nd ed.). Eugene, OR: Author.

ISTE. (2008). *National educational technology standards for teachers* (2nd ed.). Eugene, OR: Author.

ISTE. (2009). *National educational technology standards for administrators.* Eugene, OR: Author.

Jaschik, S. (2009, May 27). Special sauce for ESL. *Inside Higher Ed: News.* Retrieved from http:// www.insidehighered.com/news/2009/05/27/esl

Jewell, M. (2006). Real world contexts, skills, and service learning. In E. Hanson-Smith & S. Rilling (Eds.), *Learning languages through technology* (pp. 175–214). Alexandria, VA: TESOL.

Jobbings, D. (2005). *Exploiting the educational potential of podcasting.* Retrieved from http:// recap.ltd.uk/articles/podguide.html

Karayan, S. S., & Crowe, J. A. (1997). Student perceptions of electronic discussion groups, *T.H.E. Journal, 29*(9), 69–71. Retrieved from http://thejournal.com/Articles/1997/04/01/ Student-Perceptions-of-Electronic-Discussion-Groups.aspx

Kassen, M., Lavine, R., Murphy-Judy, K., & Peters, M. (Eds.) (2007). *Preparing and developing technology-proficient L2 teachers.* San Marcos, TX: CALICO.

Kelly, C. & Kelly, L. (1997-2010). *Interesting things for ESL students.* Retrieved from http://www .manythings.org/.

Kennedy, T. J. (2006). Making content connections online via the GLOBE program. In E. Hanson-Smith & S. Rilling (Eds.), *Language learning through technology* (pp. 83–107). Alexandria, VA: TESOL.

Kern, R. (2006). Perspectives on technology in learning and teaching languages. *TESOL Quarterly, 40*(1), 183–210.

Kessler, G. (2006). Assessing CALL teacher training: What are we doing and what could we do better? In P. Hubbard & M. Levy (Eds.), *Teacher education in CALL* (pp. 23–42). Amsterdam: John Benjamins.

Kessler, G. (2007). Formal and informal CALL preparation and teacher attitude toward technology. *Computer Assisted Language Learning, 21*(3), 173–188.

Kessler, G. (2009). Student initiated attention to form in wiki based collaborative writing. *Language Learning & Technology, 13*(1), 79–95.

Kessler, G. (in press). Language teacher training in technology. In Chapelle, C. (Ed.), *Encyclopaedia of applied linguistics.* Oxford: Wiley-Blackwell.

Kessler, G., & Plakans, L. (2008). Does teachers' confidence with CALL equal innovative and integrated use? *Computer Assisted Language Learning, 20*(2), 269–282.

Kolaitis, M., Mahoney, M., Pomann, H., & Hubbard, P. (2006). Training ourselves to train our students for CALL. In P. Hubbard & M. Levy (Eds.), *Teacher education in CALL.* Amsterdam: John Benjamins.

Krashen, S. (1981). *Second language acquisition and second language learning.* Retrieved from http://www.sdkrashen.com/SL_Acquisition_and_Learning/index.html

Lamy, N.-L., & Klarskov Mortensen, H. J. (2010). *Using concordance programs in the modern foreign languages classroom. ICT4LT Module 2.4.* Retrieved from http://www.ict4lt.org/en/en_mod2-4.htm#_Toc481294153

Language Learning & Technology, 6(2). (2002). Retrieved from http://llt.msu.edu

Lave, J., & Wenger, E. (1991). *Situated learning: Legitimate peripheral participation.* New York: CUP.

Ledlow, S. (2001). *Using Think-Pair-Share in the college classroom.* Retrieved from http://clte.asu.edu/active/usingtps.pdf

Lee, C. (2002). Literacy practices in computer-mediated communication in Hong Kong. *The Reading Matrix, 2*(2). Retrieved from http://www.mediensprache.net/archiv/pubs/2925.pdf

Levy, M., & Stockwell, G. (2006). *CALL dimensions: Options and issues in computer assisted language learning.* Mahwah, NJ: Lawrence Erlbaum.

Lewis, Tim. (2003). Integrating autonomous learning into the curriculum: The tandem learning module at the University of Sheffield. In T. Lewis & L. Walker (Eds.), *Autonomous language learning in tandem* (pp. 169–176). Sheffield: Academy Electronic Publications.

Liang, M. Y. (2010). Using synchronous online peer response groups in EFL writing: Revision-related discourse. *Language Learning and Technology, 14*(1), 45–65.

Lightbown, P., & Spada, N. (2006). *How languages are learned* (3rd ed.) Oxford: Oxford University Press.

Linden Research. (2010). *Second Life.* Retrieved from http://www.secondlife.com

Macrorie, K. (1988). *The I-Search Paper.* New York: Heinemann.

Martin, B., Jr., & Carle, E. (Illus.) (1967, 1970). *Brown bear, brown bear.* New York: Henry Holt.

Marzio School. (2010). *Real English.* Retrieved from http://www.real-english.com

Merriam-Webster. (2010). *Visual dictionary online.* Retrieved from http://visual.merriam-webster.com

Meunier, L. (1997). Personality and motivational factors in computer-mediated foreign language communication (CMFLC). Unpublished manuscript, University of Tulsa.

Microsoft. (2004). *Windows Movie Maker 2.1.* Retrieved from http://www.microsoft.com/windowsxp/downloads/updates/moviemaker2.mspx

Microsoft. (2007). *Microsoft 2007 Office Tutorials.* Retrieved from http://www.officetutorials.com/ (to download)

Microsoft. (2010a). *Microsoft PowerPoint.* [Computer software]. Redmond, WA: Microsoft.

Microsoft. (2010b). *Microsoft Word 2010.* [Computer software]. Redmond, WA: Microsoft.

Migration Policy Institute. (2010). *E pluribus unum prizes: McDonald's Corporation English under the arches—Oakbrook, IL.* Retrieved from http://www.migrationinformation.org/integrationawards/honorablemention2010.cfm

Mnemograph. (2010). *TimeGlider.* Retrieved from http://timeglider.com

Moodle.org. (2010). *Moodle.* [Computer software.] Available at http://moodle.org

Multnomah County Library. (2010). *Social issues.* Retrieved from http://www.multcolib.org/homework/sochc.html

Murphy-Judy, K., & Youngs, B. L. (2006). Technology standards for teacher education, credentialing, and certification. In P. Hubbard & M. Levy (Eds.), *Teacher education in CALL* (pp. 45–60). Amsterdam: John Benjamins.

Najarian, J. (n.d.). *Internet Safety: Using our seat belt online.* Retrieved from http://questgarden.com/81/47/9/090502174626

National Council of Teachers of English. (2010). *Stapleless book.* Retrieved from http://www.readwritethink.org/classroom-resources/student-interactives/stapleless-book-30010.html

National Forum on Education Statistics. (2006). *Forum guide to the privacy of student information: A resource for schools (NFES 2006–805).* Retrieved from http://nces.ed.gov/pubs2006/2006805.pdf

Nico's workday. (2007). Retrieved from http://www.youtube.com/watch?v=99IYG_xsAYA

Nuance Communications. (2010). *Dragon Naturally Speaking.* [Computer software]. Burlington, MA: Nuance Communications.

Oddcast. (2010). *Voki.* Retrieved from http://www.voki.com

O'Dowd, R. (2006). *Telecollaboration and the development of intercultural communicative competence.* Munich, Germany: Langenscheidt-Longman.

O'Dowd, R., & Ware, P. (2009). Critical issues in telecollaborative task design. *Computer Assisted Language Learning, 22*(2), 173–188.

Office of Science Education, U.S. National Institute of Health. (2004–2010.) *LifeWorks.* Retrieved from http://science.education.nih.gov/LifeWorks.nsf/Interviews

Ohlrogge, A. & Lee, H. (2008) *Research on CALL and distance learning: A briefly annotated bibliography.* Retrieved from http://www.calico.org/DistanceEdBiblio.pdf

Online Tutoring World. (2006). *TEFL guide to teaching with Skype.* Retrieved from http://www
.onlinetutoringworld.com/technology/teflskype.htm

Openoffice.org. (2010). *OpenOffice.* [Computer software]. Available from http://www.open
office.org

Organisation for Economic Co-operation and Development. (2000). *Knowledge management in
the learning society.* Paris: Author.

OTAN. (2003). *English for all.* Retrieved from http://www.myefa.org

OTAN. (2010a). *U.S.A. learns.* Retrieved from http://www.usalearns.org

OTAN. (2010b). *U.S.A. learns webcast.* Retrieved from http://www.usalearns.org/teacher
/webcast.html (requires free teacher registration).

Oxford, R., with Jung, S. (2007). National guidelines for technology integration in TESOL
programs: Factors affecting (non)implementation. In M. Kassen, R. Lavine, K. Murphy-
Judy, & M. Peters (Eds.), *Preparing and developing technology-proficient L2 teachers* (pp.
51–66). San Marcos, TX: CALICO.

Palabea. (2009). *Palabea.* Retrieved from http://www.palabea.net

Papert, S. (1980). *Mindstorms.* New York: Basic Books.

Payne, J. S., & Whitney, P. J. (2002). Developing L2 oral proficiency through synchronous
CMC: Output, working memory, and interlanguage development. *CALICO Journal,
20(1),* 7–32.

PBworks. (2010). *PBworks.* Retrieved from http://www.pbworks.com

Pennington, M. (1996). *The power of CALL.* Houston, TX: Athelstan.

PodOmatic. (2010). *PodOmatic.* Retrieved from http://www.podomatic.com

Prensky, M. (2001). Digital natives, digital immigrants. *On the Horizon, 9*(5), 1–2. Retrieved
from http://www.marcprensky.com/writing/Prensky%20-%20Digital%20Natives,%20
Digital%20Immigrants%20-%20Part1.pdf

Public Agenda. (2010). *Public agenda for citizens.* Retrieved from http://www.publicagenda
.com/citizen

QuestGarden. (2010). *QuestGarden.* Retrieved from http://questgarden.com

Quia. (2010). *Quia.* Retrieved from http://www.quia.com/web

ReadPlease Corp. (1999–2005). *ReadPlease.* Retrieved from http://www.readplease.com

Reed, A. (2010). *Simple concordance program.* [Computer software]. Available from http://www
.textworld.com/scp

Reinders, H. (2006). Portable language learning: Creating materials for the iPod. *English
Teaching Professional, 46.* Retrieved from http://www.hayo.nl/article%20-%202006%
20-%20English%20Teaching%20Professional%20-%20portable%20language%20
learning.doc

Reinders, H. (2007). Podquests: Language learning on the move. *ESL Magazine, 58.* Retrieved
from http://www.innovationinteaching.org/docs/article%20-%202007%20-%20ESL%20
Magazine%20-%20podquests.pdf

Renshaw Internet School of English. (2009). *TOEFL iBT speaking practice tests.* Retrieved from
http://www.english-itutor.com/TOEFL_iBT_speaking_tests.html

Rickard, A., Blin, F., & Appel, C. (2006). Training for trainers: Challenges, outcomes, and principles of in-service training across the Irish education system. In P. Hubbard & M. Levy (Eds.), *Teacher education in CALL* (pp. 203–218). Amsterdam: John Benjamins.

Robb, T. (2006). Helping teachers to help themselves. In P. Hubbard & M. Levy (Eds.), *Teacher education in CALL* (pp. 335–347). Amsterdam: John Benjamins.

Safronoff, R. (2007). *Learn basic computer skills: How to burn a CD in Microsoft Windows.* Retrieved from http://www.youtube.com/watch?v=EXn3ha6X3Vg

Sakai Foundation. (2010). *Sakai.* Retrieved from http://sakaiproject.org

San Juan College. (2008). *Research on best practices: Course structure and content.* Retrieved from http://www.sanjuancollege.edu/pages/2850.asp

Sauro, S. (2009). Computer-mediated corrective feedback and the development of L2 grammar. *Language Learning and Technology, 13*(1), 96–120.

Schrock, K. (2007). *Software evaluation form.* Retrieved from http://kathyschrock.net/1computer/page4.htm

SeaWorld Parks & Entertainment. (2010). *Animal sounds library.* Retrieved from http://www.seaworld.org/animal-info/sound-library/index.htm

Selfe, C. L., & Hawisher, G. E. (2004). *Literate lives in the information age: Narratives of literacy from the United States.* Mahwah, NJ: Lawrence Erlbaum.

Shi, M., Bonk, C. J., & Magjuka, R. J. (2006). *Time management strategies for online teaching.* Retrieved from http://itdl.org/journal/feb_06/article01.htm

Siskin, C.B. (2005). *Selected bibliography for CALL.* Retrieved from http://www.edvista.com/claire/callbib.html

Skype Technologies. (2010). Skype. Retrieved from http://www.skype.com

Slaouti, D., & Motteram, G. (2006). Reconstructing practice: Language teacher education and ICT. In P. Hubbard & M. Levy (Eds.), *Teacher education in CALL* (pp. 81–97). Amsterdam: John Benjamins.

Smith, B. (2003). Computer-mediated negotiated interaction: An expanded model. *The Modern Language Journal, 87*(1), 38–57.

Smith, B. (2010). Eye-tracking as a measure of noticing in SCMC. CALICO Conference, Amherst, MA.

SnapGrades. (2010). *SnapGrades.* Retrieved from http://snapgrades.com

SRI International. (2010). *Tapped in.* Retrieved from http://www.tappedin.org

Stannard, R. (2010). *TTV (Teacher Training Videos).* Retrieved from http://www.teacher trainingvideos.com

Stockwell, G. (2010). Using mobile phones for vocabulary activities: Examining the effect of the platform. *Language Learning & Technology, 14*(2), 95–110.

Sundar, V. (n.d.). *Timelinr.* Retrieved from http://veerasundar.com/timelinr

SurveyMonkey. (2010). *SurveyMonkey.* Retrieved from http://www.surveymonkey.com

Tanner, M. W., & Landon, M. M. (2009). The effects of computer-assisted pronunciation readings on ESL learners' use of pausing, stress, intonation, and overall comprehensibility. *Language Learning & Technology, 13*(3), 51–65.

TE Editor (2002). *Self-access: A framework for diversity.* Retrieved from http://www.teaching english.org.uk/think/articles/self-access-a-framework-diversity

Teachertube. (2010). *Teachertube.* Retrieved from http://www.teachertube.com

Teachnology. (2010). *Rubrics and rubric makers.* Retrieved from http://www.teach-nology.com /web_tools/rubrics

TESOL. (2003). *Standards for adult education ESL programs.* Alexandria, VA: TESOL.

TESOL. (2006). *PreK–12 English language proficiency standards.* Alexandria, VA: TESOL.

TESOL. (2008). *Technology standards framework document.* Alexandria, VA: TESOL.

TESOL. (2010). *Online education programs.* Retrieved from http://tesol.org/s_tesol/seccss .asp?CID=244&DID=1716

TESOL CALL Interest Section. (2010a). *Electronic Village online (EVO).* Retrieved from http:// evosessions.pbworks.com

TESOL CALL Interest Section. (2010b). *Home page.* Retrieved from http://www.call-is.org/info

TESOL Journal. (2010). Retrieved from http://www.tesol.org >Publications >TESOL Journal.

TextHelp Systems. (2010). *BrowseAloud.* [Computer software]. Available from http://www .browsealoud.com/page.asp

Time and Date. (2010a). *World clock.* Retrieved from http://www.timeanddate.com

Time and Date. (2010b). *World clock meeting planner.* Retrieved from http://www.timeanddate .com/worldclock/meeting.html

Tools for Educators. (2010). *Tools for educators.* Retrieved from http://www.toolsforeducators .com

Twurdy.com. (2010). *Twurdy.* Retrieved from http://www.twurdy.com

UCAR Community Programs. (2010). *The GLOBE program (Global Learning and Observation to Benefit the Environment).* Retrieved from http://www.globe.gov

UNESCO. (2008a). *ICT competency standards for teachers: Competency standards modules.* Paris: UNESCO.

UNESCO. (2008b). *ICT Competency standards for teachers: Implementation guidelines.* Paris: UNESCO.

UNESCO. (2008c). *ICT competency standards for teachers: Policy framework.* Paris: UNESCO.

U.S. Department of Education. (2000). *E-learning: Putting a world-class education at the fingertips of all children.* Washington, DC: U.S. Government Printing Office.

Verdugo, D. R., & Belmonte, I. A. (2007). Using digital stories to improve listening comprehension with Spanish young learners of English. *Language Learning and Technology, 11*(1), 87–101.

Verschoor, J. (2010). *Internet safety for teenagers.* Retrieved from http://jenverschoor.wordpress .com/2010/07/29/internet-safety-for-teens-through-games

Vimeo. (2010). *Vimeo.* Retrieved from http://vimeo.com

VOA special English: Text and mp3 files. Retrieved from http://www.manythings.org/voa/scripts

Ware, P. D. (2005). "Missed" communication in online communication: Tensions in a German-American telecollaboration. *Language Learning and Technology, 9*(2), 64–89.

Ware, P., & Warschauer, M. (2006). Electronic feedback and second language writing. In K. Hyland & F. Hyland (Eds.), *Feedback in second language writing: Contexts and issues* (pp. 105–122). New York: Cambridge University Press.

Warschauer, M. (1996). Motivational aspects of using computers for writing and communication. In M. Warschauer (Ed.), *Telecommunication in foreign language learning: Proceedings of the Hawaii symposium* (pp. 29–46). Honolulu: University of Hawai'i, Second Language Teaching & Curriculum Center.

Warschauer, M., & Healey, D. (1998). Computers and language learning: An overview. *Language Teaching, 31,* 57–71.

Warschauer, M., & Kern, R. (2000). *Network-based language teaching: Concepts and practice.* Cambridge, England: Cambridge University Press.

Warschauer, M., Shetzer, H., & Meloni C. (2000). *Internet for English teaching.* Alexandria, VA: TESOL.

Weather Channel Interactive. (2010). *The weather channel.* Retrieved from http://www.weather.com

Webheads in action. (2010). Retrieved from http://webheadsinaction.org

Wikimedia. (2010). *Wiktionary.* Retrieved from http://www.wiktionary.org

Wikipedia. (2010a). *Comparison of screencasting software.* Retrieved from http://en.wikipedia.org/wiki/List_of_screencasting_software

Wikipedia. (2010b). *Cultural faux pas.* Retrieved from http://en.wikipedia.org/wiki/Faux_pas

Winke, P., & Goertler, S. (2008). Did we forget someone? Students' computer access and literacy for CALL. *CALICO Journal, 25*(3), 482–509.

Witbeck, M., & Healey, D. (in press). Technology and the language program administrator. In F. Stoller & M. A. Christison (Eds.), *A handbook for language program administrators.* Alexandria, VA: TESOL.

WordPress. (2010). *WordPress.* Retrieved from http://wordpress.com

Wright, A. (2003). *Creating stories with children.* Oxford: Oxford University Press.

Yahoo.com. (2010a). *Flickr.* Retrieved from http://www.flickr.com

Yahoo.com. (2010b). *Yahoo Messenger.* Retrieved from http://messenger.yahoo.com

Yamada Language Center. (2010). *ANVILL (A National Virtual Language Lab).* Retrieved from https://anvill.uoregon.edu/anvill2

Yeh, A. (2007). Blended learning. In E. Hanson-Smith & J. Egbert (Eds.), *CALL environments: Research, practice, and critical issues* (2nd ed., pp. 404–420). Alexandria, VA: TESOL.

YouTube. (2010). *YouTube.* Retrieved from http://www.youtube.com

Witbeck, M., & Healey, D. (n.d.). Technology and the language program administrator. In M. A. Christison & F. L. Stoller (Eds.), *A handbook for language program administrators* (pp. 253–274). Provo, UT: Alta Books.

Zeinsteijer, R. (2006). *CAE B's podcast.* Retrieved from http://caeb2006.podomatic.com

Zhao, Y. (1997). The effects of listener's control of speech rate on second language comprehension. *Applied Linguistics, 18*(1), 49–6.

Zhao. (2003). Recent developments in technology and language learning: A literature review and meta-analysis. *CALICO Journal, 21*(1): 7–28.

Online References by Website Name

Academic vocabulary journal. Retrieved from http://kms.sdcoe.net/getvocal/89.html

Academic word list. Retrieved from http://www.victoria.ac.nz/lals/resources/academicwordlist/default.aspx

Animal sounds library. Retrieved from http://www.seaworld.org/animal-info/sound-library/index.htm

ANVILL (A National Virtual Language Lab). Retrieved from https://anvill.uoregon.edu/anvill2

Archiseek: Online architecture resources. Retrieved from http://www.archiseek.com

A to Z teacher stuff. Retrieved from http://www.atozteacherstuff.com

Audacity. Retrieved from http://audacity.sourceforge.net

Blackboard. Retrieved from http://blackboard.com

BreakingNewsEnglish. Retrieved from http://www.breakingnewsenglish.com

BrowseAloud. Retrieved from http://www.browsealoud.com/page.asp

Dimdim. Retrieved from http://www.dimdim.com

Dragon Naturally Speaking. Information retrieved from http://nuance.com/dragon/index.htm

easyWhois. Retrieved from http://www.easywhois.com

Educational activities for children. Retrieved from http://www.dltk-teach.com

Electronic Village Online. (EVO). Retrieved from http://evosessions.pbworks.com

Elluminate. Retrieved from http://www.elluminate.com

Enchanted Learning. Retrieved from http://www.enchantedlearning.com/Home.html

EnglishClub. Retrieved from http://www.englishclub.com/esl-exams/ets-toefl-practice-speaking.htm

English for all. Retrieved from http://www.myefa.org

ESL flashcards. Retrieved from http://www.eslflashcards.com

Facebook. Retrieved from http://www.facebook.com

Flickr. Retrieved from http://www.flickr.com

Freemind. Retrieved from http://freemind.sourceforge.net

GGeo Education Homepage. Retrieved from http://www.google.com/educators/geo.html

Gimp. Retrieved from http://www.gimp.org

GLOBE program (Global Learning and Observation to Benefit the Environment). Retrieved from http://www.globe.gov

Google Docs. Retrieved from http://docs.google.com

Google Earth. Retrieved from http://earth.google.com

Google Phone. Retrieved from http://gmail.com/ >Call phone

Google Scholar. Retrieved from http://scholar.google.com

Google Sites. Retrieved from http://sites.google.com

Hopelink Education. Retrieved from http://www.eastsideliteracy.org/tutorsupport/Tech /TechTips.htm

Hot Potatoes, Ver. 6. Retrieved from http://hotpot.uvic.ca

HowJSay. Retrieved from http://www.howjsay.com

IATEFL Learning Technologies Special Interest Group. (2010). Retrieved from http://groups .yahoo.com/group/LearningTechnologiesSIG

iEARN (International Education and Resource Network) Collaboration Centre. Retrieved from http://www.iearn.org

iMovie. Retrieved from http://www.apple.com/ilife/imovie

Internet movie database. Retrieved from http://www.imdb.com

Kidspiration, Ver. 3 Information retrieved from http://www.inspiration.com/Kidspiration

Language Learning & Technology. Retrieved from http://llt.msu.edu

LexTutor. Retrieved from http://www.lextutor.ca

LifeWorks. Retrieved from http://science.education.nih.gov/LifeWorks.nsf/Interviews

ManyThings.org. Retrieved from http://www.manythings.org

MERLOT (Multimedia Educational Resource for Learning and Online Teaching). Retrieved from http://www.merlot.org/merlot/index.htm

Merriam-Webster's Visual Dictionary Online. Retrieved from http://visual.merriam-webster .com

Microsoft PowerPoint. Information at http://www.microsoft.com

Microsoft Word 2010, in Microsoft Office. Information at http://office.microsoft.com/en-us /word

Microsoft 2007 Office Tutorials. Retrieved from http://www.officetutorials.com

Moodle. Retrieved from http://moodle.org

OpenOffice. Retrieved from http://www.openoffice.org

Palabea. Retrieved from http://www.palabea.net

PBL Checklist. Retrieved from http://pblchecklist.4teachers.org/checklist.shtml

PBworks. Retrieved from http://www.pbworks.com

Photoshop Express. Retrieved from http://www.photoshop.com

Picasa. Retrieved from http://picasaweb.google.com

PodOmatic. Retrieved from http://www.podomatic.com

Poets.org. Retrieved from http://www.poets.org

Public agenda for citizens. Retrieved from http://www.publicagenda.com/citizen

QuestGarden. Retrieved from http://questgarden.com

Quia. Retrieved from http://www.quia.com

Randall's Cyber ESL listening lab. Retrieved from http://www.esl-lab.com

Range. Retrieved from http://www.victoria.ac.nz/lals/resources/range.aspx

ReadPlease. Retrieved from http://www.readplease.com

Real English. Retrieved from http://www.real-english.com

Rubistar. Retrieved from http://rubistar.4teachers.org

Sakai. Retrieved from http://sakaiproject.org

Second Life. Retrieved from http://www.secondlife.com

Simple concordance program. Retrieved from http://www.textworld.com/scp

Skype. Retrieved from http://www.skype.com

SnapGrades. Retrieved from http://snapgrades.com

Stapleless Book. Retrieved from http://www.readwritethink.org/classroom-resources/student-interactives/stapleless-book-30010.html

SurveyMonkey. Retrieved from http://www.surveymonkey.com

Tandem Server Bochum. Retrieved from http://www.slf.ruhr-uni-bochum.de/index.html

Tapped In. Retrieved from http://www.tappedin.org

Teachertube. Retrieved from http://www.teachertube.com

Teachnology. Rubrics and rubric makers. Retrieved from http://www.teach-nology.com/web_tools/rubrics

TESOL Journal. Retrieved from http://www.tesol.org >Publications >TESOL Journal.

TimeGlider. Retrieved from http://timeglider.com

Timelinr. Retrieved from http://veerasundar.com/timelinr

TOEFL iBT Speaking Practice Tests. Retrieved from http://www.english-itutor.com/TOEFL_iBT_speaking_tests.html

Tools for educators. Retrieved from http://www.toolsforeducators.com

TTV (Teacher Training Videos). Retrieved from http://www.teachertrainingvideos.com

Twurdy. Retrieved from http://www.twurdy.com

U.S.A. Learns. Retrieved from http://www.usalearns.org

Vimeo. Retrieved from http://vimeo.com

VOA Special English: Text and MP3 Files. Retrieved from http://www.manythings.org/voa/scripts

VocabProfiler. Retrieved from http://www.lextutor.ca/vp

Voki. Retrieved from http://www.voki.com

WayBackMachine. Retrieved from http://www.archive.org

Weather Channel Interactive. (2010). The weather channel. Retrieved from http://www.weather.com

WebQuest.Org. Retrieved from http://webquest.org/index.php

Wikipedia. Retrieved from http://en.wikipedia.org

Wiktionary. Retrieved from http://www.wiktionary.org

Windows Movie Maker 2.1. Retrieved from http://www.microsoft.com/windowsxp/downloads/updates/moviemaker2.mspx

WiZiQ. Retrieved from http://www.wiziq.com

WordPress. Retrieved from http://wordpress.com

World clock. Retrieved from http://www.timeanddate.com

World clock meeting planner. Retrieved from http://www.timeanddate.com/worldclock/meeting.html

XWord Interactive Crossword Puzzles. Retrieved from http://vlc.polyu.edu.hk/XWord/xword.htm

Yahoo Messenger. Retrieved from http://messenger.yahoo.com

YouTube. Retrieved from http://www.youtube.com

Glossary

Key Words	Descriptions/Definitions
Accessibility	a quality in a website, program, or hardware tool that makes it more usable by people with physical disabilities, such as deafness, weak vision, or limited movement (see *adaptive technology* and *assistive devices*)
Adaptive technology	hardware and software that increases the usability of technology for those with physical disabilities; examples include text to speech, speech recognition, and Braille keyboards (see *accessibility* and *assistive devices*)
Application	a software program, including language software, web browsers, word processors, and games
Assistive devices	hardware that increases the usability of technology for people with physical disabilities; examples include TDD and Braille keyboards (see *accessibility* and *adaptive technology*)
Autonomy	self-motivation and independence in learning (not necessarily solitary study)
Bandwidth	the carrying capacity of the Internet, usually in a specific location, or the amount of Internet capacity required by a website or an Internet tool, such as Flash. Low-bandwidth locations (those without a lot of carrying capacity) may not be able to use high-bandwidth applications, such as streaming video.
Blended learning	teaching and learning using a standard classroom setting plus online or computer activities; also known as hybrid learning (see *hybrid course*)
Blog	a web log; a kind of online journal, where postings are in reverse chronological order and readers can add comments
Browser	a program used to view websites and other Internet-based resources; common examples are Internet Explorer and Firefox. Also referred to as a web browser.

CALL	computer-assisted language learning; the use of computers and other digital technology to enhance language instruction
CD/CD-ROM	compact disc or compact disc–read only memory; a storage device for audio (CD) and for compressed data, usually files or images (CD-ROM); gradually being replaced by *DVD*s and *memory sticks*
Clip art	digital illustrations, often line drawings, that are available for cutting and pasting
Collaborative (language) learning	learning that takes place in groups with social aspects that enhance impact
Communication styles	modes of communicating with others, such as informal, business-formal, or abbreviated (as with chat); always culture-specific
Communication technologies	tools such as email, instant messenger, chat, voice mail, web logs (blogs), and podcasts; ways of interacting with others
Community of practice	a group of people who are linked by common interests, including work, and who learn from each other in a collaborative way
Computer-mediated communication (CMC)	any communication that is accommodated by the use of computers or computer networks (e.g., text chat, voice chat, email, discussion boards, audio- and videoconferencing)
Course management system (CMS)	a software system designed to help teachers with online and hybrid course administration and delivery; typically includes discussion boards, text chat, email, grade books, and quizzes (see *learning management system*)
Courseware	software designed to serve as the core "text" or significant portion of a course; sometimes used to refer to any software designed for instructional purposes
Curriculum	objectives and learning outcomes for a series of classes or courses leading to a learning goal that is larger than what is covered in a single class
Digital	available in electronic form
Digital competence	knowledge about creating, modifying, and managing digital information
Digital file exchange	moving digital information from one format to another or one location to another
Digital literacy	basic understanding of and ability with computer functions, including Internet use
Discussion board	a form of asynchronous, computer-mediated communication used for maintaining extensive discussions; also referred to as a bulletin board or discussion forum
DVD	digital video disc or digital versatile disc; a second-generation storage device for audio, video, or computer data (see *CD/CD-ROM*)

Effectiveness (of specific student uses of technology)	how well technology works in achieving educational outcomes; determined based on the instructor's goals and reasons for using technology
Electronic feedback	responses submitted or added to existing work through the use of technology
E-list	software (e.g., Listserv and Majordomo) that creates an electronic list of users, protected by registration with a password for privacy; it sends messages to all users simultaneously (see *email*)
E-portfolio (electronic portfolio)	a collection of work maintained in digital form
Email	electronic mail; can be routed to a specific set of users through e-list software (see *e-list*)
Embedded media	audio and video files that may be heard or viewed directly on a web page or in a presentation (rather than by following a linked URL)
Embedded technology	computer chips and communication devices that are part of devices other than stand-alone computers, such as in an interactive whiteboard
Emerging technologies	new ways of using digital devices and media that have not yet been fully developed
English as a foreign language (EFL)	English language taught in countries where English is not generally spoken as a first language and not used routinely by a substantial portion of the population, resulting in learners having limited access to speakers of the language
English as a second language (ESL)	English language taught in countries where English is spoken as a common language by a substantial portion of the population, allowing learners routine access to speakers of the language in a range of settings
English for Specific Purposes (ESP)	English instruction focused on a particular academic discipline or workplace need, e.g., English for business or English for medical transcription
English language learner	used in this book to refer to a learner of English in either an ESL or an EFL context; commonly used to refer to students in U.S. elementary and secondary schools whose first language is not English
Exercise	the simplest form of language practice; it usually focuses on a limited grammar point or vocabulary items (in contrast, see *task*)
File-naming convention	a set of elements required and prohibited in computer file names, such as extensions for Windows (*.doc*, *.txt*, and the like), and including a prohibition on the slash and colon in Windows and Macintosh operating systems, respectively
Formal instruction	a planned teaching and learning situation; used in this book to address face-to-face instruction as well as online instruction

Formative assessment	ongoing evaluation of progress, often used to help learners understand what else they need to know (in contrast, see *summative assessment*)
Forum (electronic or online)	see *discussion board*
Foundational knowledge (and skills)	Basic information (and abilities) needed to perform all other tasks
Hardware	physical equipment, such as a computer, projector, and monitor
Hybrid course	a course taught using a combination of face-to-face and online instruction (see *blended learning*)
In-service	currently teaching (often used to describe courses or workshops for practicing teachers)
Instant messaging (IM'ing)	text chat, generally, although audio and video chat are also possible; a notice pops up on an IM subscriber's screen when a message is received
Intensive English program (IEP)	an instructional program for adult students learning English, generally in an academic setting; students are usually in class 4–6 hours daily
Interactive learning	activities and tasks that require social collaboration; tasks in which the computer adjusts activities based on user input
Interactive whiteboard (IBW)	a whiteboard that is linked to a computer and serves as a computer input device (e.g., the teacher projects a web page onto the whiteboard, annotates it, and follows links)
International Society for Technology in Education (ISTE)	an organization that publishes journals and standards for technology use. The ISTE standards are most commonly used in the United States
Internet resources	web, email, podcasts, and related technologies
Internet telephony	applications that allow people to place phone calls using a computer with an Internet connection and a headset
Jump drive	see *memory stick* and *portable memory device*
Lab	laboratory; in this book, a computer lab (i.e., a room that contains several computers and is set aside specifically for computer use or instruction)
Language learning competence	Understanding of how to learn a language
Learning management system (LMS)	a software system designed to help teachers with online and hybrid course administration and delivery; typically includes discussion boards, text chat, email, grade books, and quiz applications (see *course management system*)
Lesson planning	making decisions about what to do in a specific class lesson in order to achieve learning objectives

Levels of language proficiency	see Appendix B for descriptors
Lifelong learning	continuing to study topics of interest after completing formal schooling
Mailing list	a way to send a single message to a group of people simultaneously, usually via email
Malware	overall term for programs that are designed to damage a computer, including viruses, spam-enabling software, and Trojan horses
Memory stick	a small storage device for digital files, usually in USB format; also known as a jump drive, flash drive, USB drive, thumb drive, or pen drive; it is one form of portable memory device (see *jump drive* and *portable memory device*)
Mind-mapping tool	software or website that creates graphic organizers that visually link topics or ideas
Mobile devices	portable hardware such as personal digital assistants (PDAs), cell phones, MP3 players, and laptop computers
MP3 player or recorder	a device that stores and plays or records MP3 files; short for "MPEG-2 Audio Layer 3," MP3 is a widely used audio file format designed by the Moving Picture Experts Group to store audio in a compressed format
Netiquette	etiquette used on the Internet; generally includes rules such as not being rude or "flaming" on an e-list, respecting others' rights to differing opinions, and not including long quotes or extraneous matter in replies
Offline	not connected to the Internet
Online	connected to the Internet
Pedagogical approach	teaching style based on awareness of methodology, research, and theory
Peripherals	equipment attached to a computer (e.g., joystick, external drive, printer)
Personal digital assistant (PDA)	a portable device used to record addresses, appointments, and notes (e.g., a Palm Pilot)
Placemark	a digital thumbtack showing a location on a map, typically in Google Maps
Plug-in	a small program that can be installed into another program; generally used to add functions to a browser
Podcast	an online recording that can be stored online or automatically sent to a list of users. As a verb, to create this type of online recording.
Podquest	a group project created by learners using audio information from podcasts

Portable memory device	a small electronic tool such as a removable digital camera card, an external hard drive, a USB drive, or a memory stick that can easily transfer files to and from computers (see *memory stick*)
Presentation program	software that allows users to easily combine audio, video, and text to create an attractive, page-by-page (slide-by-slide) display (see also *slideshow*)
Pre-service	learning to teach (often used to describe courses or workshops for education students or teacher candidates)
Productivity tools	software used for office tasks, such as a word processor, presentation program, spreadsheet, and database
Professional practice	how people do their jobs according to the accepted norms and standards of the field
Proficiency	see Appendix B for descriptors
Register	a variety of language used in particular situations or contexts, characterized by linguistic elements such as vocabulary choice and level of formality
Research perspectives	ways of conceptualizing how to ask questions and look for answers in research (e.g., qualitative and quantitative, ethnography and critical theory)
Resources	materials used for teaching and learning, such as worksheets, computers, books, software, and markers (see also *Internet resources*)
RSS (Really Simple Syndication) feed	technology that allows a user to subscribe to a website, blog, podcast, or other "RSS-enabled" page and automatically receive updates as they occur
Schemata	assumptions about the world, culture, language, etc., already understood by learners
Screencast	a video of a series of actions that take place on the computer screen, commonly used to teach about computer use
Screen reader	a program or device that interprets text on the screen and turns it into speech, primarily for those with vision difficulties (see *accessibility*, *adaptive technology*, and *assistive devices*)
Screenshot	a digital picture of an open window or of the whole computer screen at a particular moment in time
Slideshow (online)	a web application that allows the user to combine digital photos, text, and sometimes graphics in a display that mimics a physical slideshow (see *presentation program*)
Smart phone	a mobile device that includes applications such as camera, video, GPS, calendar, personal assistant software, etc., in addition to telephony (e.g., an iPhone or Android phone)
Software	programs that enable computers to perform specific tasks; includes the computer's operating system (OS)

Spam	unsolicited and unwanted email messages; the online equivalent of junk mail (also used as a verb meaning to send such messages)
Stakeholders	people who have an interest in an educational outcome, such as teachers, parents, students, administrators, and community members
Strategies	ways in which learners approach a given task; often divided into cognitive, metacognitive, and socioaffective
Summative assessment	final evaluation (in contrast, see *formative assessment*)
Task	relatively complex activity with an end goal; often requires collaboration (in contrast, see *exercise*)
Technological resources	different kinds of electronic equipment and media that may be used for language instruction, including hardware, communication technologies, digital material, and courseware
Technology	systems that centrally involve computer chips, digital applications, and networks in all their forms
Technology-based activities	learning-related tasks that use technology as a fundamental component
Technology-based language skill-building tools	resources (e.g., programs and websites) that are designed to enhance specific areas of language learning, such as reading, writing, listening, speaking, grammar, and pronunciation
Technology-based productivity tools	see *productivity tools*
Technology-based research tools	software and hardware used to collect, analyze, and present data and research findings
Technology environments	the various contexts in which technology may be used for instruction, including computer lab, online, independent use, and one-computer classroom
Technology integration	using technology in the classroom in a way that is meaningful and connected to the goals of the class
TDD (telecommunications device for the deaf)	a device that converts text to audio transmission for communication with deaf and hearing-impaired people; sometimes referred to as text telephony, text telephone, or TTY
Telecollaboration	use of computer-based collaborative tools and web resources for curricular purposes (see *Web 2.0*)
TESOL	Teachers of English to Speakers of Other Languages, an international professional association for such teachers
Turn-taking	cooperative behavior in the classroom or online, in which one person stops and another starts talking
URL (uniform resource locator)	an Internet address, generally given in http://… format

USB	universal serial bus; a type of hardware used to connect a computer to a wide variety of devices such as cameras, headsets, microphones, and memory sticks
Voiceboard	a discussion board that allows users to record audio and sometimes video to share with a group
Web 2.0	web technologies that foster social interaction or user contributions to collaborative endeavors on the Internet
Webcam	a camera designed to be used online, generally as part of a video chat or web conference
Web conferencing	meeting on the Internet using audio or video distance conferencing software, which often has additional capabilities such as an electronic collaborative whiteboard, polling, recording, web touring, and desktop sharing (see *webinar*)
Webinar	an online workshop, generally including web conferencing; may also include email and a discussion forum
WebQuest	an activity learners complete by undertaking a directed Internet search (often, for safety, to specific sites designated by the teacher)
Wiki	a website (e.g., Wikipedia) designed to be easily edited through a browser by anyone given access to it; typically used for collaborative purposes
Wikipedia	The world's largest online encyclopedia, contributed to by volunteer users

Appendix A: The TESOL Technology Standards for Language Learners and Language Teachers

This appendix provides a list of the goals, standards, and Performance indicators without the vignettes. It is intended for use as a quick and handy reference.

Technology Standards for Language Learners

Goal 1: Language learners demonstrate foundational knowledge and skills in technology for a multilingual world.

Standard 1: Language learners demonstrate basic operational skills in using various technology tools and Internet browsers.

Performance indicators

- Language learners can perform basic functions on digital devices present in their learning environment: desktop computers, mobile/laptop computers, electronic whiteboards, mobile phones, MP3/video players (e.g., turning the device on and off; opening, closing, and resizing software windows; saving, editing, and organizing files and folders; copying, cutting, and pasting elements within a document; recognizing file types; launching and exiting software applications; and similar universal tasks).

- Language learners can perform basic browser functions (e.g., recognize hyperlinks, navigate forward and back, type in an address, use bookmarks, recognize the format of a URL [universal resource locator]).

- Language learners can recognize the format of an email address.

- Language learners can restart the digital device.

- Language learners recognize when they are and are not online.

- Language learners can use accessibility options as needed (e.g., zoom for visually impaired students, TDD, or telecommunications device for the deaf, Braille keyboard).

Standard 2: Language learners are able to use available input and output devices (e.g., keyboard, mouse, printer, headset, microphone, media player, electronic whiteboard).

Performance indicators
- Language learners demonstrate understanding of the layout of a standard English keyboard.

- Language learners can change the keyboard layout between different languages as needed.

- Language learners demonstrate understanding of where available media, devices, and other peripherals go (e.g., CDs go into slots or CD drives, jump drives go into USB ports, cables connect only where they fit and work).

- Language learners can operate available peripherals (e.g., printers and scanners) at a basic level.

- Language learners can operate relevant classroom technologies (e.g., data projectors, electronic whiteboards) and personal technologies (PDAs, mobile phones, MP3/video players) at a basic level.

Standard 3: Language learners exercise appropriate caution when using online sources and when engaging in electronic communication.

Performance indicators
- Language learners are cautious when opening attachments and clicking on links in email messages.

- Language learners have security software running on their own computers and other devices and keep it current (e.g., antivirus and firewall software).

- Underage students do not provide personal contact information except as directed by the teacher; adult students exercise caution.

- Language learners exercise caution in computer-mediated communication (CMC) (e.g., log out/off when leaving an email account or a public computer; protect personal information).

- Language learners demonstrate their understanding of the fact that placing any information or content online can become part of a permanent record.

- Language learners identify examples of false and potentially malicious information that exists online.

Standard 4: Language learners demonstrate basic competence as users of technology.

Performance indicators

- Language learners can perform basic troubleshooting operations (e.g., check for power, see if the monitor is turned off, restart safely, check the volume on media).

- Language learners can search for a file.

- Language learners can access a help menu, where available.

- Language learners ask for technical help when appropriate.

- Underage students call an adult when they have found offensive or inappropriate material, turning off the monitor if on a computer; adult students realize that they may need to turn off the computer to exit some websites.

Goal 2: Language learners use technology in socially and culturally appropriate, legal, and ethical ways.

Standard 1: Language learners understand that communication conventions differ across cultures, communities, and contexts.

Performance indicators

- Language learners identify similarities and differences in local and global communication.

- Language learners demonstrate understanding of multiple ways that computer-mediated communication (CMC) can be (mis)interpreted (e.g., using appropriate register, turn-taking, respecting expected length and content of messages, considering literal versus rhetorical meaning).

- Language learners show sensitivity to their use of communication conventions, according to the context (e.g., not using all caps [capital letters], waiting for lag time in synchronous communication, using turn-taking cues, checking spelling).

- Language learners conform to current social conventions when using technology in communication (e.g., social conventions in the classroom may restrict cell phone use).

- Language learners can identify cultural variables at play in interpreting and responding to a message.

Standard 2: Language learners demonstrate respect for others in their use of private and public information.

Performance indicators

- Language learners demonstrate their understanding that public information in one community may be considered private in other communities.

- Language learners demonstrate their understanding that images may carry different connotations in different communities (e.g., pigs as symbols of prosperity vs. unclean animals).

- Language learners use communications and digital media tools ethically and responsibly (e.g., they don't secretly videotape others and post the videos on public sites).

- Language learners practice legal, responsible, and ethical use of technology systems, information, and software (e.g., they don't make and distribute illegal copies; they document sources as appropriate).

- Language learners accommodate different communication styles online.

Goal 3: Language learners effectively use and critically evaluate technology-based tools as aids in the development of their language learning competence as part of formal instruction and for further learning.

Standard 1: Language learners effectively use and evaluate available technology-based productivity tools.

Performance indicators

- Language learners use technology-based productivity tools as aids in production (e.g., word processing, presentation software, and web-design software; associated applications such as spell-checkers and thesauri; templates for preparing presentations, newsletters, and reports; tools to assist in brainstorming and creating graphic organizers).

- Language learners use technology-based productivity tools as aids in comprehension (e.g., translators, electronic dictionaries).

- Language learners apply criteria to evaluate the appropriate use of particular technology tools for specific language learning tasks.

- Language learners use technology-based productivity tools collaboratively and individually in order to enhance their language learning competence.

Standard 2: Language learners appropriately use and evaluate available technology-based language skill-building tools.

Performance indicators

- Language learners employ age- and proficiency-appropriate vocabulary and pragmatics/body language during collaborative work that uses technology.

- Language learners demonstrate that they know when to ask for help in order to achieve their language learning objectives when using technology.

- Language learners decide when to use language software and devices as available and appropriate to enhance specific skill areas (e.g., vocabulary, grammar, and pronunciation practice software; MP3 recorders).

- Language learners critically evaluate Internet resources as available and appropriate to enhance their language learning (e.g., web-based listening exercises, online sentence jumbles).

Standard 3: Language learners appropriately use and evaluate available technology-based tools for communication and collaboration.

Performance indicators

- Language learners communicate in appropriate ways with those from other cultures and communities using digital tools.

- Language learners actively encourage others to fully participate in conversations that use technology-based tools in a language learning context (e.g., simulations, mobile phones, CMC [computer-mediated communication] tools).

- Language learners use criteria to determine which technology tools function best as a means of collaborating with others for specific types of language learning (e.g., comment function in word processors, wikis, interactive whiteboards, CMC tools).

- Language learners use and critically evaluate the use of particular digital resources to communicate ideas effectively to peers or a wider audience (e.g., blogs, podcasts, movie-making tools).

- Language learners use available technology individually or collaboratively to create content to share with peers or a wider audience, online or offline.

Standard 4:   Language learners use and evaluate available technology-based research tools appropriately.

Performance indicators

- Language learners employ technology to locate and collect information from a variety of sources.

- Language learners employ strategies to evaluate online information.

- Language learners document source material appropriately.

- Language learners determine which technology tools to use to organize information from research (e.g., moving information around in the word processor, using a database or spreadsheet).

Standard 5:   Language learners recognize the value of technology to support autonomy, lifelong learning, creativity, metacognition, collaboration, personal pursuits, and productivity.

Performance indicators

- Language learners select the most appropriate available technology for independent language learning and can provide reasons for their choices.

- Language learners demonstrate the ability to set language learning goals and objectives that employ technology, with a teacher's support or independently.

- Language learners can use technology to monitor their progress (e.g., record keeping within programs, electronic portfolios), with a teacher's support or independently.

- Language learners can express themselves using technology (e.g., creating digital media as works of art).

- Language learners provide reasons for the value of technology in maintaining communication for personal and professional purposes and having access to authentic material that supports their language learning.

- Language learners use technology to work in English more effectively (e.g., using an electronic dictionary when it is more efficient than using a paper dictionary).

Technology Standards for Language Teachers

Goal 1: Language teachers acquire and maintain foundational knowledge and skills in technology for professional purposes.

Standard 1:   Language teachers demonstrate knowledge and skills in basic technological concepts and operational competence, meeting or exceeding TESOL technology standards for students in whatever situation they teach.

Performance indicators

- Language teachers perform basic functions with available digital devices in order to accomplish instructional and organizational goals (e.g., turning the device on and off; opening, closing, and resizing software windows; saving, editing, and organizing files and folders; copying, cutting, and pasting elements within a document; recognizing file times; launching and exiting software applications; and similar universal tasks).

- Language teachers prepare instructional materials for students using basic technology tools (e.g., word-processing software, presentation software, and software that creates Internet resources).

- Language teachers exercise appropriate caution when using online sources and when engaging in electronic communication. (See Learner Standards Goal 1 Standard 3 for some examples.)

Standard 2:   Language teachers demonstrate an understanding of a wide range of technology supports for language learning and options for using them in a given setting.

Performance indicators

- Language teachers identify appropriate technologies to support a range of instructional objectives.

- Language teachers use evaluation tools to analyze the appropriateness of specific technology options.

- Language teachers share information about available technology with colleagues.

- Language teachers use online technology as available to deliver instructional or support material.

- Language teachers locate and can adapt a variety of digital resources.

Standard 3: Language teachers actively strive to expand their skill and knowledge base to evaluate, adopt, and adapt emerging technologies throughout their careers.

Performance indicators

- Language teachers utilize technology tools to expand upon a conventional activity.

- Language teachers keep up with information through a variety of sources (e.g., books, journals, mailing lists, conventions).

- Language teachers participate in a relevant community of practice.

- Language teachers explore the possibilities inherent in emerging technologies with a critical eye.

Standard 4: Language teachers use technology in socially and culturally appropriate, legal, and ethical ways.

Performance indicators

- Language teachers demonstrate sensitivity to the similarities and differences in communication conventions across cultures, communities, and contexts.

- Language teachers show an awareness of their role as models, demonstrating respect for others in their use of public and private information.

- Language teachers show awareness and understanding when approaching culturally sensitive topics and offer students alternatives.

- Language teachers conform to local legal requirements regarding the privacy of students' personal information.

- Language teachers conform to local legal requirements regarding accessibility.

- Language teachers conform to local legal requirements regarding fair use and copyright.

- Language teachers follow local guidelines regarding the use of human subjects for research.

- Language teachers demonstrate awareness that electronic communication is not secure and private, and that in some localities, email may be subject to "open records" laws.

- Language teachers seek help in identifying and implementing solutions related to legal requirements.

- Language teachers protect student privacy (e.g., not inappropriately putting student email addresses, biodata, or photos online; fully informing students about public sharing of blogs and websites; using password-protected sites when possible).

- Language teachers respect student ownership of their own work (e.g., not sharing student work inappropriately; not requiring students to post their work publicly).

Goal 2: Language teachers integrate pedagogical knowledge and skills with technology to enhance language teaching and learning.

Standard 1: Language teachers identify and evaluate technological resources and environments for suitability to their teaching context.

Performance indicators

- Language teachers identify the technological resources (e.g., hardware, communication technologies, digital material, courseware) and limitations of the current teaching environment.

- Language teachers identify appropriate technology environments (e.g., lab, one-computer class, online, independent use) to meet specific learning/teaching goals.

- Language teachers evaluate technology environments for alignment with the goals of the class.

- Language teachers evaluate technological resources for alignment with the needs and abilities of the students.

Standard 2: Language teachers coherently integrate technology into their pedagogical approaches.

Performance indicators

- Language teachers demonstrate understanding of their own teaching styles.

- Language teachers review personal pedagogical approaches in order to use technology to support current teaching styles.

- Language teachers demonstrate their understanding of the potential and limitations in technology.

- Language teachers embed technology into teaching rather than making it an add-on.

- Language teachers engage regularly in professional development related to technology use.

- Language teachers evaluate their use of technology in teaching.

Performance indicators, expert level of technology

- Language teachers work around the limitations in available technology to achieve instructional goals.

- Language teachers support peers in their professional development with technology. (Informal support may be unpaid; formal support should be paid.)

Standard 3:   Language teachers design and manage language learning activities and tasks using technology appropriately to meet curricular goals and objectives.

Performance indicators

- Language teachers demonstrate familiarity with a variety of technology-based options.

- Language teachers choose a technology environment that is aligned with the goals of the class.

- Language teachers choose technology that is aligned with the needs and abilities of the students (e.g., language learning-focused software, productivity tools, content tools).

- Language teachers demonstrate awareness of students' level of digital competence.

- Language teachers ensure that students understand how to use the technology to meet instructional goals (e.g., teach students how to evaluate online resources).

- Language teachers enable students to think critically about their use of technology in an age-appropriate manner.

Performance indicators, expert level of technology

- Language teachers adapt technology-based activities and tasks to align with the goals of the class and with the needs and abilities of the students.

- Language teachers create an appropriate technology environment to meet specific teaching and learning goals.

- Language teachers operate with an understanding of the underlying structure of the technology in use.

- Language teachers demonstrate the ability to draw on a wide range of functions in technological resources.

- Language teachers identify more than one approach to achieve an objective (e.g., a backup plan for when the technology is not working).

Standard 4: Language teachers use relevant research findings to inform the planning of language learning activities and tasks that involve technology.

Performance indicators

- Language teachers demonstrate familiarity with suggestions from research for classroom practice using technology.

- Language teachers use a variety of avenues for getting information about research related to technology use (e.g., communities of practice, conferences).

- Language teachers demonstrate understanding of the temporal nature of research findings related to technology use (i.e., that technology changes over time, so older research may not be applicable to current settings).

- Language teachers demonstrate awareness of multiple research sources and perspectives that inform technology use.

- Language teachers discern which findings about technology use are most appropriate for their situation.

- Language teachers share relevant research findings about technology use with others.

- Language teachers identify the context and limitations of research about technology use and do not apply findings inappropriately.

Performance indicators, expert level of technology

- Language teachers demonstrate their understanding of relevant research findings related to technology use for language learning.

- Language teachers identify gaps in current research about technology use.

- Language teachers help others recognize the context and limitations of research about technology use.

- Language teachers produce and disseminate research related to technology use.

Goal 3: Language teachers apply technology in record keeping, feedback, and assessment.

Standard 1: Language teachers evaluate and implement relevant technology to aid in effective learner assessment.

Performance indicators

- Language teachers demonstrate familiarity with a variety of forms of assessment that employ technology.

- Language teachers employ appropriate record-keeping tools and techniques (e.g., software-based classroom management tools, electronic grade books, reports to stakeholders).

Performance indicators, expert level of technology

- Language teachers use computer-based diagnostic, formative, and summative testing where feasible.

- Language teachers use technology to illustrate learner progress (e.g., graphic representations of scores over time, revision history).

- Language teachers provide feedback through digital file exchange (e.g., review tools in writing; annotated comments in speaking).

Standard 2: Language teachers use technological resources to collect and analyze information in order to enhance language instruction and learning.

Performance indicators

- Language teachers demonstrate familiarity with research-based principles related to technology-enhanced assessment.

- Language teachers use technology-enhanced assessment results to plan instruction.

- Language teachers interpret computer-based test scores for stakeholders (e.g., TOEFL, other standardized tests).

- Language teachers elicit student feedback in order to improve teacher use of technology.

Performance indicators, expert level of technology

- Language teachers apply research findings related to technology-enhanced assessment.

- Language teachers collect student output for analysis (e.g., concordancer to analyze lexical complexity, chat logs).

- Language teachers use digital resources to document teaching for further analysis (e.g., digital recording of lectures and class interactions, digital logs of interactions).

Standard 3: Language teachers evaluate the effectiveness of specific student uses of technology to enhance teaching and learning.

Performance indicators

- Language teachers use appropriate procedures for evaluating student use of technology (e.g., rubrics, checklists, matrices—which may evaluate enjoyment).

- Language teachers elicit student feedback in order to improve student use of technology.

Performance indicators, expert level of technology

- Language teachers develop and share procedures for evaluating student use of technology.

- Language teachers examine student outcomes that result from use of technology (e.g., examining chat logs for more complex language).

Goal 4: Language teachers use technology to improve communication, collaboration, and efficiency.

Standard 1: Language teachers use communication technologies to maintain effective contact and collaboration with peers, students, administration, and other stakeholders.

Performance indicators

- Language teachers draw on resources (lesson plans and teaching ideas) for language teachers that are posted online.

- Language teachers implement lesson plans obtained from other teachers via the Internet.

- Teachers belong to online communities (e.g., mailing lists, blogs, wikis, podcasts) with other language teachers.

- Language teachers share their email address with students and peers.

Performance indicators, expert level of technology

- Language teachers maintain an electronic forum (e.g., web page, blog) to post information for students about the class.

- Language teachers view and comment on students' electronic work (e.g., electronic portfolios, project work, websites).

- Language teachers advise administration on the use of online technology to improve communication.

- Language teachers share instructional material digitally.

Standard 2: Language teachers regularly reflect on the intersection of professional practice and technological developments so that they can make informed decisions regarding the use of technology to support language learning and communication.

Performance indicators

- Language teachers take advantage of professional development related to technology integration (e.g., conferences, journals, mailing lists, communities of practice).

- Language teachers select technology resources that promote appropriate language use.

- Language teachers demonstrate awareness of multiple sources and perspectives that inform technology use.

- Language teachers discern which findings are most appropriate for their situation.

Performance indicators, expert level of technology

- Language teachers stay informed about how to use new technologies for instructional and professional purposes (e.g., podcasts for listening and speaking, blogs for writing and reading).

- Language teachers integrate technology in innovative ways.

- Language teachers engage in research (including classroom-based) and share the results.

- Language teachers advise decision-makers about appropriate technology resources and environments.

Standard 3: Language teachers apply technology to improve efficiency in preparing for class, grading, and maintaining records.

Performance indicators

- Language teachers use electronic resources to locate additional materials for lesson planning and classroom use.

- Language teachers demonstrate understanding of various methods of providing electronic feedback on student work (e.g., email, insert comments).

- Language teachers have a system to collect, organize, and retrieve material and student data.

Performance indicators, expert level of technology

- Language teachers maintain a resource that allows students to locate and retrieve material.

- Language teachers use electronic methods, as appropriate, for formative and summative assessment.

- Language teachers encourage students to use electronic methods to document their own progress.

Appendix B: Proficiency Descriptors

This appendix defines the performance definitions (language proficiency levels) for primary and secondary English language learners that are used in the vignettes in Chapters 3 and 4. Three sets of descriptors are included:

1. TESOL's *Standards for Adult Education ESL Programs*, used by adult educators in the United States

2. TESOL's *PreK–12 English Language Proficiency Standards*, familiar to elementary and secondary teachers in the United States

3. the Common European Framework of Reference (CEFR), which provides a standard used in Europe and other parts of the world

Each learner goal vignette in Chapter 3 begins with a ***Learner profile*** that includes the type and age of the students followed by the TESOL Technology Standards label, the descriptor from the TESOL adult education standards, and finally the alphanumeric levels from both the TESOL PreK–12 standards and the CEFR standards (Council of Europe, 2010). Figure B1 provides an example learner profile with these elements labeled.

In the vignette tables in Appendix C, the **Targeted Group** column lists the same information but oriented vertically, as shown in Figure B2.

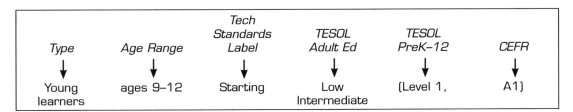

Figure B1. Learner Profile Descriptors at the Start of Each Vignette

Setting	ESL (child)
Type, Age Range	Young learners, ages 9–12
Tech Standards Label / TESOL Adult Ed	Starting / Low Intermediate
(TESOL PreK–12, CEFR)	(Level 1, A1)

Figure B2. Targeted Group Descriptors in Vignettes

It should be noted that the CEFR descriptors include a higher level of proficiency than do the preK–12 standards, and the standards for adult education descriptors provide for a lower level of proficiency than either of the other two. Thus, occasionally, one of the descriptors will not be applicable and will be omitted. To simplify, the TESOL Technology Standards labels bridge the gaps. (See Table B1.) Since the vignettes come from teachers around the world and describe a wide range of students, the use of the CEFR descriptors in addition to TESOL's descriptors seems appropriate. (For more information about the CEFR and more detailed descriptors for each level, see European Language Portfolio [Council of Europe (2010)], http://www.coe.int/T/DG4/Portfolio/?L=E&M=/main_pages/levels.html.)

Teachers wishing to adapt a particular vignette to another setting may wish to use the learner profile descriptors as a rough guideline. The descriptors also assist teachers of languages other than English in deciding on an appropriate level of activity.

In each teacher goal vignette in Chapter 4, the teacher is described in the *Teacher profile*, followed by descriptors for the students being taught, using the system shown in Figure B1. The vignette table for the teacher standards in Appendix C is set up as shown in Figure B2.

Table B1. Descriptors for the Learner Profiles

Adult = Educational functioning level descriptors and outcome measure definitions for ESL (TESOL, 2003, pp. 151–156); ESL adult learners/workplace

PreK–12 = English proficiency definitions PreK–12 (TESOL, 2006, p. 39); ESL young learner/child/teen

EFL/ESP/IEP = Common European Framework of Reference (Council of Europe, 2010); EFL/academic/ESP/IEP

Source	Descriptor
TESOL Technology Standards Label: Mastery	
Adult	
PreK–12	
EFL/ESP/IEP	**Proficient User (C1–C2)** C2: Mastery Can understand with ease virtually everything heard or read. Can summarise information from different spoken and written sources, reconstructing arguments and accounts in a coherent presentation. Can express him/herself spontaneously, very fluently and precisely, differentiating finer shades of meaning even in more complex situations.
TESOL Technology Standards Label: Bridging	
Adult	
PreK–12	Level 5—Bridging . . . . a wide range of longer oral and written texts and recognize implicit meaning. . . . . technical academic vocabulary and expressions. . . . . a variety of sentence lengths of varying linguistic complexity in extended oral or written discourse. . . . . oral or written language approaching comparability to that of English-proficient peers.
EFL/ESP/IEP	C1: Effective Operational Proficiency Can understand a wide range of demanding, longer texts, and recognise implicit meaning. Can express him/herself fluently and spontaneously without much obvious searching for expressions. Can use language flexibly and effectively for social, academic, and professional purposes. Can produce clear, well-structured, detailed text on complex subjects, showing controlled use of organisational patterns, connectors, and cohesive devices.

(Continued on p. 266)

Table B1 (continued). Descriptors for the Learner Profiles

Source	Descriptor
TESOL Technology Standards Label: Expanding	
Adult	**High Advanced ESL** — Individual can understand and participate effectively in face-to-face conversations on everyday subjects spoken at normal speed; can converse and understand independently in survival, work, and social situations; can expand on basic ideas in conversation, but with some hesitation; can clarify general meaning and control basic grammar, although still lacks total control over complex structures. — Individual can read authentic materials on everyday subjects and can handle most reading related to life roles; can consistently and fully interpret descriptive narratives on familiar topics and gain meaning from unfamiliar topics; uses increased control of language and meaning-making strategies to gain meaning of unfamiliar texts. The individual can write multiparagraph essays with a clear introduction and development of ideas; writing contains well-formed sentences, appropriate mechanics and spelling, and few grammatical errors. — Individual has a general ability to use English effectively to meet most routine social and work situations; can interpret routine charts, graphs, and tables and complete forms; has high ability to communicate on the telephone and understand radio and television; can meet work demands that require reading and writing and can interact with the public. The individual can use common software and learn new applications; can define the purpose of software and select new applications appropriately; can instruct others in use of software and technology.
PreK–12	**Level 4—Expanding** . . . language in both concrete and abstract situations and apply language to new experiences. . . . specialized and some technical academic vocabulary and expressions. . . . a variety of sentence lengths of varying linguistic complexity in oral and written communication. . . . oral or written language, making minimal errors that do not impede the overall meaning of the communication.
EFL/ESP/IEP	**Independent User (B1–B2)** B2: Vantage Can understand the main ideas of complex text on both concrete and abstract topics, including technical discussions in his/her field of specialisation. Can interact with a degree of fluency and spontaneity that makes regular interaction with native speakers quite possible without strain for either party. Can produce clear, detailed text on a wide range of subjects and explain a viewpoint on a topical issue giving the advantages and disadvantages of various options.

(Continued on p. 267)

Table B1 (continued). Descriptors for the Learner Profiles

Source	Descriptor
TESOL Technology Standards Label: Developing	
Adult	**Low Advanced ESL** — Individual can converse on many everyday subjects and some subjects with unfamiliar vocabulary, but may need repetition, rewording, or slower speech; can speak creatively, but with hesitation; can clarify general meaning by rewording and has control of basic grammar; understands descriptive and spoken narrative and can comprehend abstract concepts in familiar contexts. — Individual is able to read simple descriptions and narratives on familiar subjects or from which new vocabulary can be determined by context; can make some minimal inferences about familiar texts and compare and contrast information from such texts, but not consistently. The individual can write simple narrative descriptions and short essays on familiar topics, such as customs in native country; has consistent use of basic punctuation, but makes grammatical errors with complex structures. — Individual can function independently to meet most survival needs and can communicate on the telephone on familiar topics; can interpret simple charts and graphics; can handle jobs that require simple oral and written instructions, multistep diagrams, and limited public interaction. The individual can use all basic software applications, understand the impact of technology, and select the correct technology in a new situation.
PreK–12	**Level 3—Developing** . . . language to communicate with others on familiar matters regularly encountered. . . . general and some specialized academic vocabulary and expressions. . . . expanded sentences in oral or written communication. . . . oral or written language, making errors that may impede the communication but retain much of its meaning.
EFL/ESP/IEP	**B1: Threshold** Can understand the main points of clear standard input on familiar matters regularly encountered in work, school, leisure, etc. Can deal with most situations likely to arise whilst travelling in an area where the language is spoken. Can produce simple connected text on topics which are familiar or of personal interest. Can describe experiences and events, dreams, hopes and ambitions and briefly give reasons and explanations for opinions and plans.

(Continued on p. 268)

Table B1 (continued). Descriptors for the Learner Profiles

Source	Descriptor
TESOL Technology Standards Label: Emerging	
Adult	**High Intermediate ESL** — Individual can understand learned phrases and short new phrases containing familiar vocabulary spoken slowly and with some repetition; can communicate basic survival needs with some help; can participate in conversation in limited social situations and use new phrases with hesitation; relies on description and concrete terms. There is inconsistent control of more complex grammar. — Individual can read text on familiar subjects that have a simple and clear underlying structure (e.g., clear main idea, chronological order); can use context to determine meaning; can interpret actions required in specific written directions; can write simple paragraphs with main idea and supporting detail on familiar topics (e.g., daily activities, personal issues) by recombining learned vocabulary and structures; can self- and peer edit for spelling and punctuation errors. — Individual can meet basic survival and social needs, can follow some simple oral and written instruction, and has some ability to communicate on the telephone on familiar subjects; can write messages and notes related to basic needs; complete basic medical forms and job applications; can handle jobs that involve basic oral instructions and written communication in tasks that can be clarified orally. The individual can work with or learn basic oral computer software, such as word processing; can follow simple instructions for using technology.
PreK–12	**Level 2—Emerging** . . . language to draw on simple and routine experiences to communicate with others. . . . high-frequency and some general academic vocabulary and expressions. . . . phrases or short sentences in oral or written communication. . . . oral or written language, making errors that often impede the meaning of the communication.
EFL/ESP/IEP	**Basic User [A1–A2]** A2: Waystage Can understand sentences and frequently used expressions related to areas of most immediate relevance (e.g., very basic personal and family information, shopping, local geography, employment). Can communicate in simple and routine tasks requiring a simple and direct exchange of information on familiar and routine matters. Can describe in simple terms aspects of his/her background, immediate environment and matters in areas of immediate need.

(Continued on p. 269)

Table B1 (continued). Descriptors for the Learner Profiles

Source	Descriptor
TESOL Technology Standards Label: Starting	
Adult	**Low Intermediate ESL** — Individual can understand simple learned phrases and limited new phrases containing familiar vocabulary spoken slowly with frequent repetition; can ask and respond to questions using such phrases; can express basic survival needs and participate in some routine social conversations, although with some difficulty; has some control of basic grammar. — Individual can read simple material on familiar subjects and comprehend with high accuracy simple and compound sentences in single or linked paragraphs containing a familiar vocabulary; can write simple notes and messages on familiar situations, but lacks complete clarity and focus. Sentence structure lacks variety, but shows some control of basic grammar (e.g., present and past tense), and consistent use of punctuation (e.g., periods, capitalization). — Individual can interpret simple directions and schedules, signs and maps; can fill out simple forms, but needs support on some documents that are not simplified; can handle routine entry-level jobs that involve some written or oral English communication, but in which job tasks can be demonstrated. Individual can use simple computer programs and can perform a sequence of routine tasks given directions using technology (e.g., fax machine, computer).
PreK–12	**Level 1—Starting** . . : language to communicate with others around basic concrete needs. . . . : high-frequency words and memorized chunks of language. . . . . : words, phrases, or chunks of language. . . . . : pictorial, graphic, or nonverbal representation of language.
EFL/ESP/IEP	**A1: Breakthrough** Can understand and use familiar everyday expressions and very basic phrases aimed at the satisfaction of needs of a concrete type. Can introduce him/herself and others and can ask and answer questions about personal details such as where he/she lives, people he/she knows, and things he/she has. Can interact in a simple way provided the other person talks slowly and clearly and is prepared to help.

(Continued on p. 270)

Table B1 (continued). Descriptors for the Learner Profiles

Source	Descriptor
TESOL Technology Standards Label: Beginning	
Adult	**Beginning ESL** — Individual can understand frequently used words in context and very simple phrases spoken slowly and with some repetition; there is little communicative output and only in the most routine situations; little or no control over basic grammar; survival needs can be communicated simply, and there is some understanding of simple questions. — Individual can read and print numbers and letters, but has a limited understanding of connected prose and may need frequent rereading; can write sight words and copy lists of familiar words and phrases; may also be able to write simple sentences or phrases such as name, address and phone number; may also write very simple messages. Narrative writing is disorganized and unclear; inconsistently uses simple punctuation (e.g., periods, commas, question marks); contains frequent errors in spelling. — Individual functions with difficulty in situations related to immediate needs and in limited social situations; has some simple oral communication abilities using simple learned and repeated phrases; may need frequent repetition; can provide personal information on simple forms; can recognize common forms of print found in the home and environment, such as labels and product names; can handle routine entry-level jobs that require only the most basic written or oral English communication and in which job tasks can be demonstrated. There is minimal knowledge or experience using computers or technology.
PreK–12	
EFL/ESP/IEP	
TESOL Technology Standards Label: Literacy	
Adult	**Beginning ESL Literacy** — Individual cannot speak or understand English, or understands only isolated words or phrases. — Individual has no reading or writing skills in any language, or has minimal skills, such as the ability to read and write own name or simple isolated words. The individual may be able to write letters or numbers and copy simple words, and there may be no or incomplete recognition of the alphabet; may have difficulty using a writing instrument. There is little or no comprehension of how print corresponds to spoken language. — Individual functions minimally or not at all in English and can communicate only through gestures or a few isolated words, such as name and other personal information; may recognize only common signs or symbols (e.g., stop sign, product logos); can handle only very routine entry-level jobs that do not require oral or written communication in English. There is no knowledge or use of computers or technology.
PreK–12	
EFL/ESP/IEP	

TESOL Technology Standards: Description, Implementation, Integration

Appendix C: Vignette Tables: Quick Reference to Proficiency Levels, Skills, and Resources for Learners and Teachers

The tables in this appendix provide details about the learner proficiency levels, skill areas, and technology resources addressed in the vignettes presented in Chapters 3 and 4. The tables organize the vignettes by goal and standard and may serve as a quick reference when the reader is seeking to target a specific learner, teacher population, or type of activity.

The vignettes are designed to illustrate the standards and give examples in action of how teachers and students successfully integrate technology to improve their teaching and learning. The vignettes included in this book were collected as the result of an international call for contributions. The Vignette Team (Sophie Ioannou-Georgiou, Elizabeth Hanson-Smith, and Paige Ware) selected and edited the vignettes for consistency and clarity in illustrating the performance indicators and technical competencies.

The vignettes aim to help the reader visualize the standards in his or her own context. English language teachers work in widely varied contexts, from small village schools with minimal resources to large suburban schools affluent in technology. The vignettes show that the standards and goals are achievable in all contexts, regardless of levels of technology access. In order to achieve exemplary power, each vignette focuses on a particular teaching context (e.g., EFL classroom, ESL classroom, vocational education, online) and explains the teacher's background and aims as regards technology use (e.g., meeting curricular objectives, professional development, assessing students). The vignette then shows how teachers working with different levels of technology and resources can achieve the specific indicators. Despite the specific contexts of the vignettes, the concepts and practices they illustrate can be applied over a much wider set of classroom and laboratory contexts. Readers are encouraged to envision how the technologies and activities illustrated in particular vignettes can apply in their own settings.

Every effort has been made to represent different teacher populations (e.g., teachers of young learners, teacher trainers, tertiary language teachers). Most teachers, as well as teacher educators and administrators, will find vignettes in which they will recognize themselves and their context. We hope this familiarity will help make the standards more meaningful. At the same time, educators should imagine how these practices can enrich their own. Although not all vignettes will be relevant to every educator, we believe that they will still enable the visualization of the performance indicators and offer ideas that can easily be transferred to other contexts.

We encourage those who are working with technology in various contexts to continue to contribute their own vignettes to help expand the knowledge base available to educators. Follow the vignettes provided in this book as a template for organizing your vignette. Vignettes can be emailed to Deborah Healey, dhealey@uoregon.edu, for inclusion in an online repository.

Table C1 focuses on the vignettes from Chapter 3, Technology Standards for Language Learners, while Table C2 covers the vignettes from Chapter 4, Technology Standards for Language Teachers. Both tables list the vignettes by goal and standard and provide their titles and contributors. The following information is also included for each vignette in Table C1:

Targeted Group:

> *Setting* includes EFL/ESL/IEP designation, commercial school, blended, or all online.

> *Age* is the students' age range in years.

> *Level* is the language proficiency level of the students, using four descriptors (see Appendix B for detailed level descriptors):
>> TESOL Technology Standards label
>> TESOL adult education standards level
>> TESOL preK–12 standards level
>> Common European Framework of Reference (CEFR) level.

> *Skills Addressed* includes the language skills practiced and the approach.

> *Technologies Used* lists the most important CALL tools used. In general, all the technologies used in settings with fewer resources and lower access to technology can be used in settings with more resources and access.
>> L = low-resource, low-access setting
>> M = medium-resource, medium-access setting
>> H = high-resource, high-access setting

Table C1. Levels, Skills, and Resources for Language Learners Vignettes

Targeted Group Setting Age Tech Standards/TESOL Adult Ed Level (TESOL PreK–12, CEFR Level)	Skills Addressed	Technologies Used
Goal 1: Language learners demonstrate foundational knowledge and skills in technology for a multilingual world.		
Goal 1 Standard 1: Language learners demonstrate basic operational skills in using various technology tools and Internet browsers.		
Each One Teach One		
EFL teen Teenagers, ages 13–18 Emerging/High Intermediate (Level 2, A2)	Computer literacy Writing	L—Word processor M—Email system, WebQuest, browser H—Bookmarking
Computer Basics		
ESL, Adult education Adults, ages 17+ Starting–Emerging/Low–High Intermediate (Level 1–2, A1–A2)	Computer literacy Media literacy Writing	L—Word processor M/H—Presentation software, screencast/video
Goal 1 Standard 2: Language learners are able to use available input and output devices (e.g., keyboard, mouse, printer, headset, microphone, media player, electronic whiteboard).		
Favorite Song		
ESL Teenagers, ages 13–18 Developing–Expanding/Low–High Advanced (Level 3–4, B1–B2)	Speaking Computer literacy Media literacy	L/M—CD-ROM, USB devices, recorder, MP3 player, headset, presentation software H—Blog
Goal 1 Standard 3: Language learners exercise appropriate caution when using online sources and when engaging in electronic communication.		
Internet Safety for Children		
ESL (child) Young learners, ages 9–12 Emerging–Developing/High Intermediate–Low Advanced (Level 2–3, A2–B1)	Reading Writing	L/M/H—Browser & bookmarking, WebQuests, international collaborative projects

(Continued on p. 274)

Table C1 (continued). Levels, Skills, and Resources for Language Learners Vignettes

Targeted Group
  Setting
  Age
  Tech Standards/TESOL
    Adult Ed Level
  (TESOL PreK–12, CEFR
    Level)
	Skills Addressed	Technologies Used

Goal 1 Standard 4: Language learners demonstrate basic competence as users of technology.		
Restaurant Employees		

ESL adult workplace
Adults, ages 18+
Developing–Expanding/Low–High
  Advanced
(Level 3–4, B1–B2)
	Computer literacy
	Reading
	Writing
	Listening
	Speaking
		L—Word-processing, CD
		  typing program
		M—Wiki or blog
		H—Video/web conferencing

Basic Troubleshooting and Safety		

EFL
Teenagers, ages 13–18
Emerging–Developing/High
  Intermediate–Low Advanced
(Level 2–3, A2–B1)
	Computer literacy
	Reading
	Writing
		L/M/H—Browser &
		  bookmarking, international
		  collaborative projects

Goal 2: Language learners use technology in socially and culturally appropriate, legal, and ethical ways.		
Goal 2 Standard 1: Language learners understand that communication conventions differ across cultures, communities, and contexts.		
Cross-Cultural Communication		

ESL
Teenagers, ages 13–18
Developing/Low Advanced
(Level 3, B1)
	Listening
	Speaking
	Reading
	Writing
	Cultural literacy
	Media literacy
		L—Presentation program,
		  audio/video devices, digital
		  camera
		M—Wikis, blogs, mind-
		  mapping tools, CD burning
		H—Networked lab

Social Interactions		

ESP in EFL settings
Adults, ages 19+
Developing–Expanding/Low–High
  Advanced
(Level 3–4, B1–B2)
	Listening
	Speaking
	Cultural Literacy
	Tandem learning
		L—Recorder, desktop
		  recorder
		M—Audio/video online,
		  podcast
		H—Social language learning
		  sites

(Continued on p. 275)

TESOL Technology Standards: Description, Implementation, Integration

Table C1 (continued). Levels, Skills, and Resources for Language Learners Vignettes

Targeted Group
  Setting
  Age
  Tech Standards/TESOL
    Adult Ed Level
    (TESOL PreK–12, CEFR
      Level)
	Skills Addressed	Technologies Used

Goal 2 Standard 2: Language learners demonstrate respect for others in their use of private and public information.		
Think-Pair-Share		
EFL Teen/adult, ages 13+ Developing/Low Advanced (Level 3, B1)	Listening Speaking	L/M—Audio recorders, mobile technology, Wikipedia H—Podcast
Peer Biographies		

ESL–IEP
Adults, ages 17+
Expanding–Bridging/High
  Advanced+
(Level 4–5, B2–C1)
	Writing
	Listening
	Intercultural skills
		L—Word processor, audio
		  recording, digital camera,
		  mobile technologies
		M/H—Timeline software,
		  graphics editing, class wiki

Goal 3: Language learners effectively use and critically evaluate technology-based tools as aids in the development of their language learning competence as part of formal instruction and for further learning.		
Goal 3 Standard 1: Language learners effectively use and evaluate available technology-based productivity tools.		
Family Stories		

ESL (child)
Very young learners, ages 6–8
Literacy–Starting/Beginning
  Literacy–Low Intermediate
(Level 1 and lower, A1 and
  lower)
	Vocabulary
	Reading aloud
	Computer/media
	  literacy
		L/M/H—Presentation
		  software
		H—Networked lab (intranet)

Goal 3 Standard 2: Language learners appropriately use and evaluate available technology-based language skill-building tools.		
Interactive Language Games and Exercises		

ESL adult education–immigrant
  (blended learning)
Adults, ages 17+
Starting–Emerging/Low–High
  Intermediate
(Level 1–2, A1–A2)
	Integrated skills	L/M—CD/DVD
		M—Online programs
		H—CMS

(Continued on p. 276)

Table C1 (continued). Levels, Skills, and Resources for Language Learners Vignettes

Targeted Group
  Setting
  Age
  Tech Standards/TESOL
    Adult Ed Level
  (TESOL PreK–12, CEFR
    Level)
	Skills Addressed	Technologies Used

E-Dictionaries		

EFL
Young learners, ages 9–12
Starting–Emerging/Low–High
  Intermediate
(Level 1–2, A1–A2)
	Vocabulary	L—Digital dictionaries (online
		  and CD/DVD), mind-
		  mapping software, word
		  processor, exercises and
		  rubric (downloaded/printed)
		M—Online exercises
		H—Online rubric

Exploring Community Resources		

ESL
Adult students (ages 17+)
Beginning–Emerging/Beginning–
  High Intermediate
(Level 1–2 and lower, A1–A2 and
  lower)
	Speaking
	Listening
	Exploring community
	  resources
		L—Mobile phone
		M—Document camera
		H—Slideshow, wiki, online
		  quizzes

Goal 3 Standard 3: Language learners appropriately use and evaluate available technology-based tools for communication and collaboration.

Technology for Collaborative Communication		

EFL
Teen/adult, ages 12+
Developing/Low Advanced
(Level 3, B1)
	Speaking
	Writing
	Thinking
	Media literacy
		L—Graphics software, audio
		  recording
		M—Online sites, podcasting
		H—Video/webcam recording,
		  digital camera, mobile
		  phone

Goal 3 Standard 4: Language learners use and evaluate available technology-based research tools appropriately

ESP for Architecture		

ESP EFL academic (online/
  blended course)
Adult, ages 17+
Bridging
(Level 5, C1)
	Writing
	Speaking
		L/M/H—Presentation
		  software, email, online
		  forum, wiki, blogs
		L—Text chat
		M/H—Audio/video chat,
		  online dictionary

Evaluating Web Sources		

ESL IEP
Adults, ages 17+
Developing/Low Advanced
(Level 3, B1)
	Reading
	Critical thinking
	Writing
		L—Teacher printouts
		M/H—Internet research,
		  rubrics
		M—Online newspapers
		H—Chat, wiki, language lab
		  chat

(Continued on p. 277)

Table C1 (continued). Levels, Skills, and Resources for Language Learners Vignettes

Targeted Group 　Setting 　Age 　Tech Standards/TESOL 　　Adult Ed Level 　　(TESOL PreK–12, CEFR 　　　Level)	Skills Addressed	Technologies Used
Goal 3 Standard 5: Language learners recognize the value of technology to support autonomy, lifelong learning, creativity, metacognition, collaboration, personal pursuits, and productivity.		
Sheltered Science Concepts		
ESL teen, Sheltered/content-based Teenagers, ages 13–18 Emerging–Developing/High Intermediate–Low Advanced (Level 2–3, A2–B1)	Content-based Listening/ 　pronunciation Vocabulary	L—Online dictionary (teacher use) M/H—Online dictionary with audio (student use)
Google Earth		
IEP Adults, ages 17+ Expanding–Bridging/High Advanced+ (Level 4–5, B2–C1)	Speaking Writing Thinking skills Grammar Media literacy	L—Graphics software M/H—Internet mapping, audio recording, online graphics, Google Earth Tour

The following information is included for each vignette in Table C2:

Targeted Group:

　Setting includes EFL/ESL/IEP designation, teacher educator, teacher trainer, blended, or all online.

　Age is the age range in years of the teacher's students.

　Level is the language proficiency level of the teacher's students, using four descriptors: the TESOL Technology Standards label, the TESOL adult education standards level, the TESOL preK–12 standards level, and the Common European Framework of Reference (CEFR) level. (See Appendix B for detailed level descriptors.)

Skills Addressed includes the language skills practiced and the approach.

Technologies Used lists the most important CALL tools used. In general, all the technologies used in settings with fewer resources and lower access to technology continue to be used in settings with more resources and access.

　　L = low-resource, low-access setting

　　M = medium-resource, medium-access setting

　　H = high-resource, high-access setting

Table C2. Levels, Skills, and Resources for Language Teachers Vignettes

Targeted Group
  Setting
  Age
  Tech Standards/TESOL
    Adult Ed Level
  (TESOL PreK–12, CEFR
    Level)
	Skills Addressed	Technologies Used

Goal 1: Language teachers acquire and maintain foundational knowledge and skills in technology for professional purposes.		
Goal 1 Standard 1: Language teachers demonstrate knowledge and skills in basic technological concepts and operational competence, meeting or exceeding TESOL technology standards for students in whatever situation they teach.		
Brown Bear, Brown Bear		
EFL Teacher of very young learners, ages 3–6 Literacy/Beginning Literacy	Reading Listening	L/M—Presentation program, MP3 recording, video recording, CD/DVD recording H—Voki
New Technology Course for Teachers		
Teacher trainer (EFL) Technology-using teacher of experienced university EFL teachers Bridging–Mastery/High Advanced (Level 5+, C1–C2)	Integrated skills (tech focus)	L—Productivity software, audio recording, graphics software, portable media, browser, e-portfolio, podcasting, online exercises, rubrics M/H—Virtual office H—Wiki
Goal 1 Standard 2: Language teachers demonstrate an understanding of a wide range of technology supports for language learning and options for using them in a given setting.		
Teaching Speaking in EFL		
EFL NNS teacher and NS aide Class for teens, ages 13–18 Expanding–Bridging/High Advanced+ (Levels 4–5, B2–C1)	Speaking Pronunciation	L—MP3 recorder, audio software M—Video on DVD H—Video online, digital camera
Goal 1 Standard 3: Language teachers actively strive to expand their skill and knowledge base to evaluate, adopt, and adapt emerging technologies throughout their careers.		
Adapting Technology for Writing Instruction		
ESL ESL teacher of teens, ages 13–18 Developing–Expanding/Low–High Advanced (Levels 3–4, B1–B2)	Tools in word processor Collaborative writing Peer editing workshops	L—Word processor, graphics program M—Audio recording, book-making site H—Video recording

(Continued on p. 279)

Table C2 (continued). Levels, Skills, and Resources for Language Teachers Vignettes

Targeted Group Setting Age Tech Standards/TESOL Adult Ed Level (TESOL PreK-12, CEFR Level)	Skills Addressed	Technologies Used
Podcasts and Podquests		

EFL
EFL teacher of teens/adults,
  ages 13+
Expanding–Bridging/High
  Advanced+
(Levels 4–5, B2–C1)
	Listening	L/M—Podcasts, portable
		  media, podquests
		H—Video/audio conferencing

Goal 1 Standard 4: Language teachers use technology in socially and culturally appropriate, legal, and ethical ways.

Compliance With Privacy Regulations		

IEP; any U.S.-based administrator
Faculty and staff at an intensive
  English program (IEP) for
  adults, ages 17+
Developing–Bridging/Low–High
  Advanced+
(Levels 3–5, B1–C2)
	Student privacy	L—Internal email system,
		  spreadsheets, intranet
		M—Site-based file sharing
		H—CMS

Goal 2: Language teachers integrate pedagogical knowledge and skills with technology to enhance language teaching and learning.

Goal 2 Standard 1: Language teachers identify and evaluate technological resources and environments for suitability to their teaching context.

Blended Learning for Adult Students		

ESL
ESL teacher of adults, ages 19+
Emerging–Expanding/High
  intermediate–High advanced
(Levels 2–4, A2–B2)
	Collaborative learning
	Integrated skills
	Grammar
	Vocabulary
		L—One-computer class, skill-
		  based software, rubrics
		  (software evaluation),
		  teacher wiki
		M—Interactive whiteboard,
		  online exercises, video
		  online
		H—Multimedia lab,
		  screencasting

Goal 2 Standard 2: Language teachers coherently integrate technology into their pedagogical approaches.

Teaching Literature With Technology		

ESL
Secondary school ESL teacher of
  teens, ages 16–17
Developing/Low Advanced
(Level 3, B1)
	Listening
	Reading
	Vocabulary
		L—MP3 audio
		M—Audio online, video online,
		  online dictionary
		H—Blog, online discussion

(Continued on p. 280)

Table C2 (continued). Levels, Skills, and Resources for Language Teachers Vignettes

Targeted Group Setting Age Tech Standards/TESOL Adult Ed Level (TESOL PreK–12, CEFR Level)	Skills Addressed	Technologies Used
Goal 2 Standard 3: *Language teachers design and manage language learning activities and tasks using technology appropriately to meet curricular goals and objectives.*		
Practice for Speaking Test		
EFL Teens/adults, ages 16+ Developing–Bridging/Low–High Advanced+ (Level 3–5, B1–C2)	Speaking Pronunciation	L/M—Audio recording, podcasting, email, mobile technology H—Moodle, e-portfolio
Workday Interviews		
IEP Teacher of adults, ages 17+ Developing–Bridging/Low–High Advanced+ (Level 3–5, B1–C1)	Integrated skills Grammar Vocabulary	L—Video online, mobile phone, audio recording M—Internet telephony, blogs/ wikis H—CMS, podcasting
Goal 2 Standard 4: *Language teachers use relevant research findings to inform the planning of language learning activities and tasks that involve technology.*		
Research in the Pedagogy of Technology		
Teacher ed; teacher trainer; secondary ESL in-service teachers of immigrant newcomers Pre-service and in-service teachers enrolled in graduate school, ages 20+ Native speakers or Bridging– Mastery (Level C1–C2)	Pedagogical research in technology uses for integrated skills	L—Online articles (possibly printed out), mobile phones, Internet telephony, e-portfolio M—Blogs, wikis H—Video recording, online file sharing, virtual office
Goal 3: Language teachers apply technology in record keeping, feedback, and assessment.		
Goal 3 Standard 1: *Language teachers evaluate and implement relevant technology to aid in effective learner assessment.*		
VESL for Shipyard Employees		
Workplace ESL Teacher of adults, ages 18+ Developing/Low Advanced (Level 3, B1)	Work-related reading, writing, grammar, vocabulary Test-taking skills	L—Desktop and online quiz software, word processor, spreadsheets, electronic grade book M/H—Digital audio, e-portfolio

(Continued on p. 281)

Table C2 (continued). Levels, Skills, and Resources for Language Teachers Vignettes

Targeted Group Setting Age Tech Standards/TESOL Adult Ed Level (TESOL PreK–12, CEFR Level)	Skills Addressed	Technologies Used
Online Integrated Skills		
Online/blended EFL teacher/ trainer EFL teacher of teens/adults, ages 17+; deaf students also Expanding–Bridging/High Advanced+ (Level 4–5, B1–C1)	Integrated skills Collaborative learning Adaptive technology	L—CMS, chat, rubrics M—Virtual office hours H—Videoconferencing

Goal 3 Standard 2: Language teachers use technological resources to collect and analyze information in order to enhance language instruction and learning.

Readability in Academic Texts		
IEP/adult Reading teacher of adults, ages 19+ Expanding–Bridging/High Advanced+ (Level 4–5, B2–C1)	Vocabulary Reading Writing	L—Concordancer, readability analyzer, word processor tools, online readings, spreadsheet M—Online search H—Wiki, CMS

Goal 3 Standard 3: Language teachers evaluate the effectiveness of specific student uses of technology to enhance teaching and learning.

Rubrics in English for Science		
ESP in EFL settings Teacher of adults, ages 19+ Expanding–Mastery/High Advanced+ (Level B2–C2)	ESP Vocabulary Grammar Research Documenting student participation in collaborative projects	L—Word processor, concordancer, online concordancer, rubrics, Google Scholar M—Multimedia presentation, slideshow, wiki, photo site H—Text chat groups in CMS or online, blogs, e-portfolio

(Continued on p. 282)

Table C2 (continued). Levels, Skills, and Resources for Language Teachers Vignettes

Targeted Group Setting Age Tech Standards/TESOL Adult Ed Level (TESOL PreK–12, CEFR Level)	Skills Addressed	Technologies Used
Goal 4: Language teachers use technology to improve communication, collaboration, and efficiency.		

Goal 4 Standard 1: Language teachers use communication technologies to maintain effective contact and collaboration with peers, students, administration, and other stakeholders.

E-Mentoring		
Teacher ed and teacher programs and supervisors (online interaction) Teacher educators supervising pre- and in-service teachers, adults, ages 17+ Native speakers or Bridging–Mastery (Level C2–C1)	Pedagogy of ESL Community of practice	L—Online forum, email, blogs, wiki, text chat, virtual conferencing M—Audio chat, Internet telephony, instant messaging, mobile phone H—Videoconferencing

Goal 4 Standard 2: Language teachers regularly reflect on the intersection of professional practice and technological developments so that they can make informed decisions regarding the use of technology to support language learning and communication.

CALL Professional Development—Expert Level		
CALL teacher/trainer (expert level)—ESL or EFL CALL teacher trainer who works with EFL or ESL teachers, adults, ages 19+ Expanding–Mastery/High Advanced+ (Levels 4–5+, B2–C2)	Pedagogy and CALL	L—Website, blog, wiki, mailing list, digital camera/webcam M—Instant messaging, chat, screencast, videoconferencing H—Virtual world, emerging tech

Goal 4 Standard 3: Language teachers apply technology to improve efficiency in preparing for class, grading, and maintaining records.

Grading and Record Keeping		
ESL middle school Experienced classroom teacher of ESL young learners, ages 11–12 Developing–Expanding/Low–High Advanced (Level 3–4, B1–B2)	Integrated skills Writing	L—CMS (teacher use), grade book M—Word processor, spreadsheet, wiki H—Blog, discussion forum

About the Authors
and Contributors

Jennifer N. Brown, *vignette contributor*
Jennifer N. Brown (jennifer.brown@esl.gatech.edu) is an ESL instructor and the online coordinator at the Language Institute of Georgia Institute of Technology, Atlanta, Georgia, USA.

Dafne González, *vignette contributor*
Dafne González (dygonza@yahoo.com), an ESP/EFL teacher at Universidad Simon Bolivar, Caracas, Venezuela, is a member of Webheads in Action.

Ingrid Greenberg, *vignette contributor*
Ingrid Greenberg (ingrid_greenberg@yahoo.com), ESL assistant program chair, Continuing Education, San Diego Community College District, San Diego, California, USA, has designed and launched multilevel ESL and vocational/workplace ESL courses with corporations and public education.

Elizabeth Hanson-Smith, *Technology Standards Task Force, Vignette Team member*
Elizabeth Hanson-Smith (ehansonsmi@yahoo.com), professor emeritus, California State University, Sacramento, California, USA, is a founder and former director of the graduate TESOL Program. She has trained teachers in many countries around the world.

Deborah Healey, *Technology Standards Task Force Chair*
Deborah Healey (dhealey@uoregon.edu), senior instructor at the University of Oregon's American English Institute/Linguistics Department, Eugene, Oregon, USA, teaches in the distance education program and presents and publishes extensively on CALL.

Philip Hubbard, *Technology Standards Task Force*
Philip Hubbard (efs@stanford.edu) is senior lecturer and director of English for Foreign Students at Stanford University, Stanford, California, USA. He has published widely on using technology for language learning.

Sophie Ioannou-Georgiou, *Technology Standards Task Force, Vignette Team member*
Sophie Ioannou-Georgiou (sophiecy@yahoo.com), a teacher trainer at the Cyprus Pedagogical Institute, Latsia, Cyprus, is the coauthor of *Assessing Young Learners.* Her research interests include learner interactions, distance learning, and content-integrated language learning with young learners.

Ann Kennedy, *vignette contributor*
Ann A. Kennedy (a.akennedy@gmail.com) is a reading specialist and English language/ English teacher at Arlington Mill Hill School Continuation Program, in Arlington, Virginia, USA, and is also an adjunct in linguistics at Georgetown University, in Washington, DC, USA.

Greg Kessler, *Technology Standards Task Force*
Greg Kessler (kessler@ohio.edu) is an assistant professor of CALL at Ohio University, Athens, Ohio, USA. His research interests include CALL teacher education, teacher and student discourse in CALL environments, and the coevolution of language teaching pedagogy and technology.

Jeff Kuhn, *vignette contributor*
Jeff Kuhn (jk212509@ohio.edu), Ohio University Department of Linguistics, Athens, Ohio, USA, taught EFL in Japan and served as a teacher trainer for the Peace Corps in Mongolia. His focus is on CALL in developing countries.

Branka Marceta, *vignette contributor*
Branka Marceta (bmarceta@otan.us *and* catesol_branka@yahoo.com) is currently an OTAN technology projects coordinator and the California and Nevada TESOL coordinator of the TELL Interest Group. She has been an ESL/EFL teacher in the United States, Canada, and the former Yugoslavia.

James Perren, *vignette contributor*
James Perren (jperren@emich.edu) is an assistant professor of ESL/TESOL at Eastern Michigan University, Ypsilanti, Michigan, USA. His pedagogical and research repertoire includes ESL/EFL, service learning, CALL, and teacher training.

Steven Sharp, *vignette contributor*
Steven Sharp (ssharp66@gmail.com) is the CALL coordinator for Maryland English Institute and a doctoral student in the Department of Curriculum and Instruction at the University of Maryland, College Park, Maryland, USA.

Paige Ware, *Technology Standards Task Force, Vignette Team member*
Paige Ware (pware@smu.edu) is an associate professor at Southern Methodist University, Dallas, Texas, USA. Her research examines technology-based literacy and language instruction in secondary and post-secondary contexts.

Index

Also Available From TESOL

TESOL Classroom Practice Series
Maria Dantas-Whitney, Sarah Rilling, and Lilia Savova, Series Editors

Authenticity in the Classroom and Beyond: Children and Adolescent Learners
Maria Dantas-Whitney and Sarah Rilling, Editors

Language Games: Innovative Activities for Teaching English
Maureen Snow Andrade, Editor

Authenticity in the Classroom and Beyond: Adult Learners
Sarah Rilling and Maria Dantas-Whitney, Editors

Adult Language Learners: Context and Innovation
Ann F. V. Smith and Gregory Strong, Editors

Applications of Task-Based Learning in TESOL
Ali Shehadeh and Christine Coombe, Editors

Explorations in Second Language Reading
Roger Cohen, Editor

Insights on Teaching Speaking in TESOL
Tim Stewart, Editor

Multilevel and Diverse Classrooms
Bradley Baurain and Phan Le Ha, Editors

Pragmatics: Teaching Speech Acts
Donna Tatsuki and Noël Houck, Editors

Effective Second Language Writing
Susan Kasten, Editor

Integrating Language and Content
Jon Nordmeyer and Susan Barduhn

Using Textbooks Effectively
Lilia Savova, Editor

Classroom Management
Thomas S. C. Farrell, Editor

Teaching Listening: Voices From the Field
Nikki Ashcraft and Anh Tran, Editors

❋ ❋ ❋ ❋ ❋

T E S O L